Tales
from the
Bus Leagues

TALES FROM THE BUS LEAGUES

TALES
FROM THE
BUS LEAGUES

100 wild stories about life on the road and behind the scenes, through the eyes of a career minor leaguer

JAMIE MCKINVEN

Copyright © 2015 Jamie McKinven
All rights reserved.

ISBN-13: 978-1490333007
ISBN-10:
1490333002

All rights reserved. No part of this publication may be reproduced, distributed, or transmitted in any form or by any means, including photocopying, recording, or other electronic or mechanical methods, without the prior written permission of the publisher, except in the case of brief quotations embodied in critical reviews and certain other non-commercial uses permitted by copyright law.

This book is dedicated to the best teammates a guy can ask for. Jasmine and Cleo have brought peace to my life and remind me each day about what is truly important.

Tales from the Bus Leagues

CONTENTS

A Note from the Author	i
Cover Story: Around the World in 80 Games	v
Junior Hockey	**1**
Respect Your Elders	2
Super Rookie	4
The Best Accidental Prank Ever	6
The Curious Case of Peter Kennedy	8
College Hockey	**11**
Where Did They Find This Guy?	12
Perfect Place to Run Out of Gas	13
Game-Plan Glitch	15
The Lynah Faithful	17
Your Friendly Neighborhood Appleby's	18
Cornell Fans Sign Trickery	21
Momentum Shift	22
Mascot Down	24
Ticket Gate Campout	25
Clarkson vs. SLU Rivalry	26
UNH Student Stampede	27
Banned From the Providence Mall	28
The Chicken Man	33

The ECAC All-Ugly Team	34
The Walk-On Massacre of 2003	36
How I Became the Team Barber	39
Deputy Dummies	40
Airport Follies in Minnesota	41
Guns and Guts	44
A Keg From Craig	46
The Weighted Run	47
Deadman's Hill	50
Practice Scraps	53
NBA Jam	55
One Bad Edge	57
Das Boot	59
Welcome to the Colgate Inn	63
Mean Jean	65
Ice Bath Therapy	67

PRANKS 70

Hide the Poop	71
The Weighted Stick	72
Super Rookie Wet Suit	74
The Leaner to End all Leaners	75
Skate-Lace Hotel Prank	78
Shoe Check	80

Helmet Name Tag Prank	82
The Gatorade Shower	83
Kangaroo Court	84
Anyone Seen My Car?	88

PRO HOCKEY — 91

Welcome to Pro Hockey	92
Missing at Midnight in Mississippi	95
Clifford the Brown Recluse	97
Do You Remember Where the Apartment Is?	99
The Wild, Wild East	101
Ne Dryer, Nema Problem	107
Lost in Translation	109
Partizan Payday	111
Wet Gear in Belgrade	113
Gypsies	116
That's Why They Call It The Cage, Baby!	118
Shake and Bake	120
My Key Won't Work	122
First-Line Treatment	125
Egypt or Snowboarding	129
Motorcade and Armed Escort in Zagreb	132
Choke the Czech	136
Euro-Style	139

The Day I Was a Jerk to Novak Djokovic	142
The Brothers Jankovic	145
Sleepless in Frankfurt	150
The World of a Pro Goalie	152
A Real Pisser of a Goalie	154
The Goepf-Man Strikes Again	155
Masterful Experience	158
Masters Week Parking Fiasco	161
Wet Jeans	165
Giving Back and Getting Back	168
The Dreaded Green Jacket	172
Amarillo by Morning	174
No Luck in Lubbock	178
Scariest Night in My Hockey Career	180
Pick on Someone Your Own Size!	181
Jonny No-Elbows	184
Credit Card Roulette	185
Professional Tourist/Hockey Player	187
The Mike Sgroi Experience	191
Off-Season Blues	194
The Hierarchy of Professional Hockey	201
The Ever-Changing Landscape of the Minor Leagues	206

The Toughest Job in Pro Sports	211
Fergie-isms	214
24 Hours in the Life of a Minor Leaguer	217
Bus League Bad Habits	229
Minor League Cost-Savers	234
Requiem for a Hockey Dream	239
Moustache Boy	248
American Guns	249
Being a Healthy Scratch Sucks	252
The Midnight Rodeo	262
Meeting a D-List Hero	265
The Player to be Named	268

Hockey Tidbits — 271

Hockey Players Are a Superstitious Bunch	272
Hockey Nicknames	274
Every Team's Got One	277
The Legend of Gunner Garrett	281
Acknowledgements	288
Index	291
Other Books by this Author:	299
Author's Blog:	301

TALES FROM THE BUS LEAGUES

A Note from the Author

Picking up a laptop and deciding to hack away about my journeys in hockey was entirely based on the idea of keeping a diary or a journal. With multiple knocks to the head, I knew that one day I was going to forget it all and I wanted to make sure I had some stories to tell my kids and grandkids.

The first book happened by accident as I began charting my travels through hockey's rocky path. I had been reading a book by George Gmelch, *The Inside Pitch*, and I was blown away. George was a former minor league ballplayer who decided to pull back the curtain on what life was like making the arduous, sometimes unsavory climb through the minor pro ranks. After reading *The Inside Pitch*, I decided I would try to format my journey into a mild exposé of what life is like for a struggling pro hockey player.

After completing the book, I had no clue how to go about getting it published. I read book after book on how to promote and publish a book and followed all the advice right down the line. I tried to find a literary agent to take on my project and was basically laughed at without a word being read. Fair enough, I suppose, since I wasn't exactly Sidney Crosby or Wayne Gretzky.

What was frustrating about it all was that I felt I had a unique story to tell. I wasn't writing inspirational stories about perfection and how rosy the world of hockey is. I was telling a story from the perspective of a struggling pro who lived out of his suitcase and spent every morning scouring the transaction lists in the AHL and NHL to make sure his job was safe. I talk about drug issues and what middle of the pack pro hockey players go through in order to keep the dream alive.

With this perspective, I felt there was a story to be told that the everyday hockey fan and families, who shell out tens of thousands of dollars each year to put their kid through competitive hockey, could learn from.

Eventually, after dozens of rejections from literary agents I decided I needed to explore other options. One agent in particular told me that I was a "Nobody" and that he was already promoting a book by this phenomenal goalie and didn't have time for somebody like me. I remember thinking: "I know that goalie and I scored on him in pro. If I scored on him, he definitely wasn't that phenomenal." All this did was fuel me to push harder.

The very next rejection came with some sound advice. The gentleman said: "For your first book or two, you should consider self-publishing and building your platform that way." So with that, I set forth and self-published my first book, *So You Want Your Kid to Play Pro Hockey*, and was pleasantly surprised at the success it had. Shortly after publishing, I had companies looking to promote it on their websites, media outlets asking for interviews, and even a couple of articles written about the book. In reality, I would have been happy if just one person bought the book and was able to take something away from it.

Going through this experience and dealing with frustration and rejection along the way was exactly what I was used to and was always something I had used as motivation to work harder. My whole life I had been an underdog, so why should my writing career be any different. All it takes is for one person to say that it isn't possible. That one person then becomes a focal point for my inner ire—a villain in a quest to overcome the odds.

With my second book, I wanted to simulate a conversation you might have with a buddy over a few beers. I wanted to break it up into small stories that, when added together, paint a picture of what life is like for a journeying minor pro as he moves from town to town and level to level. This book is more light-hearted in nature than *So You Want Your Kid to Play Pro Hockey* and takes the reader deeper into the culture and traditions that are engrained within the game of hockey.

Writing the two books has given me an even bigger gift than I could have ever imagined. Through telling my tales, I have been able to take a step back and really look at where my journey has taken me and why. This perspective has allowed me to understand what might have held me back and also to see what might hinder my personal development moving forward. I have not only been able to look within myself and my experiences and discover what has shaped me for good or bad, but it has allowed me to look at hockey as a whole and see what is right and wrong in the whole mechanism. My only hope is that readers can learn something about themselves, about life in general or about their connection to the game of hockey.

Cover Story: Around the World in 80 Games
with Hockey Beauty Jay Latulippe

You may have noticed the interesting picture on the cover of this book. Maybe it's what sparked your interest, urging you to peel back the cover, or click the mouse (for all you e-readers). This fine young broth of a lad is none other than colorful journeyman hockey player Jay Latulippe, a legend of his era amongst bus leaguers the world over.

Looking at the picture, you may have guessed that Jay plays the game with a certain passion, an "edge", as it is affectionately referred to in the hockey world. This isn't something that usually comes easily or naturally to players who are 5 foot 10 and 180 pounds, but Jay isn't your typical player. There's something unique about him. Some may even say that he's "not right in the head", a phrase I've heard more times than I can remember while immersed in battles alongside Jay. These qualities, and believe me, for a hockey player these are qualities, are what has enabled Jay to enjoy a successful career spread across two continents, 7 countries, five U.S. states, and 10 leagues.

The first time I met Jay was in Potsdam, NY in August of 2003, my freshman year at Clarkson University. I was accompanying some of my new teammates to a sorority party off-campus and we were walking through the house to the backyard. One of my new teammates was telling me some stories to get me excited for the upcoming season. "Oh man, you're gonna love it here. This is gonna be a fun season man. You have no idea how much fun we're gonna have," he said.

I nodded my head as I walked through the party past beer pong tables, a guy doing a keg stand, two girls making out and a fat guy, passed out on the floor wearing only a pair of tighty-whitey underwear. Everything seemed to be business as usual, as far as college parties go. This wasn't my first rodeo.

As soon as I walked outside and caught a glimpse of the situation, my head began to tilt and my brow began to furrow. The first thing that caught my eye was a 21-year-old man swinging 20 feet above the ground from a willow tree, screaming the lyrics to Styx's "Mr. Roboto" at the top of his lungs. Everyone in the yard was chanting and laughing while looking up at him. All of a sudden, the branch he was swinging from snapped and he came crashing down, landing on his back on a picnic table with a loud thud. Plastics cups full of stale beer went flying everywhere. I thought for sure he was dead. After a moment, he sprang to his feet on top of the picnic table, grabbed a full cup of beer and dumped it on his head. He then reached out his hand to me and said: "What's up rook? I'm Jay Latulippe."

Over the next three years, I had the pleasure of calling Jay my teammate. Whether it was 8:15 p.m. on a Saturday night in the far corner of Cheel Arena or 2:30 a.m. outside of a bar that same night, he was always right by your side, willing to go to bat for you. A perfect blend of skill, fearlessness and a wicked sense of humor, Jay epitomized what being a hockey player was all about.

As mentioned earlier, Jay's career has taken him all over the world. From downtime skiing in the Chamonix Mountains of France to castle-hopping in Sheffield, England, Jay's hockey career has provided him with priceless opportunities and opened the doors to a global network. He represents the spirit of the career minor leaguer. He's living proof that hockey doesn't have to be million-dollar contracts and an all or nothing mentality.

He's proof that the dream doesn't have to die below the NHL level.

When Jay finally does hang up the blades for good, he will do so with a university degree in his back pocket, paid for by hockey, as well as worldly experiences that cannot be bought. This is the reason I chose his picture for the cover of this book. He's an inspiration to the 99.9% of all hockey players who fail to reach the dream of playing in the NHL and to everyone who ever picked up a stick and put on a pair of skates. He has captured the spirit of hockey like no other player I have ever seen.

Some players transform themselves to fit into a specific role or culture. For most players, this is often the case. Jay never had to transform or "work at it." He is the culture. He is the player that everyone hates to play against, but wants on their team. In hockey, these type of characters have an honorable name: "Beauty." And it is these "beauties" that set the game of hockey apart from all of the other major sports.

Jay's Particulars

Birthyear:	1982-03-12	**Birthplace:**	Saratoga, NY, USA
Age:	32	**Nation:**	USA
Position:	LW	**Shoots:**	L
Height:	178 cm / 5'10"	**Weight:**	83 kg / 183 lbs

Jay's Career to Date (Sept. 11, 2014)

Season	Team	League	GP	G	A	PTS	PIM
2000-01	Northwood Prep	USHS	37	28	35	**63**	-
2001-02	Clarkson Univ.	NCAA	33	8	17	**25**	48
2002-03	Clarkson Univ.	NCAA	33	7	4	**11**	68
2003-04	Clarkson Univ.	NCAA	40	14	17	**31**	71
2004-05	Clarkson Univ.	NCAA	39	16	20	**36**	62
	Johnstown Chiefs	ECHL	5	0	1	**1**	2
2005-06	Dayton Bombers	ECHL	52	12	21	**33**	62
	Augusta Lynx	ECHL	12	2	4	**6**	12
2006-07	Elmira Jackals	UHL	2	0	0	**0**	0
	Laredo Bucks	CHL	3	0	2	**2**	4
	Odessa Jackalopes	CHL	51	17	25	**42**	91
2007-08	Odessa Jackalopes	CHL	20	2	2	**4**	20
	Corpus Christi	CHL	45	12	30	**42**	58
2008-09	Cardiff Devils	EIHL	50	26	34	**60**	187
2009-10	Cardiff Devils	EIHL	68	18	50	**68**	130
2010-11	Dundee Stars	EIHL	31	16	21	**37**	89
2011-12	Tilburg Trappers	NL	43	31	65	**96**	145
2012-13	Chamonix	France	26	12	23	**35**	54
2013-14	Kristianstads IK	Div 1	42	14	41	**55**	85
2014-15	Sheffield Steelers	EIHL	1	0	0	**0**	2

Awards/Achievements

- 1999-2000 EJHL Most Valuable Player
- 2004-2005 Bill Harrison, Clarkson MVP Award
- 2006-2007 Odessa Jackalopes (CHL) 7th man award
- 2008-2009 Cardiff Devils Player Of The Year
- 2010-2011 Dundee Stars Website Player Of The Year
- 2011-2012 Netherlands All-Star Game

Junior Hockey

The period in time in every hockey player's life when he becomes a man. Parents say goodbye to their little boy as he learns to survive amid the wolves.

Respect Your Elders

In my third career junior A game, I learned two very valuable lessons. I had just finished a season in junior C where we had to wear full face masks and the stick work was abundant. I was now in Tier II junior A hockey where everyone wore half-visors. Not only was the level of hockey a significant jump, but there was a new set of rules I would have to learn, mostly the hard way.

So here I was in my third game of the season and we were on the road in Cobourg, Ontario. I was standing in front of the net, trying to clear a highly respected 20-year-old out of the way. I was having a tough time with this guy since I was all of 160 pounds at the time, so I decided I'd give him the ol' "Face Wash". At the time, I didn't realize that the face wash, where you take your hand and grab the face of your opponent, was a major show of disrespect, especially coming from a pipsqueak rookie, like me. After I wiped my stinky, sweaty palm in his face, the guy turned around and cross-checked me straight in the face. I dropped like a sack of potatoes.

Lesson No. 1 learned: Respect your elders.

As I lay in a heap in front of our net, a point shot was blocked by our winger and he took off on a breakaway from our blue line all the way in. The referee blew the whistle to the stop the play because we had possession of the puck with an injured player down on the ice. The trainer came out and put a towel on my face and helped me off. As I neared the bench, I could hear our coach Steve Tracze's voice getting louder and louder. He was really letting me have it. He continued to let me have it for the next couple of minutes. Traczer was a great coach and was only 23 years old at the time, which was unheard of for a head coach at the junior A level. He had played in the Ontario Hockey League (OHL) for the Belleville Bulls and had his promising career cut short by a bad shoulder injury. He understood the code and unwritten rules of hockey.

Traczer was pissed at me because I stayed down on the ice when I could have gotten off on my own. By staying down on that play, I potentially cost us the go-ahead goal and ultimately what could have been the game. If I had have gotten up and gone to the bench, we probably would have scored on the breakaway and sealed the win.

Lesson No 2 learned: Don't stay down if you can make it to the bench.

That's what makes hockey players so great. It's their toughness and the respect for the sacred code. For hockey players, you are either injured or you are hurt. If you're hurt, you can still play; if you are injured, you can't. Most ailments for true hockey players fall under the category of hurt. Hockey's the one sport in which you see players playing with separated shoulders, broken ribs, facial fractures, broken hands, broken fingers and knee sprains. There is a lot of honour and respect in hockey. Players are always banged up with the physicality of how the game is played and the frequency of the games.

Have you ever noticed during mid-season in the NHL when a rookie gets called up from the AHL or in the spring when a major junior or college guy makes his debut? They always come in flying and have a lot of success right out of the gate. The reason for this is because they're fresh and healthy. Everyone else is playing hurt. After four or five games, the rookie always cools off because the grind gets to him and now he's banged up in one way or another.

Hockey is most closely comparable to football in its physicality. However, in hockey you play as many as 82 regular season games a year plus playoffs, not 14 to 18 games like they do in the NFL. Often, hockey players are playing back-to-back nights while traipsing all over North America. In my last year in the minors, we played 21 games in the month of March, often travelling up to 14 hours between games.

Super Rookie

In hockey, there are rookies who follow the rules and respect the code and there are rookies who think they are above everything. These are what are called "Super Rookies". In my last year of junior, while playing with the Ottawa Jr. Senators of the Central Junior Hockey League, we had the ultimate super rookie. His daddy was kind of a big deal and the kid was young and didn't really have a good grasp of the code.

All year long we had to hear about how he didn't have to pack the bus and he didn't have to pick up pucks. He would get up before the veterans and get off the bus first, which was considered to be a complete show of disrespect to the elder statesmen of the team. He wouldn't toe the line and wanted to flaunt it in our faces. At the start of the season, we went to Nova Scotia and played two exhibition games. I had just joined the team and was just getting a feel for things. We won our first game against the Antigonish Bulldogs and dropped a close game, 4-2, in Halifax two nights later to the eventual Royal Bank Cup champions, a team we would face three more times that year in playoff action.

One thing I have always hated is losing, especially when you know it was a close one. After the game, we were pretty glum about the loss and a bunch of us got on the bus to sulk in peace. All of a sudden, Super Rookie got on the bus and started goofing around with the microphone. I got up and told him to sit down and shut up. I grabbed the microphone from him and he proceeded to throw a hissy-fit. As I was putting the microphone back on its holder, Super Rookie took a swing at me. In a quick reaction I shoved him and he tripped backwards on the front step of the bus and crashed into the windshield. The windshield cracked from center to edge like a spider web. Immediately, I knew I was in deep.

Super Rookie took off running into the rink, proclaiming that he was going to tell. I went back and sat in my seat. Everyone was dead quiet. Ten minutes later, our coach, Freddie Parker, got on the bus and growled: "Whoever did this just got a one-way ticket out of town." I stood up and said that it was me. Immediately, other players began stepping up and defending me and explaining what had happened.

I thought for sure that I was done. I had just joined that team and didn't really know anyone. To make matters worse, I was playing like shit. Parker pulled me off the bus and took me around back to talk to me. He said: "Jamie, the kid is young and doesn't get it yet, I know this. If I were in your shoes, I probably would have done the same thing. I'm going to have to suspend you for a game. I have to show everyone that we need to tighten things up and I know you understand that."

That meant a lot to me coming from Freddie. A lot of coaches would have used the opportunity to dump an unproductive player. He knew how to best manage tough situations. I always had a lot of respect for him and how he managed the interpersonal side of the game, which is often the most neglected.

Repairs to the windshield cost $2,000, and our owner, the late Art Neilsen paid for it out of his own pocket. He never mentioned it to me and never held it over my head. Art was a passionate hockey man. He spent the better part of his life giving kids like me opportunities to reach their dreams. His generosity was endless. He was a first class guy.

That incident was over, but it wouldn't be the last regarding Super Rookie.

The Best Accidental Prank Ever

During my last season of junior hockey, three of us lived in the basement of our coach's house because we were low on billets that year. We were all in our last year of junior hockey and were prone to getting into mischief. One night, nearly the whole team went out and got into one at a local bar. About five of us came back to the house and ended up passing out on the floor of the basement.

At the time, a few of us were taking part-time courses at the local University while our captain, "Cappy" was working part time for the city hydro company. Cappy had to be to work the next day for a half-day shift from noon to 5 p.m. This is where the story began to get pretty funny. You see, Cappy ended up getting pretty drunk that night and passed out first. While he was passed out, the rest of us thought it would be pretty funny to draw funny and perverted pictures on his face with a marker. This was a pretty common procedure amongst drunk hockey players. It was usually either that or shaving off eyebrows.

We had an alarm clock in the basement at our coach's house that had bright digital numbers on the face. One of the guys on the team had to be up at 10 a.m. and in a drunken stupor, began trying to set the alarm in the dark. Instead of setting the alarm, he accidentally advanced the time by four hours.

The next morning, Cappy woke up and panicked when he saw that the clock read 11:50 a.m., even though it was actually only 7:50 a.m. He had to be to work at noon and jumped up and scrambled out the door.

Cappy drove a Toyota Corolla that was getting a bit long in the tooth. The car had electrical problems, so the digital clock didn't work. He was also missing his rear-view mirror, which had fallen off.

So, in his state of panic, Cappy was out the door and in his car without looking in a mirror. He screeched into work at what he thought was 15 minutes late and in a huff told his boss that he was sorry about being late and that traffic was insane. At this point, his boss looked at him strangely: One, because it was only 8:15 a.m.; and two, because he had pictures of male genitalia drawn all over his face.

Cappy's co-workers were cracking up as his boss told him what the real time was and to go home, shower, get a couple hours of sleep and come back in for his shift at noon. I still remember Cappy coming back home that morning and wrestling with everyone. We all laughed non-stop for hours after that one.

The Curious Case of Peter Kennedy

In my last year of junior, I was fortunate enough to play for a first class organization in the Ottawa Junior Senators. Our owner was Art Neilsen, who was a legend in the Central Junior Hockey League, known for his generosity, kindness and never-ending contributions to junior and youth hockey in eastern Ontario. That year, I had the pleasure of playing with an immensely talented and highly recruited defenceman from Brookfield, N.S. named Peter Kennedy.

"Snake", as we affectionately called him, due to his uncanny resemblance to the like-named character from "Degrassi Junior High", was being recruited by at least 30 Division 1 programs that year, including the University of Minnesota Golden Gophers, the crème-de-la-crème of NCAA hockey.

Snake being on Minnesota's radar was highly unusual and spoke to the prospect and potential of his game. No Canadian had been recruited and played for the Gophers since a young goaltender by the name of Frank Pietrangelo back in 1982. We're talking 20 years between Canadians!

Eventually, Snake said, "Thanks, but no thanks", to a laundry list of D1 programs such as Boston College, Maine and Harvard, and signed a letter of intent at the "U". Minnesota was just coming off an NCAA national championship and was a perennial contender. His roommate for his freshman year was going to be Thomas Vanek. What wasn't there to be excited about?

The problem with going to a program like Minnesota as a true freshman was that you had to compete with guys like Keith Ballard, Paul Martin and Alex Goligoski for ice time. Snake was an offensive-minded defenceman who excelled on the power play. He had to try to steal ice time away from future NHL power play quarterbacks who were two to three years older than he was.

Even though the Golden Gophers repeated as national champions in Snake's first year, he was only able to get into 10 games. The next year, he played in 35 games and looked as though he was going to start reaching his potential. In his junior year, he suffered a serious hip injury that required surgery and lost nearly a whole season. By his senior year, he was still hampered by the injury and was limited to just seven games.

After Snake's freshman year, we attended a summer development camp for defensemen run by former NHL standout defensemen and Bowling Green teammates Gary Galley and Dave Ellett. At the camp were NCAA and OHL kids, with some already-drafted NHL prospects such as Marc Methot, Kyle Wharton, Grant Clitsome and Mitch Maunu. Even with the talent being what it was that week, everybody was in awe of Snake. He was just that much better than everyone.

I remember Methot being ultra-competitive and being irked at the fact that everyone was marveling over Snake. Here was Methot, who had just been drafted by the Columbus Blue Jackets, on his way to winning a Memorial Cup with the powerhouse London Knights and he was playing second fiddle to Snake.

After college, Snake played a few years of pro hockey in the Central Hockey League but never really reached the potential that everyone thought he could. In sports, it's all about situation and timing. Had Snake chosen Harvard and gone on to play more minutes and develop, we may very well have been watching him in the NHL. It's hard to say with any certainty, and hindsight is always 20-20, but sometimes when choosing the path you want to take, you need to put a lot of consideration into which one will be most suitable to harvest your talent and help you reach your potential.

The fact is, there is no way to predict the future in hockey. Between injuries, situational setbacks and coaching changes, players can peak or dive at any given time. Like anything in life, hockey is all about timing, opportunity, and a little bit of luck.

College Hockey

You're no longer playing simply for the love of the game. It is the first time you are essentially owned and owe a debt of servitude. Start to perform or someone else will.

Where Did They Find This Guy?

My proudest moment in hockey was accepting a full scholarship to Clarkson University and signing my letter of intent. I had dreamed my whole life about playing in the NCAA, ever since hearing stories of my cousin, Kevin Scott, who played on a full-ride at Western Michigan. I couldn't wait to get down there and start the season. I was almost afraid they'd change their mind.

As a player, I was always picky about my gear. I hated new gear. I wore my skates until they literally fell off my feet. I wore the same elbow pads from major peewee all the way to the end of my pro days. I liked small shoulder pads, low-cut gloves and smaller shin pads. Skating was my strength and I didn't want anything to slow me down.

When I showed up on campus for my first captain's practice I still remember the look on everyone's faces when I walked in carrying my dad's old "OV Hockey" bag. They were looking at me cockeyed as if to say, "Is this a joke?" I looked like I just got off the ice from a beer-league game and walked into the wrong dressing room.

My good friend Mac Faulkner always laughs when he recounts first meeting me. He says: "I remember when you walked in with that old beer league hockey bag with the broken zipper. You had these old work-boot skates with torn eyelets, cracked shin pads, tiny shoulder pads, a cage from the 1980s, and the old-school Gretzky aluminum sticks. I couldn't stop laughing. I turned to the guys and said, 'Look at this fuckin' guy.' It was priceless!"

After the first few practices, Coach must have gotten some comments about me because he walked right up to my stall with a new pair of shoulder pads and shin pads in his hands and said, "You're wearing these from now on."

Pretty soon the season began and I started using one-piece sticks and brand new gear. I looked like everyone else, except for that 1980s cage. I wouldn't give that baby up. It was a classic and I loved the way it felt. The boys used to call it "The Todder", because they figured it was still around the equipment room from the days when former NHLer Todd White graced the Clarkson green and gold.

Perfect Place to Run Out of Gas

During my freshman year we were on a road trip to play Colgate and Cornell. It was a grey, rainy weekend and our play was as equally sloppy as the weather. We gave up the lead in both games and lost on terrible mistakes, the types of blunders that make coaches pull their hair out.

After the Saturday night game at Colgate, our coach really tore a strip off us. No one was looking forward to the four-hour trip back to school or the guaranteed bag-skate on Monday.

About two hours outside of Hamilton, N.Y., the bus was deathly silent. There were nothing but blank looks outside of a window on a desolate stretch of dark highway. All of a sudden, the bus shuddered to a halt. If you could believe it, we were out of gas! There we were, at the end of a horrific road trip where we dropped two crucial games to conference rivals and our bus driver forgot to fill up the tank for the trip home. Needless to say, our coaches, who were already on edge, were not too pleased with Bussy.

The funny thing about it all was the fact that we had run out of gas in the middle of a one-street village that had about six places of business, only one of which was open at 12:30 a.m. The gas station was closed. The grocery store was closed. The bank, hair salon and thrift store were all shut up tight. The only place of business with a light on was the local tavern. In our dejected state, this place looked like an oasis in the middle of the desert.

Coach turned to the rest of the bus and said, "Everyone sit tight," and then disappeared into the bar. He emerged about three minutes later and told us we could go into the bar and have one beer but not to have more than that.

We couldn't believe it! I don't think I've ever moved faster in my life, trying to belly up to that bar. It was as if they opened the chute gates to the trough on the pig farm.

It turned out that Coach went into the bar to ask who owned the gas station and they had to call the guy and wake him up at home. It was probably going to be anywhere from a half-hour to an hour before this poor old guy could get here to open up the gas station so we could fill up and hit the road again. The tavern was a tiny hole in the wall, but it may as well have been Studio 54 that night. We were so happy to have something to laugh about rather than sit staring out a bus window.

We all broke the one-beer maximum limit that Coach had set, but he didn't seem to care. I think he took one look at us and saw how much fun we were having and how close-knit we were and realized that maybe this was the turning point we needed.

When we boarded the bus that night, we were refueled, both literally and figuratively. Everyone had a smile on their face. Sometimes teams need a strange turn of events in order to break out of a slump. Our bus running out of gas outside of a bar in the middle of nowhere was a saving grace for us that season. I'm not entirely sure if our record improved dramatically after that road trip, but I do know we went on quite a successful run that year in the playoffs, enjoying vengeance against both Cornell and Colgate when it counted most. I still remain close with a lot of the guys I played with at Clarkson and we still love to reminisce about that night.

Game-Plan Glitch

Hockey has evolved in every way imaginable over the years. One major evolutionary aspect is the influx of technology into the game. Coaching staffs spend hours upon hours analyzing and breaking down video of both their opponents and their own team to hone system play and correct mistakes. Most teams at higher levels even staff a full-time video coach due to the large body of work that is required in this field.

When I was playing in the NCAA, we had a student video coach who assisted the coaching staff using the

"Steva" video breakdown system. Each week, the coaching staff would analyze the teams we were going to face during the coming weekend. Teams were mandated to share video with their opponents, turning over their previous week's games to allow for fair system preparation. The staff would break-down the video and dissect everything from power-play breakouts to controlled fore-checks in order to prepare and tweak our systems. It was all very scientific and was quite similar to how football teams prepare week to week.

One week, we were getting ready to host Yale and Princeton and the coaches had us prepping all week for the Yale game. We never had much trouble with Princeton, so the main focus was to shut down Yale. All week we were studying their breakouts and power-play setups. We watched video of how they would try to attack us in all situations and then spend our practices working on how to conquer their systems. We're talking about hours and hours of hard work and preparation. We were ready for them!

So, Friday comes along and it's 5:30 p.m., the time we always had our pre-game video session for one last run-through. We're doing an overview of their systems one last time with the video we have been watching all week, when all of a sudden one of our guys blurts out: "Hey, which team is Yale on the video again?"

Everyone looked at him like he is from Mars. I can distinctly remember flinching and thinking, "Oh shit, he's done. The first pre-game scratch I've ever seen is coming up." Coach just looked up with an annoyed look and said, "Blue, you dummy!"

Then the player said, "I'm pretty sure that's UConn, Coach." Coach started to snap back with, "No, you idiot, UConn is in the wh---," and then paused as he looked more carefully at the monitor. The player was right!

The video was always a bit grainy and nobody thought to look closely before. All week we were prepping for what we all thought were Yale's systems when in fact they were UConn's!

To this day, I'll never forget the reaction from Coach once he realized we'd just prepped all week for the wrong team. He stood up, turned to us, threw his clipboard in the air and said: "Alright boys. Forget about systems tonight. Let's just make sure we score more goals than them."

It was priceless! We were all in stitches.

The Lynah Faithful

Cornell University has a rich tradition in hockey. Hockey legend and big-bodied goaltending pioneer Ken Dryden donned the pads for the Big Red. Later, multiple Stanley Cup-winner Joe Nieuwendyk would sport the classic red and white. Lynah Rink, home of the Big Red, is as legendary as the success of its program. It seats 4,267 and the Cornell crowds are some of the rowdiest in all of college hockey. During a Cornell home game, the fans stand the entire game and participate in chants led by the famous Big Red student band.

The first time I experienced Lynah Rink in all its glory was in my freshman year at Clarkson. The Big Red was ranked No. 4 in the nation that season and had a big, strong and highly skilled team. That 2003-04 Cornell team featured future NHLers Matt Moulson, Ryan O'Byrne, Mike Iggulden, Byron Bitz and Ryan Vesce, and many other players who would go on to successful pro careers in Europe and the minors. It was intimidating enough just looking at the lineup sheet.

The veteran players had already warned me about what it was like playing at Lynah. The atmosphere was electric. I was ready for a crowd that would tear the roof off that place when I hit the ice. So, it was a major surprise to me that when we hit the ice prior to the start of the game, it was deathly silent.

We emerged from the dressing room onto the ice and all you could see and hear were thousands of ruffling newspapers. The entire crowd was holding up newspapers in front of their faces as we took to the ice as if to say we weren't worth looking at. As soon as the Big Red hit the ice after us, the entire crowd erupted, crumpled up the newspapers into balls and threw them at us as we skated around. It was hilarious!

It took rink workers five minutes to clear all the newspapers off the ice before the national anthem could be started. I had never seen anything like it. It is a great tradition that has been carried on since the early years of the program.

I think we ended up losing that game 5 – 0. However, we got the last laugh that season. We went into Lynah as major underdogs and ousted the highly ranked Big Red in a best-of-three playoff thriller.

Your Friendly Neighborhood Appleby's

At the end of my freshman year, we ran into the Cornell Big Red who were ranked No. 4 in the country. Big Red was an understatement. Other than a couple of players, the entire team was over six-foot-three and 200 pounds. Overall, they had 11 NHL draft picks in their lineup and a finalist for the Hobey Baker Award in nets in David McKee. Going into this series, we were David and they were certainly Goliath.

During the regular season, we faced them twice and never came close, losing both games in embarrassing fashion. In Game 1 of the best of three series, we were steamrolled 5-0. I can remember after the game, we were all on the phone trying to figure out where we were going for spring break the next week.

Saturday night, we came out and played our hearts out. We were rewarded with a hard fought, physical 5 – 4 victory. All of a sudden, we were in a dogfight. We could actually win this!

The play on the ice in the first two games was fast-paced and mean. It was clear we hated them and they hated us. Guys were chirping each other and the hits were hard and often. Guys weren't just separating the man from the puck; we were all trying to separate heads from bodies. The refs basically sat back and let us decide it for ourselves. I remember it was like we were teleported back to the late '70s, early '80s with all the clutching and grabbing. It was a fun series!

After the Saturday night game, my roommate and I decided to go grab dinner at the nearby Appleby's. What better place to unwind and relax, right?

Wrong.

Shortly after we sat down, Cam Abbott and Chris Abbott, twin forwards from Cornell, and what seemed like their entire extended family entered the restaurant and sat down at a nearby table. They were glaring at us as they walked in and we were glaring right back.

My roommate that year was Matt Nickerson, who was public enemy No. 1 wherever we played. He was six-foot-five and 265 pounds and was a third-round NHL draft pick of the Dallas Stars. He was tough and he could play. He skated really well for a big guy and had unbelievable hands.

That season, Big Nicks set an NCAA record for most penalty minutes in a season. He loved to play hard and fans loved to razz him wherever we went. That series against Cornell, the fans at Lynah made signs reading "Nickerson Eats Babies" and some other things I don't want to repeat, even in a book revealing pretty much everything! There were insults and slurs hurled at him that would make Harvey Keitel cringe. They harassed him to no end. During warm ups in the playoffs, one nutty fan even tried to throw a puck at his head.

So back to Appleby's.

Here we were trying to unwind, and the whole time we were sitting at our table, these Abbotts were shooting us looks. Knowing Nicks could get pretty riled up, I decided nothing good could come of this, so I said, "Let's get out of here, pal." We settled our bill and headed to the exit. As we passed by the Abbott table, one of the twins muttered something at Big Nicks. The next thing you know, I was tripping over Grandma Abbott to try to pry Big Nicks' bear hands from around one of the twins' necks. Poor Grandma was sprawled out on one side of the booth and I think the dad was pulling at my neck. Eventually, I was able to get Big Nicks to cool down and we headed back to the hotel.

The next day, we went out and spanked the Big Red 5-1 and eventually advanced all the way to the ECAC finals. What an experience it was to walk into that legendary rink against such a heralded team and upset them on their own ice. I've never seen that place as silent as it was that Sunday afternoon.

At the end of the game, as we celebrated, the loyal Big Red fans kindly reminded us that we "still sucked" and that "we don't care, that's OK, we're still Ivy anyway".

Cornell Fans Sign Trickery

The next season, we went into play Cornell again in the playoffs. The Big Red wanted vengeance for what we did the year before in the playoffs, knocking them off when we had no business being on the ice with them. They were strong again, returning all of their big guns and hungry for revenge.

This was around the time when Facebook was in its early years of existence and was only available to U.S. colleges and universities. Before the series began, one of the Cornell fans thought they would be clever and created a fake Facebook account, posing as a cute blonde girl who supposedly attended Cornell. This fake girl requested several of our players who had Facebook accounts to add her as a friend in order to gain access to photo albums.

Once they were added and access to the accounts

and photo albums were granted, the Cornell fans got creative. They were able to find some photographs that were posted on one of our players' accounts and created a poster the size of a standard door. The poster had a picture of my good friend Nathan Beausoleil, freshman forward Matt Isbister and me.

We had been goofing around in the trainer's room one day after practice and we tried to see if we could all fit into a cold tub at once. One of the guys took a picture and posted it on his Facebook page. We never thought much of it. We were always goofing around at the rink after practices and people were always taking pictures.

Now, several months later, while standing along the boards during warmup, I hear banging on the glass. When I turned my head I saw a massive poster of Nate, Matt and me, all sitting in a cold tub with the words "Plays Well With Others" plastered across the top.

That one provided fodder for a lot of ribbing from the boys for quite some time. I have to admit though, it was pretty clever and they obviously put a lot of planning and hard work into it.

Momentum Shift

Hockey, like almost all sports, is all about momentum. The team or individual that has the most momentum in a game tends to have the most success. In hockey, momentum builds and shifts in many different ways. Coaches try to do their best to maintain momentum or shift it, depending on the situation of the game, using strategies and line combinations.

For example, if the other team scores two quick goals and secures definitive momentum, a coach may send out his fourth line to try to stir things up and get the momentum back with a big hit or a fight. This is why every player on a hockey team is valuable, no matter how much they play or what type of role they have. Grinders and muckers are just as important in hockey as scorers.

One time during my freshmen year we were playing at Cornell, where we always had heated and physical affairs, and I was going back hard for a puck with a man bearing down on me. Greg Hornby was a grinder with Cornell and was built like a brick shithouse. Hornby was five-foot-eleven and weighed a solid 220 pounds. He resembled a running back on skates and loved to hit and get the Lynah crowd going. He used to creep in on the fore-check, down the weak-side wall and prey on unsuspecting defensemen as they circled the net on the breakout.

So, I was going back hard and had a step on the fore-checker chasing me. I gained the net and quickly saw Hornby salivating as he was charging toward me looking for the big hit. I shifted at the last second and snapped a tape-to-tape pass across the ice to the far wall for a crisp breakout. I had trapped all their fore-checkers on the strong side by passing across to the weak side.

A moment after I completed the pass, Hornby absolutely annihilated me. It sounded like two cars colliding in a head-on collision. I remember the ringing in my ears as if it was yesterday, like I was a tuning fork vibrating after being struck. I popped up and skated to the bench trying not to look like it hurt at all. I even smiled at the Cornell bench as they hurled chirps at me as I skated by.

When I got to the bench, I felt pretty good about making that great pass and taking a big hit to make the play, but I could tell from the glare from our captain and not receiving a pat from our coach that not everyone was as thrilled as I was. After the hit, the Cornell crowd went bonkers and began a chant that lasted five whole minutes. They were stomping their feet and screaming in unison, "Hornby! Hornby! Hornby!" It was deafening.

It was then that I realized what I had done. I had put myself in a bad situation and allowed Greg Hornby to do what he does best. His big hit had jump-started the Cornell crowd and created a huge buzz that lit a fire under the Cornell bench. For the next five minutes, we couldn't get out of our zone. I hadn't just taken a hit to make a great play; I had given them momentum, which is an invaluable commodity. Hockey is a game of momentum. Momentum breeds victory.

Mascot Down

Mascots have been a part of sports for decades. At baseball games, they provide endless entertainment for young fans during the many breaks and lulls in the game. In hockey, you really don't see much from mascots except for at the NCAA and minor pro levels.

When I was at Clarkson University, we were the Golden Knights, so we had a mascot who was a knight decked out in golden armour, wielding a stick. He skated around before the game as we came out to take to the ice. Each year, they would hold tryouts for the mascot position, which usually ended up being someone from the student body.

In my freshman year, we had this really energetic mascot. The first game of the season, he came tearing out of the tunnel and onto the ice and was really giving it his all. We took the ice after him and began a leisurely warm up skate just prior to the start of the second period.

I remember circling in our own end when all of a

sudden the mascot went flying by me and slammed into the end boards right in front of the student section. There was a 15-minute delay because they had to get the stretcher to get this guy off the ice. Turns out that the mascot separated his shoulder and broke his arm and jaw. And you think it's just hockey players who are tough. Our mascots are just as tough!

Ticket Gate Campout

Rivalries in sports are the greatest thing going. In the NHL, there are some great rivalries, such as the classic Boston Bruins and Montreal Canadiens rivalry, or the battle of Alberta with the Calgary Flames and Edmonton Oilers. In the NCAA, every team has a "travel partner", which is another in-conference university that is your closest opponent and usually doubles as your rival. Travel partners hit the road in tandems and play another set of travel partners on Fridays and Saturdays.

When I was at Clarkson, our travel partner was St. Lawrence University (SLU). When we hit the road to play the University of Vermont and Dartmouth University, who were also travel partners, we played Vermont on Friday night and SLU would play Dartmouth. Then on Saturday we flip flopped.

Our rivalry with SLU was intense. Our campuses were just 10 minutes apart, with us in Potsdam, N.Y., and SLU in Canton, N.Y. When we played SLU at home, the attendance for the game was dangerously beyond fire code. If you didn't have a ticket months in advance, you weren't getting in. The rule with the student section was that you could get in for free with your student card but it was first come, first served. Therefore, you had to get there early if you wanted to secure yourself a ticket for the game.

On game days, we had a morning skate at 11 a.m., so we were at the rink around 10 a.m. When we cruised through the concourse at 10, we were stepping over masses of students who were camped out with sleeping bags, blankets, board games and books. The gates opened up for the game at 6:30 p.m., so the students would camp out front early in the morning to make sure they could get the seat they wanted for the game that night, which started at 7:30 p.m. It was wild.

We were always excited for those games because you knew you were going to be playing in front of a plus-capacity crowd. We set a record one year with 4,127 fans which was pretty damn good for a rink that holds 3,300. The atmosphere was electric for those rivalry games.

Clarkson vs. SLU Rivalry

The rivalry between Clarkson University and St. Lawrence University is deep-seeded and traditional. The fans really got into it when we played each other. When we made the 10 minute trek down the road to play SLU, we pulled into the back (players) entrance about two hours before puck drop. When we arrived, there was always a rowdy group of SLU fans waiting for our bus to pull in so they could hurl insults and sometimes objects at us as we exited the bus.

The fans all wore white shirts with the inscription "Cluck Farkson" on the front. Their rink, Appleton Arena, was a classic old barn with wooden rafters and the crowd felt like it was right on top of you. Playing at

SLU was like playing in a shoebox with nowhere to go.

Our goalies despised playing there because it was so dark and it was hard to pick up high shots and dump-ins. If you look back over the years, not too many SLU goalies went on to play in the NHL. It was a goalie's nightmare to play in that rink.

One thing about playing in the midst of heated rivalries was that you really came to hate your opponents. When I was at Clarkson and we played against SLU, I can remember hating every one of them.

After university, I went on to play against a bunch of SLU guys in the minors and I still hated them. That rivalry gets engrained deep in your soul and you just put everything into wanting to win.

UNH Student Stampede

One of the nicest places to play in college hockey was the Whittemore Center Arena at the University of New Hampshire (UNH). The Whittemore Center has the largest ice surface in college hockey, 200 x 100 feet. Regulation rinks are 200 x 85, so there was a lot of extra room to maneuver out there. UNH used this to their advantage when recruiting and always had some speedsters who would run wild on the pond-sized sheet. Whittemore Center held about 6,500 and pretty much packed it out for every home game.

One season, we went in there to play a weekend set and I can remember sitting up in the stands before the Friday night game, taping my sticks and looking over the crisp, cool ice. I used to love to sit in the stands before games when they hadn't turned up the lights yet and look out over the rink. There is a misty haze that sits over the ice and a unique smell in the air. It's magical. I didn't have a lot of superstitions or routines before games and I always hated being there so early. I usually would just go and sit in the stands before to relax and think about the game.

All of a sudden, the gates from the lobby opened and about 1,000 stampeding UNH students came charging into the rink. The student section was at one end of the rink, right behind where the opposing team's net was for the first and third periods. This way, the fans could heckle the opposing goalie for two periods of the game.

The fans were screaming and trampling each other in order to get the seats they wanted. The students got in for free, so there wasn't assigned seating for them. It was first come, first served, so you had to scratch and claw once the gates opened up to the public. Watching those fans sprinting down the stairs in the aisles and hurdling over seats in the stands was like watching the running of the bulls in Pamplona.

Banned From the Providence Mall

During my freshman season, we played in the Providence College Christmas Tournament in Providence, R.I. on Dec. 27 and 28. We played against St. Cloud and Harvard that weekend and ended up splitting with a win Saturday night. Since we beat Harvard on the Saturday night, Coach let us go out and blow off a little steam. Any time you're on the road and the coach gives you the green light, it's like telling a kid it's Christmas.

We were staying in the Westin Hotel, which was attached to the Providence Mall, so we decided to stay local and hit up the Dave and Busters, located at the other end of the mall. Dave and Busters is like a Chuck E. Cheese for adults. In order to get to the D&Bs, we had to walk through the mall, where all the stores were gated up for the night. We had a good group of guys and everything was going great.

Once half of us were in, we got a call from a player who forgot his ID. He looked similar enough to me, so one of the guys distracted the doorman and I slipped him my ID from inside. He successfully used my ID to get in and the crisis was averted. I didn't grab the ID from him right away because he had to wait in line for a few minutes before he could get in.

We ended up having a pretty good night and tipped back quite a few wobbly pops. At about 12:30 a.m., a group of us decided to head over to another bar while a large portion stayed behind at Dave and Busters, including the team mate using my ID.

This is where things got interesting.

Later on, we all met up at the hotel in a room and recounted stories from the night. The group that stayed behind at Dave and Busters ended up having some trouble with mall security on their way back to the hotel. The guy who borrowed my ID had to take a leak in the middle of the long walk through the mall back to the hotel. All the bathrooms were locked, so he decided to take a leak in a nearby plant.

Just as he was in mid-stream a security guard approached him and demanded to see some ID. For fear of being arrested, and because he was too drunk to run away, the guy reached into his wallet and handed the security guard my ID! The security guard went to his office and made photocopies of my ID. The picture of my ID ended up making the "Banned Patrons" book, listing the people who are never to set foot in the Providence Mall again.

The Invention of Beer Darts

During my senior year at Clarkson University, I was introduced to a wonderful game called "Beer Darts" by a fun group Potsdam State University hockey players. We were all hanging around together after both our seasons had ended and one of the Potsdam players invited us over to play a drinking game they had recently discovered. One of the players, who was from British Columbia, had come across the game during a ferry ride from Vancouver Island to the mainland.

Beer darts is a game that at first glance seems like a dangerous mixture of sharp objects and alcohol, but is really a lot of fun. Here's how it's played: Four people play, two versus two, with teammates sitting beside each other, facing their opponents, who sit at a distance of 10 feet away. Between the teammates' chairs sits a cooler full of beer at each end. In front of the cooler, on the ground, sits a full, unopened beer can that has been shaken up to increase the pressure of the can.

The object of beer darts is that you have to throw a dart at the pressurized beer can to score points. If the can is punctured on the side, the opposing player at the end containing the can must grab the can quickly and drink half of the beer and then pass it to his teammate who drinks the other half. One point is awarded for a "Side-Shot". If the dart punctures the top of the can, the opposing player must drink the entire beer while his teammate grabs another full beer from the cooler and drinks it in its entirety. A "Top-Shot" or "Topper" is worth three points.

Each game of beer darts is played until one team reaches five points. Once a team reaches five points, the opposition is given a final set of rebuttal shots in order to try to extend the game. On every turn, both teammates throw a dart, to equal two shots per end. A specific rule states that while throwing a dart, your back must remain flat against the back of the chair. Absolutely no leaning is allowed. If a player is caught leaning, their shot is voided and they lose their attempt.

Points are only awarded if the can is punctured. If a dart grazes a can and does not puncture it, no points are awarded. A team can call for a "Shake" if they believe that a can was slightly punctured by a grazed dart. A "Shake" consists of the can being shaken up and closely listened to in order to determine if there is a hissing sound, in which points would be awarded. If a "Shake" is called for following an attempt and it is determined that there is no puncture, the team that called for the "Shake" must split a full beer as penalty for a failed challenge.

Before a new beer is introduced into the game, it must be thrown "Around the Horn." Around the horn consists of shaking the beer and tossing it around so that each player touches the can. This pressurizes the can and readies it for entry into the game. Once the can is juiced, you are ready to let loose.

The season that we got hooked on beer darts was in the spring of my senior year at Clarkson. We played for the first time with the boys from Potsdam State and had a blast on a hot, sunny Saturday. We had decided that beer darts was our new favorite drinking game and that we were going to play every chance we got. So the next weekend, we were all geeked up about playing beer darts when bad news struck in the form of rain. We were so excited about playing that we weren't going to let anything get in the way of our fun, so I came up with the ridiculous idea of playing in the living room of my on-campus townhouse.

My townhouse, which I shared with two other teammates, was a decent apartment with a nice spacious living room. I figured, why not just move the game inside, we had plenty of room. It started off great, but it didn't take long for the carpet in our living room to become soaked through to the concrete. The next morning when I woke up with the usual Sunday morning booze blues and slunk downstairs, I was met with a nice soggy stroll across the living room to my Cheerios in the kitchen.

That carpet took 10 days to fully dry out and had a nice stale beer smell that I bet would have lingered for years. I was told that at the end of the year, the university had to cut up the carpet and put a new one down.

Classy tenants we were.

The Chicken Man

There was a tradition that was set at Clarkson University many years ago by the men's hockey team that stated that one or more players must perform the "Chicken Man" at every party attended by the team throughout the year. No one quite knows when the tradition was created, but it was rumored to be an ages-old ritual.

We had heard at alumni events legendary Chicken Man stories dating back into the 1970s, so we knew it was legit.

The Chicken Man consisted of a hockey player stripping down naked in a bathroom at a party and covering himself from head to toe in shaving cream. Once he was caked with shaving cream, the player would exit the bathroom and run wild through the party, tackling girls as he went along.

After running amok for a period of time and creating pandemonium, the Chicken Man would slip back into the bathroom, shower up and emerge back into the party as if nothing had ever happened. The ideal Chicken Man would perform the prank without anyone really knowing who was caked in the shaving cream. This was a tough feat to pull off because once you tackled a couple of girls, the shaving cream would smear off and identities were often exposed.

The most paramount Chicken Man prank of all time was rumored to be performed by an unmentionable former Clarkson Hockey great who went on to a successful NHL career. This unnamed legend allegedly caked himself in shaving cream and stormed the school library during exam time and escaped undetected and without repercussion or punishment. The library at exam time is like a can of sardines. Everyone and their dog are trying to cram to make the grade. To pull off a successful Chicken Man in a place like this was epic.

We often spoke of this rumored event in awe and stated that one day one of us would repeat that performance and honor our past Clarkson Hockey greats. On the night of my last exam at school, we celebrated at a local on-campus pub, with a few merry beverages and set out to return to our campus homes.

On the way home, with a little courage in my belly, I decided I was going to replicate the legendary Library Chicken Man. The only problem was that we didn't have a can of shaving cream on us and I was hell-bent to do it right away. So without a moment's hesitation, I debriefed and wrapped my T-shirt around my head and tore off into the library where I ran laps of the crowded, two-tiered building. After causing quite a commotion, I exited the library and tore off into the woods to avoid campus security whom had assuredly been called.

Ten minutes later, I returned to our apartment wearing my T-shirt as a pair of shorts to some hoots, hollers and high-fives. I had pulled it off. It may not have been as legendary as the famous Library Chicken Man, but it was as close as it gets.

The ECAC All-Ugly Team

Each season in college hockey just before the start of the season, each team publishes their team rosters and player profiles on their respective team websites. This was a fun time of year because we'd all race to jump on our team website and then laugh hysterically at everyone's profile pictures. We'd debate over who was the ugliest player on our team and carve and ridicule them endlessly. It seems awful and mean, but that's how we always were with one another. It was part of the hockey culture. If you weren't being chirped and carved up, that meant you weren't as likable as a teammate and weren't one of the guys.

One year, we decided to scour the other teams' websites in the ECAC and come up with "The ECAC All-Ugly Team". This was a blast. We'd huddle around a computer with a few beers and howl at how ugly some of the guys were on the opposing teams. I can remember we would always put more St. Lawrence University guys on the ECAC All-Ugly Team, due solely to the fact that we were our heated rivals.

Once the team of hideous hockey players was assembled, we'd print it out and post it in our dressing room. Since the hockey world was so small and everyone had buddies on other teams in our conference, we began to email the list, complete with pictures and nicknames, to members of all of the other ECAC teams.

It was great for rivalries as well. Most of the guys laughed it off or took it in stride, but some of the other players on other teams got really angry over it. I can remember playing against teams throughout the year and partaking in the usual in-game chirping and then tossing out a chirp about the other guy being an "ECAC All-Ugly First-Teamer" and then watch as he boiled over. If anything, it ended up making the mind games that exist on the ice all the more entertaining.

The Walk-On Massacre of 2003

During my freshman year at Clarkson, we had a new set of coaches. After Mark Morris was involved in a player-hitting scandal, the university dismissed him and replaced him with his assistant coach at the time, Fred Parker. Freddie was my old coach from my junior hockey days in Ottawa and was a first rate guy. At the end of the season, the university decided to cut ties with the scandal in its entirety and elected to hire a fresh, new coaching staff that all had previous ties to Clarkson.

The new head coach was George Roll, who had just led Oswego State University to a national championship appearance at the Division III level and was a former assistant coach at Clarkson. Roll brought on board Greg Drechsel, who was also a former Clarkson assistant coach and had dipped his foot in the NHL pool over the past four years as a scout. To round out the staff, Roll hired a former Clarkson fan favorite in J.F. Houle, who had recently finished his pro playing career.

All in all, it was a well-rounded staff, but I couldn't help but feel bad for my old bench boss, Freddie Parker. Luckily, Freddie landed on his feet, serving as assistant coach to Peter Deboer with the powerhouse Kitchener Rangers of the OHL. Freddie later went on to become a scout with the Calgary Flames of the NHL.

Any time you make a coaching change at the NCAA level, it comes with a great deal of stress and unease for the players. Changes are certain with regards to team culture, team strategies and sometimes in player personnel. The problem is, not every coach builds a team in the same fashion. When recruiting players, one coach may see an invaluable piece to a future national championship team, while a different coach may see a dime-a-dozen player. So, every time a new coach takes over a team, it's like open tryouts all over again. All the players are on edge. They are all thinking: "Is he going to like the way I play? Is he going to cut back my ice time and play some freshman that he brought in over me?" It's a very stressful time.

It's no picnic for the new coaches, either. They know the players are leery and on edge and they have to try to figure out the best way to right the ship. They also have to spend three years with players on a team that they haven't entirely built themselves.

In my first year at Clarkson, I was one of a handful of freshmen who were recruited by the new staff. In those first couple of months you could cut the tension around the rink with a knife. The veteran players were all wondering what type of team we were going to have and how the new coaches were going to go about business. One of the first orders of business, one that didn't sit too well with the vets, was having "open tryouts" to begin the year.

In the NCAA, usually every team member is recruited by the coaching staff. The term "walk-on" is predominantly used to describe a player who is recruited by the coaches to play but is paying their own way and not on an athletic scholarship. A "true walk-on" is a player who just shows up out of the blue and wows a coaching staff into giving them a roster spot. This doesn't happen very often. Most teams will allow regular students who weren't recruited to try out for the team, but will hold a separate practice exclusively for the true walk-ons. This is beneficial to minimize the risk of injuring an existing team member.

In my freshman year, the new coaching staff held an open tryout where all the current team members and recruited freshmen players battled it out alongside true walk-ons. Some of these guys had clearly not played organized hockey, or if they had, it amounted to something along the lines of house league or just above. We're talking about players who were using their stick more for balance than for shooting or passing. All the while, the veterans are grumbling furiously about the whole situation. I can remember one of the guys saying: "All we need is for one of these guys who can barely skate to fall into somebody's knee and end their season." He had a valid point.

It eventually got to the point when we decided to take matters into our own hands and show the coaches that we didn't like the idea of the open tryouts. I can vividly remember one of our bigger guys absolutely annihilating these teetering true walk-ons. This player was a big dude, too, at 6-5, 235. When he would build up some speed and label a guy, it was like watching a piñata explode at a kids birthday party.

After the first day, we didn't see many of the true walk-ons come back. I think most of them realized they were way out of their league, but there were definitely a lot of kids who were flat out scared for their life or were too banged up to return. I can still remember walking past the trainer's room after practice. It looked like a triage tent in a war zone with all the kids getting iced and bandaged up. I can tell you one thing, those kids all walked out of there with a bit more respect for what hockey players go through on a daily basis.

How I Became the Team Barber

Potsdam, N.Y., is a pretty small town. In fact, the sign just as you enter reads: "The Village of Potsdam," so, it's really not even big enough to register as a town. During the summer, Potsdam has a population around 16,000, but, during the school year, that number nearly doubles with two universities lining the town on either side of the Raquette River. Needless to say, it's not quite a metropolis. With a handful of shops and restaurants, it's a nice quiet little place to live.

When I was a student at Clarkson University, there were roughly two places for a guy to get his hair cut, but only one sticks out in my mind. It was called "The Beach" and doubled as a tanning salon. The one thing The Beach had going for it was that there were three good looking blondes who cut hair there. The downside was that these blondes, strategically hired no doubt, were absolutely atrocious at cutting hair.

Even though these blondes were butchers, it never stopped the boys from lining up week after week to get their hair lopped off at the hands of the bodacious barbers. The haircuts were so bad that immediately after getting one, we'd have to run into the local old boys-style barber to get the hack job corrected.

Eventually, the costs of two haircuts began to add up. We had to come up with a better solution. Around this time, I decided that I'd help the boys out and try my hand at cutting hair. How hard could it be? I mean, I was pretty good at drawing. So began my days as the team barber.

My first few haircuts were nothing to write home about, but eventually I got pretty handy with the shears. It wasn't long before all the boys were coming to me after getting butchered at The Beach. For a long period, I actually began cutting my own hair with the help of a second mirror. It even carried on into my pro days when I was lowering the ears of my teammates on a regular basis.

Deputy Dummies

In my college days, we executed a lot of crazy pranks and stunts that, looking back, I can't believe we got away with. One season, one of our players secured a volunteer firefighter's roof light and we decided to use it in our newest prank. The new prank consisted of pulling people over on campus using the new toy and pretending to be Campus Safety Officers, which was easily a criminal offence.

The volunteer firefighter lights we had back home in Ontario were always green, but for some reason this light was a blue one. I'm not quite sure what state uses blue lights for volunteer firemen, but it couldn't have worked out better for the execution of our prank.

One night, probably a Wednesday because it was the first night of the week we were prohibited by the 48-hour rule from dipping into the booze, we decided we would drive around campus and pull people over using our new blue light. One of the guys dressed up in an old Halloween cop uniform and approached the car with a flashlight shining on the driver. He began to go through a routine, asking for their driver's license and registration with the rest of us laughing hysterically in the backseat of the "cop" car parked in rear. We would always let the panicked student go with a stern warning.

I can remember we only ran this prank once because we found out that if we had been caught, the consequences would have been pretty severe. I still don't know how we got away with it and how our coaches never found out. Maybe they did and just didn't want to accept that they had recruited a bunch of criminal meatheads.

Boredom breeds stupidity and stupidity comes with an eager entourage.

Airport Follies in Minnesota

At the start of my freshman year at Clarkson, we kicked off our season with two games in Bemidji, Minn. For us at Clarkson University, being a school located in northern New York, this was going to be quite a journey.

We started our travels packing our gear and bussing from Potsdam, N.Y., to Syracuse to board the first of three flights we would take that day. From Syracuse we would fly into Detroit and then board a connecting flight to Minneapolis. Once we touched down in Minneapolis we had to board our last flight of the day, a 35-minute cruise up to Bemidji.

The first two flights went smoothly. We touched down in Minneapolis at the largest airport in North America in the mid afternoon. After deplaning, we looked up at the airport connecting flight monitors, and found that our next flight was located at the farthest gate away from us in the terminal. It was literally a half-hour walk to get to the other end of the airport. Once we got there, the check-in attendant gasped in panic as our entourage entered the gate waiting area. She immediately got on the phone with her supervisor and began conversing frantically.

Our coach, George Roll, had already walked over to check us in and we could see he was not pleased with what he was being told. When Roll got back to the group, he informed us that we might have a complication with our next flight. What had happened was that when they book these small flights, they usually average out a weight for each passenger, according to industry standards. That way they can fill all the seats and stay at a reasonable weight for the flight. The problem was that the entire flight, other than a group of eight hunters, was composed of an NCAA hockey team with an average weight of about 200 pounds. I think the industry standard was something like 170 pounds per passenger. So, with 35 people travelling in our group, we were more than 1,000 pounds overweight for the flight.

The gate attendant began by telling Roll that we might have to stay overnight in Minneapolis and take a flight the next day. Our coach was none too pleased, to say the least, with hotels and meals already booked for that night in Bemidji. Amidst the panic, the eight hunters stepped up and volunteered to hold over and take a flight the next day, alleviating the weight issue and allowing us to continue on as planned. As I mentioned in an earlier story, coaches don't like deviating from their itineraries. Most of them, in my era, grew up on typewriters, so it's a task in itself just to create them.

With that problem out of the way, we boarded the flight. This is when it got really interesting. The plane itself looked as though it had been borrowed from the Red Baron. It was an old propeller plane with patched-up wings and a dented exterior. I couldn't believe this plane was approved to carry passengers. It looked like the plane the Cleveland Indians used in the movie "Major League."

Next up, the only flight attendant on the tiny flight was nearly nine months pregnant, days away from her due date. She was ready to pop. The airline had tried to force her into maternity leave a month ago, but she filed a grievance with the union and was allowed to continue working. The one stipulation was that she could only attend to flights her husband, a pilot, was flying. To make matters worse, I was seated in the front row on the aisle and she said to me: "If I go into labor, you're going to have to assist in the delivery." I replied: "Sweetie, if you go into labor, I'll be passed out on the floor beside you!"

Needless to say, everyone was a little nervous as we teetered away from the terminal and taxied out to the runway in the rickety rocket. After sagging a couple of times during the takeoff, we eventually pulled up and took off over the Land of 10,000 Lakes. Of all the places I've been over the years, Minnesota is one of the most picturesque landscapes to fly over.

After sweeping Bemidji in our opening series of the season, we made the cumbersome trek back to school, starting with another scary puddle-jumper flight from Bemidji to Minneapolis. The next hiccup was that the plane was delayed because it ran out of fuel and we had to wait until they trucked more in and filled up. Once we finally hit the skies, we were dangerously behind schedule. When we landed in Minneapolis, again on the polar opposite side of the airport, we had to sprint to reach the gate for our next flight to Detroit. Our associate coach, Greg Drechsel, called ahead to the gate and informed them that we were on our way. Luckily, they were nice enough to delay the flight by 15 minutes to allow us to get there.

After a 10-minute sprint where several innocent bystanders were left sprawled on the airport floor as we barged our way through, we arrived out of breath and sweaty, ready to board our next flight. I still remember the dirty looks we received when we boarded. People must have been wondering why they were waiting so long to depart. Then a sweaty group of Neanderthals amble onto the plane and take up all their elbow room.

Just because they are student-athletes, don't think that players in the NCAA are any more civilized. If our team had spent more than a couple hours in a zoo, we'd probably end up in cages.

Guns and Guts

Springtime after the college hockey season ends is the best time of the year. The sun is shining, the birds are chirping and everything is fresh and clear. This is also the time when some of the best team bonding takes place.

In my junior year, we lost out in the second round to a hated rival, Cornell. With the hockey season over, we had to find other ways to entertain ourselves. We found this solace in a series of gong show parties that were aptly named "Guns and Guts."

That year, a couple of former Clarkson hockey players came back to school after a pro career to attain their MBA. During their stay for the graduate program, they rented a place about a mile off campus that was fully loaded with an indoor pool and hot tub. Since they knew what it was like to grind out a hard-fought season in the North Country, they offered up their cozy abode to stage some wild spring parties.

Our captain/social coordinator decided that he would spearhead a party campaign entitled "Guns & Guts" and "Guns & Guts Part Deux". He even was able to persuade David Hasselhof (or at least a cardboard cut-out of The Hoff) to take time out of his busy schedule to act as our spokesperson and came up with the slogan: "Hate it or love it, the Hoff's on top." We handed flyers out all over campus, and all the social media streams were flush with promotions of the event. Guns and Guts was to be the cat's meow of social gatherings for Potsdam's finest that spring.

These parties had kegs, swimming and fun. The night always started off pretty mellow with a few people lounging in the hot tub or pool and others playing drinking games in an adjoining room. As the night continued and more and more people showed up, it would get pretty rowdy. If you showed up later to one of the parties, you had to make sure you left your keys, wallet and phone outside. Most times, if you showed up later to the party, you were immediately tossed into the pool, as is.

As the night went on, the pool looked more like a sardine can, with most people fully clothed just chatting and drinking as if they were at a bar and not nipple-deep in a pool. The grossest thing about these parties was that I don't recall many people getting out of the pool or the hot tub to go to the bathroom. In particular, I can remember one of our players spending four consecutive hours in the hot tub, where he must have consumed anywhere from 10 to 12 beers without once leaving to go to the bathroom. He'd be like, "Jamer! Come join us in the hot tub! The water's perfect!" Ya, perfect, if you work for the International Olympic Committee.

I'd reply, "I'm not going in there as long as urine there. Oops, I meant as long as you're in there."

A Keg From Craig

During the 2004-05 NHL lockout, we were extremely lucky to benefit from two former Clarkson greats. Both Erik Cole and Craig Conroy, who keep off-season homes in the North Country, practiced with us for parts of that season. Watching these guys practice was something special. If you think NHL players just go through the motions in practice, you'd be sorely mistaken. These guys pushed the pace no matter what they were doing.

You didn't really get to appreciate how good Erik Cole was until he was blazing past you on a one-on-one and dragging you like an old sack of potatoes to the net behind him. While Cole left in January to sign with the Berlin Polar Bears, Conroy ended up staying close to home and continued to practice with us and help out. He was a free agent at the time and wasn't about to go play abroad and risk an injury.

After our season ended in the spring, a bunch of us joined a friend's team in an annual beer league tournament in nearby Alexandria Bay. The rink in Alex Bay was perfect for these types of tournaments because it had a bar/restaurant right in the rink. Conroy was also playing in the tournament but on a different team.

In our first game, we pounded some team from

Cornwall 9–1. After our first game, which was at 10 a.m., we had a big break before our next game, which wasn't until 6 p.m. By the time the second game rolled around, half our team could barely walk let alone skate and we ended up losing 5-4, dressing just enough drunk players to ice a team.

The next day, which was a Saturday, we played another two games, one at noon and another at 4 p.m. We easily won the first game and were about to press repeat from the events of the previous day when Conroy came over to our table to give us a stern pep talk.

You see, Conroy was playing for "Tons Sports Bar", another Potsdam team, and these guys wanted to win. In order for them to make it to the semi-finals, they needed us to win our next game by three or more goals.

So, Conroy came over and said: "Look guys. I know you're having a party tonight back on campus. If you stay sober here and go out and win your next game by more than three goals, I'll give you the money to buy a keg for your party tonight."

A couple of beer-free hours later, we trounced some team 10–0 and celebrated as if we had just won the Stanley Cup. In our case, the Stanley Cup amounted to a keg of Bud Light, which, for a bunch of college guys, was about as close as it gets.

The Weighted Run

During my freshman year at Clarkson University, the program was in a bit of disarray. Mark Morris, who coached a pretty impressive stretch of seasons during the '90s that saw players like Todd White, Craig Conroy, Erik Cole and Willie Mitchell don the green and gold, was unceremoniously relieved of his duties and former Clarkson assistant coach, George Roll was assigned with the daunting task of rebuilding the reputation of the program.

In college hockey, when a new coach steps in, he inherits a team that has been recruited and shaped by the previous coach. It's tough enough as a coach but as a player, this is an even more confusing and frustrating time. Picture this, you are recruited by a coach who really believes in what you can do and has a specific purpose for your strengths in his system. This coach is now gone and a new coach, whom you have never met, comes in with new systems and philosophies. You are immediately going to feel cheated. Who knows if this new coach likes the way you play or has room in his system for what you bring to the table.

Change in college hockey is always met with initial resistance simply because teams are built around a coaching staff's philosophy and a culture that is harvested by recruiting players to fit a particular scheme. In college hockey, you can't be traded like in major junior or pro. Your only recourse is to try to transfer to another school, but in order to do that, you would have to sit out an entire year. This is not a common practice for obvious reasons. In the end, coaches and players have to find a way to co-exist and respect one another in order to succeed.

In his first season at the helm, Roll needed to clean up the public perception of the program and make the team his own. The first couple of months, he put a huge emphasis on discipline, specifically off-ice discipline. Morris used to give his teams a bit of rope and allow them to run a bit wild, as long as the results were there on the ice. This philosophy was about to get turned on its head.

Right off the bat, Roll cracked the whip when dealing with off-ice issues. He constantly reminded us that we were student-athletes and the key priority was to conduct ourselves with professionalism and responsibility as a member of a prestigious academic institution. He wanted to change the perception that hockey players had always been greased through at Clarkson and that they viewed themselves as superior to the rest of the student body. We were about to get a stern lesson in humility.

One of the first doses of punishment we received was for a wild party we threw at one of the campus townhouses. Campus Safety was called several times to break up what we thought was just a good old-fashioned campus shaker. The next day, the captains were front and center in coach Roll's office to hear what the punishment would be. The gavel hit the block and Monday morning we were sentenced to run three miles as a team at 6 a.m. If it happened again, that morning run would turn into a week straight of 6 a.m. runs.

Bright and early on Monday morning we dragged ourselves wearily to Cheel Arena's parking lot to pay the piper and were met by the coaching staff and a pile of weights from our weight room. Immediately we were confused.

One of the guys asked: "Coach. I thought we were doing a run?"

Roll replied: "Oh you are. You're just going to have a few items in tow while you do."

We were going to have to complete a three mile run with nearly 400 pounds of weight to lug along, and we had to complete it as a team in less than 40 minutes, with the lightest weight, a five-pound plate, crossing the line last. If we failed the task, we would have to redo it every successive morning until we completed it.

We groaned and scampered to awkwardly pick up the weights as the coaches announced that the clock had started.

In all, there were 28 of us, and for the first while it took a lot of shuffling around to figure out the best method to carry the weights while we ran. Some guys carried weights between them, sharing the load, while others worked in pairs or teams of three to each carry weight for a section of time before passing it off to another.

To make matters worse, after about three-quarters of a mile, it began to pour down rain. We trudged along in the rain and the muck and eventually, after what seemed like an eternity, we completed the task with a few minutes to spare. We were elated that we wouldn't have to come back the next morning to do it again.

In the end, the punishment didn't necessarily curb our off-ice partying, but it did show that the coaches were standing by their philosophy and it instilled in us that for every action there was going to be a reaction.

If you were willing to deal with the consequences to an action, then so be it. If there were others in the group that weren't, then you were going to have a problem on your hands. A big part of their philosophy was that if one acts out, the entire team pays. I always liked that concept because it further emphasizes the motto: "Live as a team, die as a team."

Deadman's Hill

In college hockey, after the conclusion of each season, players usually get a couple of weeks off and then dry land training starts back up in full force for all of the players eligible to return. The workouts might be weight sessions, outside runs, plyos, sprints or core workouts. This was the time to set the tone for the upcoming season and to ensure that guys didn't fall too deeply into bad habits. The motto for us was always: "Next season starts now."

One day in particular, and I'll never forget it for as long as I live, we were told we were going to be performing the day's workout on a hill on campus that led down to a lower tier parking lot. The hill was about 70 yards in length from bottom to top and was at roughly a 35 to 40-degree incline. Before the workout, we just called it "The Hill". After the workout, we renamed it to the more appropriate moniker: "Deadman's Hill".

To set the scene, the time of year was late April and it was sunny and uncharacteristically hot at a humid 28 degrees Celsius. We were split up at the bottom of the hill in a line with the forwards on one side and the defensemen and goalies on the other. All the way up the hill, at 10-yard intervals, pylons were set up. On the coach's whistle, the defensemen and goalies would take off sprinting to the first cone, 10 yards up, touch the ground and sprint back down to the bottom. On the second whistle, the forwards would do the same.

After three 10-yard intervals were completed we moved on to 20-yard intervals for three reps and then 30-yards, and so forth. This continued on until we reached 70 yards, which was the top of the hill. To sum it up, we were running 840 yards as hard as we could uphill and 840 yards downhill overall during this exercise. On top of that, we were doing it in extreme heat with no shade in sight. It was grueling and easily the hardest physical test I had ever faced. During the exercise, four members of the team lost their lunches.

Once we finally completed the last 70-yard sprints and made our way back down, we all sighed or, more accurately, wheezed in relief. I can still remember Greg Drechsel, one of our coaches, saying: "Good job boys, go take a walk around the block." Once we finished a slow walk, regaining our breath and letting the lactic acid subside in our legs, Drechsel barked out: "Alright boys, back on the line. We'll start with three sets at 70 and work our way back down from there! Defensemen and goalies on the whistle!" Tweet!

We couldn't believe it! This was the hardest thing any of us had ever done and here we all thought it was over. Now they were telling us that we were going to have to do it again?

By the time we finished the second set of intervals, working our way back down from 70 yards, everyone had thrown up at least once. Some of the guys were unable to even finish the task. We're talking about top-flight athletes with VO2 Max scores that were off the charts, some with as low as 5% body fat.

When all was said and done, we slowly made our way back to the rink. The walk back to Cheel Arena felt as though we were walking in the Sahara desert with that sun pounding down on us. As soon as I transitioned in from the hot sun to the rink and the lighting got darker and the temperature cooler, I began to faint. I was able to stop myself from going down but I had to lay down with my eyes closed to help stop the room from spinning.

For the next two days, our bodies were in recovery. It might have been the first weekend when we didn't have some sort of a party. I felt like I had the worst hangover of my life for two days straight. I didn't feel like eating and all I wanted to do was sleep. That's the hardest I had ever pushed my body, and after that I definitely knew what my limit was.

Practice Scraps

There's nothing quite like looking one of your best friends in the eye and saying, "Let's go!" Due to the stubborn and competitive nature of the sport of hockey, and the knuckleheads who are stupid enough to play it, fights in practice are inevitable. Whether it's a game or a practice, hockey players are going to want to win. And, in reality, most hockey players at high levels are sore losers and extremely proud.

At every level that I've played, there were always a few dust-ups in practice. It wasn't a negative thing by any means. In fact, as ridiculous as that may sound, I often found it helped strengthen the bond between teammates. Whether it's boxing, mixed martial arts or hockey, if you ask any athletic combatant, they will tell you that they have a great deal of respect for the guys they go toe-to- toe with.

On the whole, the male population has an amazing amount of respect and admiration for courageous public figures. We admire guys like Clint Eastwood, John Wayne and Chuck Norris for what they represent and the fictional characters they portray onscreen. You might even catch a tough guy shedding a tear when he watches an athlete like Steve Yzerman or John Elway play through horrific injuries. It's that individual toughness and character that we admire and strive to emulate.

That image and desire is thoroughly engrained in the hockey culture. You will see this when two guys face off in a hockey fight. They are governed by unwritten rules known simply as "The Code". Briefly, the code consists of rules such as: don't take advantage of a guy if he slips during a fight, and take off your helmet if you play with a visor so that the other guy doesn't hurt his hand. Also, at the end of most fights, the combatants will tap each other on the head or back and say, "good job". For these guys, respect is gained from another player showing that he has the courage to throw hands with you.

An interesting thing when it comes to practice scraps is that there are actually a lot of fights in practice in the NCAA. This is because NCAA practices are extremely intense. In the NCAA, teams carry roughly 28 players on their roster because if players go down during the season, you can't call a guy up from an affiliate or trade or sign new players. The drawback or benefit to carrying so many guys, depending on whether you are a coach or a player, is that if everyone is healthy there are a lot of healthy scratches. Since competitive athletes don't like sitting out, practices are intense as guys will be battling hard to get back into the lineup.

During my sophomore year, I spent the first month and a half of the season on injured reserve. Once I came off IR, I was in a tough position because we were playing well and I was shuffled further down the depth chart. It was tough for me because I wanted to play every game, but I knew I had to work hard, bide my time and seize the opportunity once it arose. At the same time, we had about five other guys in the same position. With so many healthy scratches, practices were like gladiator events.

On Tuesdays that season, our practices were designed with a lot of battle drills involved. We were always in situations where we were competing and battling in the corners for puck possession. One day, we were doing a two-on-two battle drill down low and our coach blew his whistle and barked at me about how I needed to do a better job pinning opposing forwards and waiting for support. The next rep, I engaged on my good buddy Lyon Porter in the corner and pinned him for what seemed like an eternity. I had just gotten reamed out and wasn't about to release and Lyon was getting really frustrated.

As I continued to pin him in the corner, Lyon began raining elbows down on the back of my head. After about four or five of these, I pushed off and we both dropped the gloves and removed our helmets. I knew this probably wasn't going to go well for me; Lyon was big and tough and knew how to handle himself. We were both filled with rage at the moment, but it wasn't at each other. We were mad about our current playing situations and that competitive habit of wanting to be at your best was spilling over. After throwing a few pillows and taking a few good shots, I was happy that I didn't come out of it in too bad of shape. He'd never admit it, but I think he took it easy on me.

After the fight, we gave each other a respectful tap and continued on in the drill. Twenty minutes after practice ended, Lyon and I were workout partners, spotting each other on the bench press in the weight room, laughing about the fight. We never once thought it was personal and, in fact, we developed a deeper respect for one another after that day.

We were both just a couple of guys getting a chance to live the dream and do what we love to do. Sometimes a good scrap between teammates can do wonders for camaraderie and morale.

NBA Jam

As mentioned in an earlier tale, when George Roll came in as head coach at Clarkson, he was aiming to clean up the program and perform a culture makeover. In the beginning, there was a lot of head-butting and growing pains but slowly we began to reach compromises. One of the issues Roll had was on-campus parties escalating and getting out of hand. He wanted to erase a black mark that had begun to emerge, depicting Clarkson hockey players as reckless hooligans and party animals. After enduring some punishment runs and workouts, we were beginning to shape up with the new season just a week away. We were about to find out, however, that a reputation was harder to shake than anything.

One autumn night on a Tuesday, we were lying low as ordered, watching an NHL game on T.V. down at one of the on-campus townhouses. All was going well, there wasn't even a can of beer cracked or consumed. All of a sudden, one of the guys dug out an old Sega Genesis video game console from the closet and we all began to get excited as we rifled through the game cartridges. One game in particular caught everyone's eye and we decided we'd have a friendly tournament to help pass the time on this low-key Tuesday night. The game was "NBA Jam".

As the night progressed, we stayed within the boundaries of acceptable behavior and stayed off the booze. Things were just starting to come together and we were gaining the trust of our new coach. The only problem was we were so caught up in the fun we were having with NBA Jam that we didn't realize we were getting louder and louder. It didn't take long for the competitive nature of hockey players to spill over and add to the rowdiness. Arguments, chirping and laughter began to escalate into a riotous crescendo.

Then came a stern knock on the door and a voice. "This is Campus Safety. Please open up." Everything became silent in a hurry. We let them into the townhouse and they began to look around. Apparently, we didn't realize how loud we had gotten and someone had called and made a noise complaint.

Campus Safety asked us questions while looking around and then left with a firm instruction to keep the noise at a minimum. All in all, it was pretty much par for the course for a typical Campus Safety drop in. We really didn't think anything of it and weren't at all worried since we were drinking Coca Cola instead of the usual party staple, Keystone Light.

The next day, the captains got called to the carpet where Coach Roll went up one side and down the other. Apparently, Campus Safety filed a report and a copy was given to Roll. In their report, they said that we were throwing a party and that drinking was involved. Those slimy bastards! I guess Campus Safety finally got sick of us making them work for the money on Saturday nights and got some payback on us.

No matter what the captains said, it didn't matter. Roll wasn't having any of it. For the next week, other than Friday and Saturday game days, we were up at 6 a.m. for three-mile runs. Monday was also an hour-long bag skate, followed by an hour of battle drills. Even trying to follow rules and be good little boy scouts, we couldn't win.

One Bad Edge

The smallest occurrence in sports can make or break a career. If you have the game of your life in front of the right people, every door you can imagine can be opened for you. Conversely, if you stink up the joint in front of important eyes, you may fall into a hole that you'll never be able to climb out of. That's why consistency and mental toughness are two of the most important attributes of a hockey player.

In my freshman year at Clarkson, I had a pretty strong year. I led our team in plus/minus, played on the second power-play unit for long stretches of the year, won ECAC Rookie of the Week honors once and was named an honorable mention for NCAA rookie of the month during the playoffs. All in all, I was proud of what I had accomplished and worked hard over the summer to build on that in my sophomore year.

At the start of my sophomore year, I struggled with a couple of injuries that put me out for the first few weeks. Once I was able to scratch and claw my way back into the lineup, Coach George Roll showed me some love and slotted me back in on the second power-play unit. I figured it wouldn't be long before I started to excel and show what I truly felt I could do. Things were going well again and I wanted to keep progressing.

In the blink of an eye, everything changed. It was a Wednesday and we were practicing our power-play breakouts and in-zone options. For some reason, tensions were high that day and Roll was irritated with our poor execution during drills. Earlier in the practice, my left skate had gone into the post during a battle drill and I completely lost my outside edge. Every time I went to turn left, the edge gave out and down I went.

Later in the practice, we started working on power-play breakouts and, wouldn't you know it, each option started with me gaining the net and wheeling up the right side, which meant I had to turn left each time. So, the first time I attempted it, I bailed. Roll blew the whistle and commanded us to do it again, slightly annoyed. So we ran it again and down I went, again. Roll was getting very irritated by now and barked at me to get it together.

One last time.

Here I went again, for some reason expecting things to be different, and my left skate slipped out once again, sending me sprawling. At this, Roll blew the whistle and told another defenceman to take my place.

At the time I didn't know it, but that would be the last time in my college career that I would ever get a shot at the power-play. That year I was six-foot-one and 190 pounds and considered myself a power play player. I felt that with my skating ability and puck handling, the power play was how I would make my mark. We already had our penalty killing units set in stone, so I wasn't going to be able to try to make that my bread and butter. You see, if you're a player who only plays even strength, your value to a team is primarily for depth. Without a true role, I was about to get lost in the shuffle.

One bad edge ultimately spawned the beginning of the end for me at the college level. After that, my confidence was down. Once a coach labels a player in his mind, it's hard to break that image. All you can do at that point is work hard, hope for another opportunity to arise and run like hell with it if it does.

Das Boot

Throughout my career at Clarkson University, I was fortunate to have access to a car. During my freshman year, I was driving a cherry red 1993 Chrysler Concorde. It wasn't the nicest car on campus—most of the kids came from pretty wealthy families and found Hummers, Beamers and Range Rovers with personalized plates in the driveway on the morning of their sixteenth birthday. I was just happy to have some wheels.

I drove that car for the first two years I was at school and it acquired a few nicknames in the process.

There were pretty self-explanatory nicknames like, "The Boat", "The Red Cherry", "The Cherry Blaster", and then there was my personal favorite: "The Squealer".

The reason my car got the nickname The Squealer was because, for the longest time, I had a loose fan belt that I was too cheap and too mechanically uninclined to fix. For the first two minutes after I started the car, it would make this high pitch, blood-curdling, unbelievably loud sound that was not unlike nails on a chalkboard through a megaphone. I would fire up The Squealer in a busy parking lot and everyone would immediately look at me with a mixed expression of: "I want to kill you with a chainsaw" and, "I just accidentally ate poop."

Teammates used to tell me that they would be walking to class, a mile away from where I parked my car on campus and could hear The Squealer starting up. They would turn to one another and say: "There's Jamer. I wonder where he's going."

It had gotten to the point that I didn't even notice it anymore because I had gone so long without getting it fixed. There were times when it wasn't as bad as others. For example, on the really cold winter days it didn't squeal as much because the belt was constricted by the freezing cold air. It was always the worst when the weather turned warm.

One time, I was going out on a date with a girl for the first time and I went to pick her up in The Squealer to take her to a movie. I pulled up to her dorm and she nearly ran back inside. All of the dorm window lights started popping on and people were lurking about at their windows trying to see what was making that god-awful sound. I jumped out of the car strutting over to the passenger door to open it up like I was "The Fonze" and this poor girl was mortified.

During my first season at Clarkson, I had a lot to

learn about possessing a car on campus. On the very first day, I went out to my car and noticed that I'd been given a parking ticket. The ticket was for $10 for parking in a university lot without a permit. I told the fellas about the ticket and asked where I could go to buy a permit. One of the veterans quickly interjected, telling me not to waste my money because Campus Safety doesn't know who owns which car unless you register and they never try and track down rogue cars. They just give out tickets and assume people will pay them.

So, the rest of the year, I threw every ticket I got in the garbage. Sometimes I would put them on a teammate's car to mess around. By the end of the year, I estimated that I had thrown away at least 90 to 100 parking tickets. At $10 a pop, that was a pretty hefty sum.

During my junior year, I was able to finagle a free parking pass from someone I knew who worked in the student council office, so my bad boy days were coming to an end. I was also driving a different car: a 2000 maroon Chrysler Concorde (another hand-me-down boat from my dad), more affectionately known as, "The Black Cherry". This car didn't have the clearly audible attributes of The Squealer but she was definitely not lacking in character.

Early on in my sophomore season, one of our freshmen, David Leggio, came in to the dressing room one day and asked where he could buy a parking pass. Remembering the sage advice I had received as a freshman the previous year, I put my hand on his shoulder, shook my head and told him not to bother. I repeated the reasoning that was passed on to me a year earlier. Leggio nodded his head and smiled.

The rest of the season, Leggio tossed away tickets left and right, laughing, as I had, in the face of authority. There was a competition going to see if he could break my parking ticket record, a feat that he easily achieved, and then some.

A year later, Leggio was a sophomore, passing on the advice to the next group of freshmen on a stroll out of the rink one day when he noticed something different about his GMC SUV. Affixed firmly (we tried everything we could do to pry it off) to the wheel of his SUV was a big, yellow car boot—Das Boot. Apparently, unbeknownst to any of us, the University had done an audit during the summer of 2005 and realized they were missing a lot of uncollected revenue from unpaid parking tickets. They were trying to track down vehicles that had large sums of unpaid fees by coordinating with the New York State Police. They had also invested in two car boots to help them recoup unpaid fees and, apparently, two vehicles where No. 1 and No. 2 on their lists. No. 1, with a bullet, was a cherry red 1993 Chrysler Concorde with Ontario plates and no. 2 was a GMC SUV with New York plates (Leggio's ride). Since The Squealer was no longer in commission, collecting moss in a car graveyard somewhere, they moved onto public enemy no. 2, and Leggio's SUV got Das Boot.

It was a shitty situation because Leggio had accumulated a crazy amount of parking tickets that had amounted to somewhere in the neighborhood of $1,200 to $1,500. Coupled with the fee to have the boot removed, Leggio was looking at around $2,000 to get his car back. I remember sitting around at lunch one day and we were trying to figure out if Leggio should just let the university keep his SUV instead of paying the $2,000 to get the boot taken off. In the end, they worked out a deal where Leggio had to pay a largely reduced fee and Das Boot was removed.

Welcome to the Colgate Inn

One of the quaintest towns in central New York state is Hamilton. Hamilton lies in the Chenango Valley, just south of the headwaters of the Chenango River in Madison County. It is plush green in the summer and pristine white in the winter. The colonial houses line the tranquil streets surrounding the picturesque campus of historic Colgate University. As soon as you set foot in Hamilton, N.Y., you develop a sudden craving for tea and crumpets and readings of the works of Robert Frost and Leo Tolstoy.

Colgate University, which accounts for 50 percent of the village of Hamilton's population, was one of our conference rivals when I played at Clarkson University. Colgate lays claim to several NHL alumni, such as Mike Milbury and Andy McDonald, as well as all five members of Broken Lizard, the creators and lead actors in cult comedy hit movies "Super Troopers" and "Beerfest." Starr Arena is a small shoebox of a rink, but it holds one distinct advantage over many of the other arenas in the ECAC, a bowling alley practically right outside of the visitors dressing rooms.

Every time we went to play at Colgate, we stayed at the Colgate Inn, which is a Dutch Colonial- style inn that opened in 1925. The inn is known for its elegant ballroom, stylish parlors and cozy rooms. It is a haven for highbrows, scholars and artisan travelers. It was hardly typical of the Red Roof Inns and Courtyard Marriotts that we normally stayed at.

The first thing I noticed about the historic inn was how narrow the hallways were. The rooms themselves looked like they belonged to Little Red Riding Hood's grandmother. I half expected to open the door and find a

90-year-old lady knitting an afghan in front of a well-stoked fire while watching reruns of "Murder She Wrote." All of the furniture, from the side tables to the chairs and beds, were teak. Rumors were that the inn was haunted, and it wasn't implausible to see why.

After unpacking some of our gear, my road trip roommate and I decided to flip on Sportscenter and relax. There was only one problem. When we flopped down on the beds, the mattresses engulfed our bodies like waves and our legs hung over the end of the bed. These "Bert and Ernie" single beds were only five and a half feet in length.

Just before the Sportscenter Top Ten came on, my roommate went into the tiny bathroom to get ready for bed. Ten minutes later he came out, just in time for the Top Ten, after which we shut off the TV and lights and went to bed.

The next morning, at about 6:35 a.m., our phone rang. I looked at the clock, saw the time and ignored the call. Our wakeup call was set for 7:30, so obviously someone had the wrong number. After ignoring the call, the phone began ringing again. This time I picked it up and groggily answered. The person on the other end of the line was a frantic inn employee. "Excuse me, sir. Is the toilet overflowing in your bathroom?"

I asked them to hold on, put down the receiver and went to the bathroom to check. When I opened the door, I saw that the floor was covered in poopy water. I woke up my roommate and said: "Hey! You clogged the shitter last night, man. Look! It's all over the floor."

Apparently, the water had been running all night and had pooled under the tile in the bathroom, leaking down into the ceiling of the ballroom below us. Our team breakfast was cancelled on account of a shit storm!

When we went downstairs, we were met with quite a

sight. The pristine ballroom ceiling was bowed down with a massive pocket of sewage. Plumbers, wait staff and bellhops were hastily moving tables and clearing off glassware and cutlery. One particular maintenance worker was on a ladder just beneath the pocket of filth, removing an elegant chandelier.

The next time we played at Colgate, we stayed outside of town at the Red Roof Inn. Hockey players, you can dress them up, but you can't take them out.

Mean Jean

My first captain's practice in college was the biggest eye-opening experience in my hockey career. Going to the NCAA, you're coming from junior hockey where you predominantly play against 16-to 19 year-olds. In the NCAA, most of the players are 20 and older. Some are as old as 24 or 25.

The sheer physicality of the jump from junior to college is astounding. Not only are college players older players, they are older players who train hard and are in better shape than anyone else you've ever played against. Immediately, in the first practice, I noticed that everyone was fast and strong. Also, the passes were a lot crisper and harder and everyone could shoot like a pro.

In college, guys were harder to contain and knock off the puck, and when possessing the puck, your window of opportunity to make a play was dramatically smaller. In junior, I could spin off guys, take more ice and pick apart the opposition to make the play I wanted in the time frame I wanted to make it in. In college if you tried that, you would end up on your back or stripped of the puck in a hurry. The level of hockey was just that much faster, stronger and more precise.

The first player that stood out to me when I went to Clarkson was a guy by the name of Jean Desrochers. This guy was unbelievable. He was big (6-2, 225) and he could move. What amazed me the most about Jean were his hands. He easily had the best hands I had ever seen. He could dangle with the best of them and his offensive instincts were off the charts. I remember asking one of the guys: "How is this guy not in the NHL right now?"

The reply was simple: "Just wait until we start playing in a system".

You see the problem with Jean was that he couldn't grasp system play. He would get confused as to where he was supposed to be and what he was supposed to be doing once he got there. Jean didn't start playing organized hockey until he was 15. Before that, he played pickup hockey on the outdoor rink or with the old boys at lunch. He didn't grow up with positional teaching, so he relied exclusively on skill and instincts.

It was sad because he had so much talent. If Jean had played in the '60s, '70s or '80s, there is no doubt in my mind that he would have been an NHLer. Since it was 2003, when hockey was, and still is dominated by system play, he didn't get a chance to realize his potential to the fullest. The problem with a guy like Jean, for a coach, is that you see so much potential that you're actually harder on him than any other player. When he can't grasp the system, you get frustrated and it's easier to bench him than deal with the disappointment. I can remember that Jean sat out five games in a row once during his senior year as a healthy scratch.

Once Jean graduated from Clarkson, he turned pro in the ECHL with the Johnstown Chiefs. Now playing pro, where system play is scrolled back a bit from what it is in college, Jean was able to rely more on his natural instincts and achieved a great deal more success. In his rookie season, Jean was named to the ECHL all-star game and received a call-up to Springfield of the AHL.

Jean would go on to play several more years in the ECHL, AHL and in Italy, experiencing success and getting a chance to see the world. As well as he did in life and in hockey, it makes me sad to think of the potential that Jean had and what might have been. I honestly believe that if he played in a different era or had begun playing organized hockey at a younger age, Jean wouldn't have just been good, he would have been great.

Ice Bath Therapy

There's nothing worse in sports than getting injured or banged up. For starters, it hurts. Secondly, you may or may not be out of the lineup for an extended period of time. If you are still able to play and gut it out, you're probably going to be struggling and operating at under 100 %. The thing about hockey players is that, due to the physicality of the game and the number of games played in a season, no one is ever truly playing at 100 %.

If you go down any professional team lineup you'll probably see a plethora of injuries that guys play through from separated shoulders to sprained knees to broken hands. Outsiders don't know about these injuries because you never want your opponent to know you're hurt. So, in order to make it more comfortable, trainers will apply several forms of therapy to speed up the healing process and minimize the pain.

One injury that is awful in hockey is a groin injury. Groin injuries are common in training camp because you're on the ice so much at the start of a season and chances are, even with year-round on-ice training, you haven't been exposed to that kind of intensity on the ice since the prior season. Also, the ice is typically softer during training camp, causing more ruts in the ice and increasing the incidents of groin injuries.

Groin injuries have a mind of their own. Sometimes you'll feel fine and then you turn quickly and a sharp pain runs straight to your brain. They're easy to re-injure and ultimately can hamper you for extended periods of time, sometimes a whole season. The problem with groin injuries is that you can usually play through them, albeit with a lot of discomfort. This means that the injury never really gets time to heal. To make playing through a groin injury tolerable, trainers will employ several remedies and treatments. One thing trainers do is wrap groins and make players wear compression shorts, which keep the groin from popping out. Another form of treatment for groin injuries is ultrasound and ice baths.

Ice baths are the worst! You sit in a cold tub filled with cold water and ice cubes at a temperature where the ice cubes don't melt away. We're talking freezing cold water! It's bad enough that you're injured and having to play through it, but now you're enduring worse pain than the injury itself in order to make pain from the injury lesser? Doesn't that sound nuts?

The first time I experienced the ice bath was when I sprained my medial collateral ligament in my right knee during my sophomore year. I remember going down to the athletic center for treatment on my knee after practices and having to sit in the ice bath. To finish each treatment session, I had to soak my knee up to my hip in the ice bath for 20 to 30 minutes. I was squealing like a pig sitting in that thing and I only had one leg in it. On the other side of the room was a girl from the soccer team who was up to her neck in the ice bath for a back injury and here I was, supposedly some tough hockey player, squealing like a stuck pig.

After that experience, I injured a disc in my back and had to start doing full-body ice baths. Now I was sitting in that torture chamber up to my neck. Your heart rate actually slows right down to a crawl when you're neck deep in those things. To put it in perspective, Navy Seals spend hours at a time in water at that temperature as part of their notorious "B.U.D.S. Hell Week" training. You'd be amazed at the words that come out of your mouth when you're sitting in water that cold.

After a few tours in the ice bath, your body begins to get used to it. By the fourth or fifth time it isn't too bad at all. Once you got used to it, you even began to take ice baths after practices and games just so you could zap all the lactic acid out of your muscles so you weren't sore the next day. As painful as they are when you're in them, ice baths make you feel like a million bucks when you walk out of them. If you're planning on making a real go of it in hockey, the ice bath becomes your best friend.

PRANKS

The embarrassment of others is what makes life tolerable. Pranks are and always have been an essential part of the hockey culture.

Hide the Poop

In my last year of junior hockey, while playing for the Ottawa Jr. Senators, we went on a pretty wild run. We finished the regular season in fifth place in a 10-team league and then ran table through the playoffs upsetting the No. 3-ranked team in Canada, the Cornwall Colts, in the league championship series. After that, we advanced through the Fred Page Cup and made it all the way to the Royal Bank Cup—Canada's Tier II junior A championship.

We had a lot of fun that year and had a great group of guys. We didn't have the most talented team, but we played hard for our coach, Freddie Parker, and hard for each other. It was the perfect blend.

As tight-knit of a group that we were, one thing we were notorious for was being ultra-tough on the rookies. The Royal Bank Cup that year was held in Halifax and we were there for eight wild days. At the hotel in Halifax during some downtime, we decided it would be fun to play a little game called "Hide the Poop" with a group of three rookies who were sharing a room.

When the three rookies went down to the pool one day, we snuck into their room and found a small garbage pail. One of our players had a bad case of the runs that day and we had them take a huge dump in the garbage pail and we hid it under the bedside table in the rookies' room. The bedside table was perfect for this prank because it was hollow below the top drawer. That meant it was covered all the way to the floor but had a hollow area when you lifted it up – a perfect spot to "Hide the Poop".

When the rookies got back to their room, all they could smell was rotting feces. It was rancid. They were looking everywhere, but because it was so strong they couldn't figure out where it was coming from. It took them three days to finally figure out where it was and what we had done. I'm pretty sure one of the boys felt bad and tipped them off. That prank was a classic.

The Weighted Stick

During my sophomore year at Clarkson, I began to settle into a position of comfort and confidence. I wasn't a rookie anymore, which meant I could partake in more tomfoolery. My partner in crime was one of my best friends, Chris Brekelmans, "Breksy". Breksy and I were in the same program in school and had a lot of the same classes and basically an identical schedule.

When we had some down time during the day, Breksy and I would head to the rink early and plot and scheme prank after prank to play on unsuspecting freshmen. One prank we used to love to bring out of our bag of tricks was one we called "The Weighted Stick." The weighted stick consisted of taking one of the two-piece sticks that some of the players used and removing the blade, filling the shaft up with dirt and then putting the blade back in. This took a bit of time because you had to use a heat gun to melt the glue that held the blade in place, go out to the back parking lot and fill up the shaft with dirt and gravel, and then melt the glue and slide the blade back into place. It was a time-consuming process.

We were very careful and meticulous when it came to running this prank. We had to carefully select our prey according to schedule and preference of stick. One of our favorite targets was then-freshman Grant Clitsome, "Clitty". We practiced Monday to Thursday at 3 p.m. and Clitty had a class that ended at 2:30 on Wednesdays.

This meant that he had to hurry to get to the rink and be on the ice on time for 3 p.m. Being late wasn't an option because it meant that the entire team had to suffer.

Most players like to get to the rink an hour before practice and lounge around a bit and take time to prep their equipment, skates and especially their sticks. Because Clitty was in a hurry on Wednesdays, he would prep his sticks Tuesday after practice so he didn't have to worry about them before practice on Wednesday. This is what made him the ideal target for the weighted-stick prank.

We couldn't run this prank very often and especially not to the same person more than once or twice in a season. When we did run it, we would have to make sure to fill all the sticks in the respective player's stall. We usually had four sticks in our stalls, so you had to make sure you were there nice and early to ensure you had time to fill all four.

The last step to the prank was to let everyone else in on it. This way, if the victim wanted to try to borrow someone else's stick, he couldn't. He would have to lug that barbell with a blade on it around all practice, flubbing passes and shots while the whole team would giggle. It was even better when the coaches would get riled up and bark at the victim about being sloppy.

My sophomore year was the last time we ever ran the weighted-stick prank, since everyone began using one-piece sticks. Technically, you could still run it by removing the plug from the top and filling the stick, but it sort of lost its luster. I can remember hearing about guys who played back in the old days of pure lumber, slightly cutting the shafts about halfway up the stick so that players would fall on their face when they went to take slap shots and one-times.

Super Rookie Wet Suit

Super Rookie struck again later in the year during my last season of junior hockey at the Fred Page Cup in Truro, N.S. He was refusing his rookie duties, as per usual, and the other rookies were really starting to get pissed off. A group of the rookies came up to us and said that something needed to be done about Super Rookie and that it wasn't fair to them that they had to pick up his slack. We thought that was plenty reasonable and devised a fun prank to get him back.

The first day of the tournament consisted of a team practice followed by a media conference where all the players got their headshot photographs taken and met with the media to answer questions. We were instructed to wear suits to the practice so that we would look presentable at the news conference afterwards.

The guys started hitting the ice and we waited until Super Rookie jumped on to set the prank in motion. Once he left the dressing room, we gathered up his suit clothes and bundled them up in a ball and taped the ball tight. We then took the ball of taped clothes and put them in the shower and turned it on. When he got off the ice from practice, he was met with a ball of soaking wet dress clothes.

This prank drew a lot of applause and laughter from the team and poor Super Rookie was left to attend the news conference in his shorts and undershirt. The coaches didn't get involved because they knew we were handling our own in-house problems. Successful teams, just like military platoons, are ones that govern themselves. That way there is more mutual respect and honor and everyone follows the code.

The Leaner to End all Leaners

In my freshman year in college, I lived with a beauty of a roommate and a great teammate in Matt Nickerson. Big Nicks and I made a great pair. We were both pretty laid back and had a lot in common despite being three years apart in age. You see, I was an old freshman who played his overage year in junior and Nicks was a true freshman, coming straight from grade 12. Coach matched us together because Big Nicks was a highly touted recruit (drafted in the third round of the 2003 NHL Entry Draft by the Dallas Stars) who could use someone mature to look out for him and help him adjust to college life. I guess because I had already taken two years of university while finishing my junior career in Canada, the coaches thought I was "mature."

Over the next year, Nicks and I went through a rollercoaster of thrills and spills. Some of the stories I will tell, but some I won't for fear of prosecution. We laughed, cried and enjoyed a lot of memorable times that I still look back on today.

To begin the tale of "The Leaner to End all Leaners", I'll need to give you a little bit of background. Big Nicks was a terrific hockey player and bona-fide NHL prospect. He was from Old Lyme, Conn., and was a monster at 6-5, 265 with an unbelievable mean streak. The kicker was that he had some of the softest hands on the ice you have ever seen and he had great mobility.

Off the ice, Big Nicks had a big heart and was one of the funniest guys I've ever had the pleasure of knowing. Big Nicks and I lived on the first floor of Reynolds House, which was a freshman dormitory on the Clarkson University campus. We lived in 127 Reynolds, located right next to the communal bathroom on the floor.

All in all, we had a pretty good group of students living on the floor and, despite having varying interests, priorities and sleep schedules; we were all able to co- exist in harmony.

Everything was great in Reynolds House except one meatball that continually acted like a jackass and had to try to make it tough for everyone else to live. He would constantly be mouthing off to people on the floor and causing disruptions during quiet hours, but it was something he did one night when he was drunk that forced Big Nicks and me to take some aggressive action. One Saturday night, we came home to a group of people in the communal bathroom moaning and groaning because the floor jackass decided to drop a deuce in one of the showers and leave it there for all to enjoy.

Big Nicks looked at me and we nodded our heads in unison. We both knew what had to be done. We were about to dole out the "Leaner to End All Leaners."

A leaner is when you take a small garbage pail and fill it up with water and lean it against the outside of a door. When someone on the other side of the door opens it, the garbage pail tips over and soaks the feet of the unsuspecting victim.

Now if we were going to perform a leaner on this douchebag, it couldn't just be any run-of-the-mill leaner. No, no, this would have to be an epic leaner. During the commotion of the groans and moans of disappointed floor mates, we quietly took the industrial-sized garbage can from the bathroom and brought it into our room. Inside the can, which already contained a decent amount of garbage, we added several urine-filled plastic bottles, which we uncorked and emptied into the garbage itself. We also did the same with several plastic bottles filled with chewing tobacco spit and added a couple of small cartons of rotten milk.

After adding all the vile contents we could muster, we returned to the bathroom and filled the rest of the garbage can with scalding hot water from the shower. We were now ready to carry out the leaner and put that jackass in his place once and for all.

In the ensuing moments, Big Nicks and I carefully waited until the hallway was dead silent and we tip-toed the garbage can and its rank contents over and propped it silently against douchebag's door. We spent another 30 seconds quietly bickering over whether or not we should just leave it or knock, until Big Nicks decided to pound loudly on the door.

We took off like rockets and flew into our room, which was only a few doors down, and made like we were lounging and watching a movie. As we quickly settled in, we heard a loud, sloshing noise. It was so hard not to burst out laughing, but we had to keep silent to not give our successful efforts away.

Douchebag went into a raging tirade, which drew almost every floor occupant into the hallway, including us. I must admit we did a superb job of acting aloof and even offered some vague explanation about seeing a couple of frat guys running out of the exit.

The best part of the story came about five minutes after all the hubbub died down. We got a knock on our door from our floor resident adviser, Luke. As soon as Nicks saw who it was through the peephole, he looked at me and said, "We're cooked, bro."

We let Luke in and he closed the door behind him and sat down. He then looked up at us, grinning, and said: "That was unreal! I saw you guys setting up that leaner. I hate that asshole and now he's going to be sniffing piss and chew spit for the next semester and a half!"

The rest of the year we would get secret winks from the rest of the hall occupants and nobody really cared if we played our music loud or had the odd late night party. We became gods of the floor.

Skate-Lace Hotel Prank

Being a hockey player on the road, you find yourself with quite a bit of free time. Sometimes you use this time to relax and prepare for the upcoming game and other times you use the time to stir up mischief. One of my favorite pranks to perform on the road was the "Skate Lace Prank." This prank is a great one to do when the team is shacked up in a hotel.

Most teams that I have been a part of operate in the same way. When you are on the road, coaches prepare itineraries to prove that they do more than just play solitaire in their spare time. The itineraries are mapped out with timelines and each event has a strict start time. A typical day in the middle of a road trip might look like this:

Saturday, January 10 - Game @ Colorado

8:00 a.m.	-	Wakeup Call
8:15 a.m.	-	Team Breakfast @ Hotel
9:00 a.m.	-	Video Session
9:45 a.m.	-	Bus Departs for Arena
11:00 a.m.	-	Pre-Game Skate
12:30 p.m.	-	Bus Departs for Macaroni Grill
1:00 p.m.	-	Pre-Game Meal @ Macaroni Grill
2:00 p.m.	-	Bus Departs for Hotel
4:45 p.m.	-	Bus Departs for Arena

5:30 p.m.	-	Team Meeting @ Arena
7:00 p.m.	-	Warm-Up
7:30 p.m.	-	Game vs. Colorado Eagles
11:00 p.m.	-	Bus Departs for Oklahoma City

Sometimes you might play a string of games in a row on the road and make one-game stops in each spot, getting most of your sleep on the overnight bus treks in your bunk. Other times, especially if you are travelling long distances, you will play two-or three-game sets in one spot before moving on to the next spot. During these sets, you'll stay in hotels.

The "Skate Lace Prank" is set up like this. Knowing that you're going to have an 8 a.m. wake-up call, set your alarm for about 7:15 or 7:30. This way, you can set up the prank just before your victims arise for the day. Now on the road, since you probably either travelled most of the night and got in at 3 a.m. or you just played a grueling first game of a set, you are going to wait until the last possible moment before getting up, grabbing a quick shower and then heading down for breakfast. So, you really don't have to get up too early to set up the prank.

For the prank to work properly, you have to find two pairs of your teammates that are staying in rooms that are directly across the hall from each other. Once you locate the two rooms, take out the skate lace, tie one end securely around one of the door handles and tie the other end around the door handle across the hall. Make sure that there is no slack and that the lace is pulled as tightly as can be.

When the two pairs of roommates wake up and have their shower and head down at 8:13 a.m. for the mandatory 8:15 breakfast, they will not be able to open their doors, no matter how hard they pull. If you happen to see a hotel employee in the hallway, be sure to let them know what you're up to so they don't call security on you or cut the lace too early and ruin the prank.

Now all you have to do is go downstairs to breakfast with the team and wait. Most coaches are pretty proud of their itineraries and take them very seriously. They set timelines and expect everyone to adhere and show up on time. Even if the coaches are lax, players police themselves with fines for being late to mandatory team functions.

After the victims of the prank finish panicking, cursing who they think got the better of them, and call down to have someone come up and cut the lace, they will enter the dining room to a round of jeers from their peers and head shakes from their coaches.

Remember, though, if you like to play the role of prankster, you better be prepared to take it as good as you give it. Athletes are proud, stubborn animals and vengeance is always the best medicine. Like the old saying goes: "Live by the sword, die by the sword."

Shoe Check

When you're on the road as a team, restaurants are a big part of the experience. You're always eating together in places like The Macaroni Grill or The Olive Garden, and if you're going to perform pranks everywhere else, why not here? One of the greatest pranks to pull at a restaurant is the "Shoe Check". It's simple, yet effectively humiliating all in one.

The shoe check is as simple as it sounds. The prankster finds a victim and pours some sort of sauce, usually ranch or ketchup, on their shoe. Once the prankster is back in their seat, they begin clinking their glass with their fork and everyone else joins in, knowing that a shoe check has taken place. At this point, everyone has to check their shoes to see who got it. The victim then has to stand up and take a bow while having buns and napkins thrown at them.

At the start of the season, the rookies have no idea what the shoe check is, so it's easy to pull off. As the season rolls on, everyone expects it to happen and is on high alert during team meals. Since it becomes more difficult, the prankster has to become slicker in their attempts. In order to pull off this prank when everyone expects it, you may have to recruit help from your teammates and devise diversions. For example, you might get a guy to come up behind someone and engage them in an animated conversation while the prankster slips under the table and nails the guy while he's being distracted.

The greatest shoe check that I was ever a part of was at my good friend and former teammate John Sullivan's wedding. The wedding was at a spectacular venue in Manchester, N.H. It was a ritzy affair at a pristine golf course and everyone seemed to be on their best behavior. During the dinner, everyone was sitting elegantly at their tables and enjoying the event. I was sitting at a table with five former teammates, all of whom played with Sully at Clarkson. We all looked at each other and smiled. We didn't even need to say a word because we knew what was on each other's minds. We were about to pull off the wedding shoe check—the ultimate of all shoe checks.

We got one of the guys to go up and chat with Sully and then Jay Latulippe slipped under the table and dumped a load of ranch dressing on Sully's slick new dress shoes. After we got back to the table, we started to clink our glasses. Now at a wedding, when someone starts clinking their glass it's usually to get the bride and groom to kiss. When we started clinking our glasses, the bride and groom started to rise and move in for a kiss and we started hollering: "No! No! No! Shoe Check! Shoe Check! Shoe Check!" Sully turned beet red and just started laughing.

Helmet Name Tag Prank

All hockey players, at one time or another, have had their name written with a marker on white stick tape plastered to the front of their helmet. Almost always this is when you are first starting out in a group of 30 ankle-biters at a learn-to-skate session. There is no shame in this at all, since it's hard for one instructor to remember all these little hellions' names.

When you're a 25-year-old professional hockey player with a name tag on your helmet that looks like it was written in crayon by a four-year-old, it's just downright funny. This is one of my favorite pranks to pull when you have some down time before a game.

Since the helmets are always put into the stalls with the backs and numbers facing out, a lot of guys don't look at the front of their helmet too closely before putting it on. Now you can't pull this trick too early, because some guys will take time to clean their visors or make adjustments to their helmets. You have to wait until about five minutes or so before warm up. You might have to do a little recon work in order to find the right victim. Pick somebody who runs into the trainer's room to get their wrist taped or to go grab some wax for their stick.

In order to prep the trick, you need to get a piece of white stick tape and write a sloppy name in big block letters on it. It works better if the sharpie is red or green because it accentuates the adolescence of the prank. Next, pick a different name than the player's that screams "four-year-old ankle biter." My go-to was either Zachary or Douglas. Once you have prepped the name tag, keep it readily available in your stall until the perfect moment arises to apply it to an unsuspecting victim's helmet.

Sometimes this prank, like many others, will be caught before it reaches the lights of the arena. But, when it is successful, it works great. It's funny to trail behind the victim in warm-up and hear the other team chirp them as they loop around the ice and to hear all your own teammates call him by his new name.

The Gatorade Shower

Another prank involving a player's helmet is the "Gatorade Shower" prank. This prank is very simple. You take a full cup of either Gatorade or water and you carefully place it in an unsuspecting player's stall just under the back lip of their helmet. As mentioned earlier with the "Helmet Name Tag Prank", the helmets are placed in the stalls on a shelf with the numbers facing outwards.

The way this prank works is that an unsuspecting victim will pull out their helmet to head out for practice and get doused in Gatorade or water as the cup catches the front of the helmet and tips over.

Kangaroo Court

Kangaroo Court is common across many sports. It is a way to police your own and, from my experiences, a great way to promote camaraderie and a light-hearted atmosphere within your team. When I was in college, Kangaroo Court was a big production every Wednesday after practice. Our team had a "Fine Master," who was basically a makeshift judge, and everyone took part in the process.

The rules were pretty simple. Rule No. 1: Rookies can't fine other players. Rule No. 2: Everyone has a right to the appeal process. Appeals are heard and judged by your peers in the same court session that the fine is announced. Rule No. 3: All fines must be paid up within the week after the fine is administered. If a fine goes unpaid in the first week, it is doubled every week thereafter.

We always looked forward to court sessions because everyone would get riled up and there were always a lot of laughs and a lot of great stories. One thing court did was recap the events of the parties on the weekend and uncover any stories or mischief that might have occurred.

During court sessions, guys would get fined for all kinds of fun stuff, from stepping on the team logo in the dressing room to leaving your stall a mess after practice. Quite often, the fines were pretty funny, like being fined a dollar for getting caught holding hands with your girlfriend in public or bringing a bad type of beer to a party.

Rookies always took a big hit when it came to court sessions. Since rookies couldn't fine, there was no retaliation for getting cut up in court. You had to grin and bear it and wait until your sophomore year when you could razz the next crop of rookies.

In my freshman year, I remember getting hammered in the first few court sessions. In the first session, I got tabbed by Chris Brekelmans, who would go on to be one of my best friends, for a dollar for taking my helmet off during the team stretch at the conclusion of a practice. Every fine came with a dollar amount and then a comment. The comment for this one was: "Who do you think you are? Bobby Orr? Have some respect and keep your helmet on so we don't have to stare at your ugly mug."

Breksy was an intense guy and he could hit like a freight train. The first captain's practice we had that year, I came around the net and made a nice pass through the seam to a guy cutting through the neutral zone. I was watching my pass with pride when all of a sudden, wham! Breksy finished a check on me and folded me up like a cheap lawn chair. I vaguely remember him barking at me as I slowly began to regain the air in my lungs and the ringing in my head began to subside.

At the end of each court session, there would be a few fines directly aimed at the rookies. One might say: "One dollar fine to all the rookie (insert pluralized, derogatory four-letter word of choice) just for being alive."

Another one might say: "One dollar fine to all rookies for being the ugliest rookie class in Clarkson University history." It was always something everyone would get a good laugh out of to end court on a good note.

Over the years, I was a part of some really funny fines. One fine in particular required a great deal of planning and co-ordination. We had one player who would always disappear and then make up elaborate stories about where he was and what he was doing. Let's call this guy Jack for argument's sake. Jack would bail out on plans with the boys, like bowling, and when we'd ask him where he was, he would say: "Oh sorry boys, I had to go help out at a soup kitchen for the evening in Massena."

One day, we decided to tail him when he backed out on a plan. We all crammed into our buddy's car and brought along a digital camera for evidence-gathering purposes. We followed Jack to a movie theatre in Canton, N.Y., which was 10 miles down the road. On the way to the theatre, Jack stopped at a house and a girl jumped into his car.

Click, click.

Jack and the girl then went to the movie theatre. We took some more pictures of Jack and the girl entering the theatre and decided we would use them as evidence with the fine we were about to lay on him.

The plan was to gather the intel and then wait until court to drop the big fine on old Jacky boy. But, since we had already gone through all the trouble to follow him, we decided we couldn't wait until the next court session to see the surprised look on his face when we caught him. So we piled out of the car and went in and bought tickets to the movie. I think it was some chick flick like "Step-Up" or "Save the Last Dance." That made it even better because it added more money to the fine.

So we went into the dark theatre and could see him and the girl sitting a few rows down, waiting for the previews to start. We quietly snuck in behind him and sat down. In a few moments one of the guys tapped him on the shoulder and asked him if he knew if this movie was supposed to be any good. Jack turned around to reply and was faced with five of his teammates grinning ear to ear. We immediately erupted in laughter and he just started laughing as he knew that he'd been caught. I felt bad for the poor girl. She must have been embarrassed. To make matters worse, since we already bought our tickets, we stayed and watched the whole movie and ruined the rest of his date.

Even though we caught him in the act and embarrassed him in public, Jack wasn't going to escape further embarrassment at the next court session. All in all, the fines amounted to: $1 for bailing on Tuesday night bowling with the boys, $1 for bailing on the boys for a girl, $1 for lying to the boys as to why you were bailing, $1 for taking a girl from another school on a formal date, $1 for going to see "Step-Up", and $1 for not offering the boys some of your large popcorn at the movie. Those fines were funny enough, but it was definitely the surveillance pictures that brought on the biggest round of laughter.

Another one of my teammates had a real rough time during his freshman year with fines. He just seemed to be getting dinged more and more for boneheaded infractions at every court session. The first court session of that year, he was fined for wearing a Boston College T-shirt to one of our workouts. I mean this was as bad as it gets. It would be like playing for the Toronto Maple Leafs and wearing an L.A. Kings T-shirt during an interview.

The next one he got nailed for was answering a call on his cell phone during a team workout. For starters, cell phones were banned in the dressing room and workout rooms. Secondly, how hard are you working when you have time to have a leisurely chat with your girlfriend on your cell phone when you're supposed to be pushing the envelope in the weight room with everyone else?

Sometimes, even though everyone knows court is supposed to be light hearted and fun, things could get pretty heated. During my freshman year, in the second or third court session of the year, things got pretty hairy. One of the veteran players fined a rookie teammate, and he didn't take too kindly to it. Everyone was laughing, but the rookie was just boiling over and I could tell right away things were about to get real. All of a sudden, the rookie snapped back that he was going to introduce himself to the veteran on the ice during next practice and stormed out of the room. Everyone looked at me as if to say: "Is he just kidding around or is he serious?" I just nodded and said: "He's not kidding."

Chirping is chirping, but all hockey players are proud and have breaking points. Sometimes, and it depends on what the player's mindset is at the time, they can take a lot of flak and other times it doesn't take much to flip the switch. The best part about blowups and feuds in the dressing room is that they are quickly forgotten and put to rest. Boys will be boys, but in the end, your team is your family.

Anyone Seen My Car?

Cars are a burden. They cost a lot of money to buy, maintain and operate, and they're worth half of what you paid for them once you drive them off the lot. We often curse the very existence of our automobiles, but at the same time, we can't live without them. Our dependence on vehicles is what makes one of my favorite pranks all the more effective.

Wherever I have played, one of the most effective pranks to play is called "Anyone Seen My Car." The first time I played this prank was when I was working at the NCAAA Hockey School in Ottawa in the summer of 2004. I was an instructor at the school and one of the other instructors was an old teammate, Sean Roche. Rochey was a beauty. He was intense and was really easy to rile up, which made him a prime candidate for various pranks, in particular this one.

In the beginning, the prank was easy. We'd steal Rochey's keys while he was on the ice and we'd go and move his mom's minivan over to the opposite side of the building. When Rochey would go out to grab his lunch out of the van after he got off the ice, he'd be running around frantically trying to figure out where it went. Of course, it wouldn't take him long to figure out that we'd pulled the slip on him, but we'd still leave him hanging trying to find it.

After getting nailed a couple times, Rochey started hiding his keys. No problem, We had lots of time on our hands. We would always find them. After a while, Rochey decided to take the keys with him wherever he went. This was the best idea he'd had yet. The problem for him was that we had taken them over to the mall earlier that morning and had a copy made. Nothing was funnier than the look he had on his face when he went out to get into his van and it was gone. He had kept the keys on him at all times and couldn't figure out how we could have done it.

When hiding the van became old, we just started piling stuff inside of it. We'd grab all the gear for soccer or baseball and fill up the back area and the seats. We would put garbage pails in there or anything we could find lying around. He would just shake his head and lug all the stuff out while we stood by like little school boys and snickered.

The next stage in the evolution of "Anyone Seen My Car?" came when I was in college. Winters in Potsdam, N.Y., were pretty wild when it came to snow. We were located right in the middle of the snow belt of northern New York State. When the plows would clear the parking lots, they would leave massive piles of snow behind.

The first Clarkson University edition of "Anyone Seen My Car?" came in the winter of 2004-05, much to the chagrin of Grant Clitsome. A few of us walked out of our place on a snowy day to see Clitty's car sitting conveniently beside a massive snow bank. We grabbed a couple of shovels from the house and began transferring the giant pile onto and around Clitty's car. By the time we were done, you would have sworn the snow pile had just moved a few feet over and that the car was never really there. Unfortunately, we had to rush to get to class and were unable to see the fruits of our prank, but later at practice we were able to razz the grinning victim.

A couple of years later, I was playing over in Belgrade, Serbia. One day, while chatting with a few of the guys, I discovered that a Yugo, a popular vehicle in Eastern Europe, could be unlocked and started by any key that was the right size to fit in the tip of the door lock and ignition. Immediately my prank bells started ringing wildly. It was time for Anyone Seen My Car, Euro edition!

On our team in Belgrade—HK Partizan—we had three brothers—Bogdan, Bojan and Beki Jankovic. The brothers just happened to own one of these prank-friendly Yugos. Throughout the season, we would see the Jankovic Yugo at our practice facility and hide it in a new parking space. Other times, we'd see their Yugo outside of their apartment and move it to another street. One time, five of us even lifted the tiny car and moved it manually.

There really was no end to the evolution of "Anyone Seen My Car", a prank that was truly an international classic.

PRO HOCKEY

It's what you have been training for and striving for all your life. It presents an opportunity to show everyone that you deserve to make a living playing hockey. Don't blink or your window of opportunity will close.

Welcome to Pro Hockey

In my first year of pro hockey, I started the season signing with the Bossier-Shreveport Mudbugs of the Central Hockey League (CHL). I signed early in the off-season, around the end of May. I remember the song and dance I got from the coach, Scott Muscutt. He told me what I wanted to hear: I was going to be in the top six on defense and he envisioned me being an impact player on the power play, yadda, yadda and all those good things. I was pretty excited about the opportunity.

I had been talking with other teams, Johnstown in ECHL and Youngstown in the CHL, but they were bluntly honest with me, saying that I'd have to come into camp and win a job. The Mudbugs were not only offering me a spot, they were saying I was going to be an impact guy.

Another bonus with Bossier-Shreveport was that it was one of the only CHL teams affiliated with an NHL club, in this case the Buffalo Sabres. So amid the excitement of beginning my pro career, I signed.

As the summer progressed, the list of signed players with Bossier-Shreveport grew. Soon, there were two more defensemen with three-plus years of pro experience signed. The next week two more defensemen with impressive resumes signed, and three more the week after that. All of a sudden, it's time to go down to camp and Bossier-Shreveport had signed nine experienced defensemen in total.

When training camp began in October, there were 15 defensemen with either pro, NCAA or OHL experience in camp battling it out for seven spots. Before I even stepped on the ice, Muscutt called me into his office and stated that he wanted to convert me to a forward, a position I had very limited experience with and zero desire to pursue. However, at that point, all the other pro teams had signed their lot and had begun camp so if I wanted to play pro hockey I'd have to learn how to play a new position and suck it up.

To add insult to injury, there were about 25 forwards in camp battling it out for 12 positions and these guys were no slouches. I was looking at an uphill battle, to say the least.

I can't really blame Muscutt for leading me on and loading up a training camp roster. He wanted to build the best team he possibly could and if the summer progresses and some top-end talent falls into his lap, what is he going to say? No, thanks? Not if he wants to win. At the pro level, winning is everything. Winning puts butts in the seats, and as a coach in pro hockey, you are only as good as your last season's record.

I ended up having a pretty good camp and advanced to the exhibition games, where I excelled with two goals and an assist in two games. I even dropped back to play defense in one game when a couple of players went down with injuries. I impressed the coaching staff enough to keep me on as an extra forward when we broke camp after the exhibition schedule, but my future looked bleak with the prospect of players being sent down from Rochester, our affiliate in the American Hockey League (AHL).

With the season set to begin, disaster struck. There had been a mix-up with the work visas of all Canadian players and we were all deemed ineligible to work in the U.S. until our visas had been declared legitimate. This meant that our team had to start the season with only eight eligible players.

In a mad scramble, the team began pulling guys out of the area like retired players, Jim Sprott and Jason

Campbell, who had settled in the area after their playing careers had ended. Some of these guys hadn't played hockey in four-plus years and were badly out of shape.

Sprott was a great pro and had a fabulous career, but he wasn't expecting to be back playing in a pro game after retiring four years earlier. He was grossly overweight at about 275 pounds and looked like he might have a heart attack in the middle of warm up.

Not all of the guys who were called for emergency duty were accomplished former pros. Some were players who played university club hockey or local recreational hockey. It was pretty scary to see some of these guys playing against hungry pros looking to make a name for themselves.

A couple of games went by with the makeshift roster and the Canadian contingent began to get antsy. We didn't know when or if this situation was going to be sorted out and the coaching staff's hands were tied as they were just as much in the dark as we were.

Personally, I could see the writing on the wall. I was playing a foreign position, currently at the back end of a group of 12 forwards, and with the impending doom of potentially four players being sent down from Rochester, I knew my days were numbered.

Then something great happened. One of the guys I met in camp, Scott Wright, came up to me one day and said that his agent from Europe called him and said he had an opportunity for two defensemen overseas. Wrighter had played the prior season in Holland and was also in a situation where he was at the back end of a volatile situation. Wrighter asked me if I wanted to go. My reply was quick and simple, "Absolutely." I didn't even ask where it was, what the pay was going to be or anything. I was just desperate to play.

Next thing you know, we were on a flight the next day

out of Louisiana and heading to Belgrade, Serbia, to begin what would be an awesome adventure. It was an exciting time and we were just flying by the seat of our pants. The pro hockey world is so unpredictable and you always have to be ready for anything. Your bags are never fully unpacked because you have to be ready to move at the drop of a hat.

Missing at Midnight in Mississippi

During the limited time I was in Bossier-Shreveport, we had a team-bonding weekend in Tallulah, Miss., at our owner's hunting camp. The hunting camp was on a massive property that had an ample supply of deer and several ponds filled with alligators. It was a great place to get away and bond with your new teammates.

The first night we were there, four of us decided to take

out four-wheelers and cruise around the trails. We were flying high and having a great time ripping around in the dirt and mud. It was pitch black out and we didn't realize how big the property actually was. The trails were like a maze and it wasn't long before we were completely lost.

We stopped and looked around to see if we could figure out where we were but there was no light in sight. While we were stopped we could hear the sloshing of some alligators in a nearby swamp. After hearing that, we decided we had better keep moving.

Soon, some light came into view in the distance and as we got closer, we realized it was coming from a hunting camp. We were saved...or so we thought! As we drew closer and the camp came into focus, we began to realize it wasn't our owner's hunting camp. Once we realized it wasn't where we wanted to be we turned back and headed the other way.

Just as we made a loop to head back, a white pickup truck came barreling up behind us with flood lights on. I was at the back of the pack of four- wheelers and this pickup was practically riding my back tires. We had the four-wheelers going full tilt, but this truck kept gaining on us. Still trying to lose him, we ducked into a side path that eventually ended with a dead end at a swamp.

As we came to a stop, the owner of the truck leapt out and cocked his shotgun and pointed it at us. At this point, my heart rate was through the roof. I was thinking: "This is it. I'm going to die in this swamp." We began to panic.

One of the guys shouted out that we were here with the hockey team and we were staying at John Madden's (not the former NFL coach) camp as part of a team bonding trip. As soon as he heard this he shouted out in his thick Cajun accent: "Well why didn't y'all say so! I thought y'all were poachers!" He then invited us back to his camp for a beer.

We went back with him and had a few beers and swapped stories, all the while laughing about our close brush with death out in the Mississippi swamp.

Clifford the Brown Recluse

Growing up in Ontario, there aren't many animals or insects that you need to worry about living in and/or around your house. The spiders, as startling as they can be, aren't going to kill you with a bite and the snakes are nothing to write "National Geographic" about. Moving to the southern states, there was a lot for me to get used to.

When I was in Shreveport, La., I shared an apartment with two other players: Austin Sutter, from Red Deer, Alta., and John Decaro from Seattle, Wash. We were pretty naive when it came to living in the south and were especially naive when it came to species of insects. Shortly after moving in, we began to notice a spider that had made a little web in the light fixture just outside the entrance door to the apartment. We would always say hello to the spider when we would come home and even gave it a name: Clifford.

One day, one of the other players who had been playing in Shreveport for the last five seasons stopped by our apartment and said: "You guys better get rid of that spider."

We laughed and said: "Come on, you're not afraid of a little spider are you? That's just our buddy Clifford. He's the bouncer."

He replied: "Well I'm not afraid of spiders, but I am afraid of brown recluses and that, fellas, is what you have living just outside the door of your apartment.

The brown recluse spider is a venomous breed of southern state spider. It is one of the most dangerous spiders in the U.S., due to the necrotic effects of its venomous bites. If not immediately treated, the brown recluse bite can become fatal. It is not exactly the type of neighbor or housemate that you generally wish to have.

After finding out who Clifford really was, I grabbed my seven-iron and the three of us played rock/paper/scissors to figure out who was going to get rid of our deadly doorman. Although it was kind of sad to kill Clifford in such a heartless manner, we were relieved that we discovered his true identity before the weather turned chillier and he decided to move in. The last thing we would want is a full-blown infestation.

After telling the boys at practice the next day, we found out it was pretty common to encounter some deadly critters day-to-day in the southern U.S. One of the elder team members, who had become a permanent resident after marrying a local girl, told us about an encounter with two black widow spiders in his garage. He had been cleaning out the garage and the two unwanted tenants popped out after he moved a garbage bag.

The next season, when I was playing in Augusta in the ECHL, there was a scary incident that landed one of our conference's top scorers on the IR. Matt Reid, of the South Carolina Stingrays, was placed on the IR after receiving a bite from a deadly copperhead rattlesnake. Reid, who owned and operated a pressure washing business on the side, was performing a job during a day off from the rink and accidentally stepped on the resting snake. Reid was rushed to hospital and received treatments for the potentially fatal bite, but had to miss nearly two weeks of action during recovery.

Do You Remember Where the Apartment Is?

When we signed our contracts to go play over in Belgrade, Serbia, my roommate, Scott Wright, and I had no idea where Serbia was. All we knew was that it was a place to play and the money was pretty good. We were 24 years old, fearless and ready for anything. You could have offered me a contract to play in Baghdad at that time and I would have signed it.

Within two days, we were touching down in Belgrade with zero idea of what to expect. All we knew was that we would be living together in an apartment close to the downtown core and that someone with a sign at the airport was picking us up. We knew we were there to play hockey and that it was somewhere in Eastern Europe and that was about it.

My first memorable experience in Belgrade was waiting at the baggage claim as all of the bags circled the conveyer belt until there were no more Samsonites making the rounds. Wouldn't you know it, right off the bat, my luggage was lost. It took two days for the airline to locate my baggage and have it rerouted. This included my hockey gear and all of my clothes. So for the first two days of practice, I watched from the stands.

The first day we arrived in Belgrade, we were dropped off at the rink to meet the team, coaches and to get certified with the International Ice Hockey Federation (IIHF). After a quick chat with the owner and coaches, Scotty and I moved into our apartment and decided we'd better get to know the lay of the land.

By this, I mean we naturally figured a pub crawl was the best way to get acclimated to our new city. We walked out the front door of the apartment building and headed left down the street. About a block and a half later, we stumbled upon a small pub called The Black Peter. This place looked like a classic Irish pub, so we headed in for a couple of stouts.

After a couple of beers and some oddly mismatched techno music, we headed to a roulette room. Scotty liked to gamble and they served free beer to anyone who was laying money on the tables. Since I wasn't much of a gambler, I laid a chip on red and a chip on black for each bet so that I always came away even. In the end, Scotty lost 20 euros and I had three free pints of Becks. Sometimes you win, sometimes you lose.

Next on our journey was a bar called the Tramvaj, which was Serbian for tramway, appropriately named since the streets of Belgrade were lined with trolley cars. With its live rock music and homemade brews, the Tramvaj became one of our favorite spots.

That night at the Tramvaj, we ran into a couple of our teammates and they took us to another bar further downtown called the Belle Epoque. It was a fancier, nightclub-type bar. As the night began to fade and Scotty and I decided we'd tossed enough back for one night, we decided to hit the streets and grab a bite before heading back home.

As we wandered the streets, laughing and recounting what was easily the longest day of our lives, we began to realize that we were completely lost. Being stubborn Canadian hockey players, we began to disguise our confusion with masked bravado. The problem was that we didn't know the street or address we were looking for, so we couldn't just ask a cabby to drop us off.

Suddenly, the buildings began to look familiar and I blurted out: "I know exactly where we are. I remember this building earlier. The apartment is this way!"

After following my errant directions for another 40 minutes, Scotty chimed in: "Wait a minute! I know where it is. It's down this street and then a right and then another left." Scotty's misleading trek would tack on another 45 minutes of aimlessness.

After nearly two hours of dizzying ignorance, our stubbornness turned to argumentation. We bickered back and forth and pushed and shoved until we both split up in a huff and decided to find the place on our own.

The sun had already broken over the horizon and it was getting close to 7 a.m. when I finally spotted the convenience store that was located on the corner of the street where our apartment was. As I sighed with relief and stumbled up to the entrance of the building, my attention was drawn to my left where Scott was doing the same thing.

We had split up after nearly ripping each other's heads off and had found the place at the exact same time from opposite directions. We both just started laughing hysterically.

The Wild, Wild East

When my roommate, Scott Wright, and I landed in Belgrade, Serbia, we were oblivious to our new surroundings. I was so oblivious, caught up in the whirlwind of radically altering my rookie pro season plans on a whim that I didn't realize that "Serbia" wasn't "Siberia" until about half-way through "Nacho Libre", our mid-flight feature movie. All we knew was that we were going to play hockey and they were going to pay us handsomely to do so. What else did we need to know?

Aside from the obvious language barrier, Wrighter and I knew things were going to be a little different than we were used to, growing up in southern Ontario. The first thing that grabbed me was the intensely strong sense of pride. Serbians, especially the men, were insanely proud people. Whether it was a debate over politics or preference of beer, these guys were passionate and stubborn. For example, a friendly game of pickup basketball could turn into an all-out donnybrook over a missed travelling call.

Considering that Serbians have been living with the constant presence of war and conflict for centuries, it makes complete sense that they would be extremely proud people. Family, religion and deep-rooted cultural values are what have guided Serbians through their darkest days. It's the foundation of their perseverance, something we, as Canadians, were lax and somewhat absentminded about. It wasn't that we didn't appreciate the importance of these values. It was more that we never had to rely on them for survival. I had never known the feeling of my heart dropping at the sound of bombing sirens or the sheer panic of scrambling to protect an infant sibling from a deadly attack. My adversaries growing up were schoolyard bullies and athletes on opposing teams. This wasn't just a different country for us. This was a different world.

The first tough lesson Wrighter and I learned was that Serbians absolutely loathe Americans. I can't say I blame them considering it was the U.S. that bombed the shit out of their country for 78 straight days in 1999, killing upwards of 4,000 civilians. It's one thing to hate a country because you don't like their soccer team. It's another thing to hate a country because their army killed your entire family. A lot of my friends in Serbia lost brothers, fathers, sisters and mothers to war and violence.

Our introduction to this passionate hatred came late one night after Wrighter and I finished up at a pizza joint in downtown Belgrade. We were walking along the Bulevar, jabbering on about past glories when we were jumped by three guys. The first shot came from behind as one of the attackers drove his fist into Wrighter's right temple from behind. I saw Wrighter tumble forward with the attacker draped over his back. As I turned to jump in, I took a right hand across my right cheekbone. We were in a battle.

Every fight I have ever been in I have always remembered the first punch or two and then have no recollection of the events of the rest of the fight until after it is over. This isn't because I've been knocked out in every fight I've been in, it's because I "blackout" when I get into fights. I'm conscious and active, but I have no memory of what happened. I can't recount punches I've thrown or whether I won or lost.

After watching Wrighter get jumped and then taking a shot in the cheek, I went into blackout mode. When I came to, I was straddling one of the attacker's chests, throwing wild punches to his face. He wasn't conscious and was covered in blood. Wrighter was prying me off of him from behind, frantically telling me that we had to get out of there. We were in front of a busy bus stop with an audience of about seven or eight bystanders who seemed like they were oblivious to what had just taken place.

The next 10 minutes was like a blur of adrenaline and bemusement. I was in shock and wasn't processing anything that had happened. Once we were able to calm down, I began asking Wrighter about what happened. We talked it out and we pieced together the events. After getting jumped, Wrighter spun his attacker around and drilled him. After getting hit, the first attacker quickly ran off, evening up the ratio. I engaged with the guy who hit me and ended up knocking him out. Wrighter took care of the third attacker, who also fled. It happened so fast and nobody who was nearby seemed to care. It was like it was business as usual.

About 20 minutes after the fight ended, my hands began to throb and all of the dings and scrapes began to hurt. Wrighter had a welt under his eye and scarred up knuckles on his right hand. Both my hands were a mess and I had blood on my shirt and pants. Wrighter's shoes were splattered in blood, as well.

After the adrenaline wore off, we began to think rationally and immediately began to worry about consequences. "Shit, do you think the cops are out looking for us?" I asked.

"I don't know, man. Maybe? I mean, you would think they would be. But, no one at the bus stop seemed to even care, eh?" Wrighter replied.

"Maybe we should go to the police station and get ahead of it. Tell them that we got jumped and were just defending ourselves." I said.

"That's a good idea. Ya, let's do that." Wrighter said.

We walked down the street and into the police station. It was confession time. When we walked in, two men were sitting at a desk with their feet up, listening to a radio, reading newspapers and smoking heavily. "Hi. Do you speak English?" Wrighter said.

One of the police officers responded without looking over at us: "Yes."

"Oh good, we were just jumped in the street on the Bulevar by three guys. We ended up defending ourselves and kind of won the fight. We just wanted to come in and give a statement as to what happened. It was self defense all the way." Wrighter said.

The police officer who spoke to us before continued to read his paper without looking over at us and replied: "OK."

"So do we have to fill out a report or sign anything? Do you want to ask us questions?" I asked.

"No. That's OK." Replied the police officer.

"So we are good to go? No problems?" Wrighter asked.

"Yes. No problems. Good night." Replied the officer.

And with that, Wrighter and I walked out of the police station and headed home.

At practice the next day I couldn't even hold my stick because my hands were so swollen. We told all the guys about the brawl and they were killing themselves laughing. "You Canadian guys are crazy," said Nikola Dunda, a 5-foot-9 domestic defenseman. Dunda was a funny guy who loved to indulge in the abundance of nightlife entertainment Belgrade had to offer.

"It was nuts, Dunda!" I replied. "I think I may have killed one of the guys."

"You know why they jumped you, right?" Dunda said.

"Why?" I asked.

"They thought you guys were Americans. We hate Americans here, Brate. You boys gotta start wearing stuff to show you are Canadian. We love Canadians, but hate, hate, hate Americans." He replied.

We told the guys about how we went to the police station to report the fight and the room erupted in riotous laughter. Some of the guys were crying they were laughing so hard. "You reported the fight to the police?" Bojan Jankovic shouted over the laughter.

"Ya, man. We didn't want to get arrested." Wrighter replied.

"They aren't going to arrest you for that. The police don't get paid enough to give a shit about that stuff." Bojan said.

Bojan was right. About two weeks later, Dunda took a bunch of us to a rave in an industrial park on the outskirts of Old Belgrade. Later that night, about six of us were crammed into a Yugo, driving back into Belgrade's downtown core when we got pulled over. I was sitting in the backseat and immediately started panicking. Our driver was pretty wasted and I thought for sure he was going to get dragged away in cuffs and charged with a DWI.

"He's fucked! Oh shit, he's fucked. What are we going to do?" I said.

"Shut up, brate. Calm down, he's not going to get charged." Dunda said.

"What do you mean? He's plastered. They're going to charge him." I said.

While Dunda tried to calm me down our driver got out of the car and walked back to meet the police officer who was getting out of his car.

"Oh shit! He's going to shoot him. Why did he get out of the car? Oh fuck!" I said.

"Relax brate! Everything is cool." Dunda reassured me.

Just then, the driver came back to the car, leaned in the window and asked if anyone had 1600 dinars, the equivalent of about 20 bucks. I eagerly reached into my wallet and handed him the cash. He walked back to meet the cop and handed him the cash. They then shook hands and the cop turned and went back to his car. Our driver hopped back in the Yugo and away we went. Dunda then explained to me that the police barely make any money and need to find ways to supplement their income. All of them are on the take and almost anything can be settled for the right amount of money.

My good friend Bojan Jankovic told me a story about a time when a police car pulled in behind him with the lights flashing, looking to pull him over. He said he felt bored at the time and decided to see if he could lose him. What happened next was a good old-fashioned 10 minute, high-speed car chase through the winding streets of downtown Belgrade. Bojan's father used to be a professional race car driver in Yugoslavia, so it was in his blood. Bojan told me about careening around tight corners into side streets, using the trams to create diversions and blazing through red lights. Towards the end of the chase, Bojan had lost the cop and backed his Yugo into a dark alley and turned the lights off. Moments later, the police car pulled up in front of the alley and the cop hopped out and shone a light on him.

Busted!

Bojan said the cop didn't arrest him but made him pay a pretty penny for his little adventure. Where else could you get to be Steve McQueen for a night, get caught and stay out of the clinker? Anything and everything was possible in the *Wild, Wild East*.

Ne Dryer, Nema Problem

The Eastern European lifestyle presents quite a few differences from the lifestyle we are accustomed to in North America. They eat a lot healthier than we do, dress a lot nicer and drive cars that would fit in your wife's walk-in closet. In Belgrade, Serbia, the citizens boast a strong sense of pride in their culture, heritage, religion and family. Serbians are passionate and patriotic.

During my first tour over in Europe during the 2006-07 season, my roommate, Scott Wright, and I lived in a beautiful old apartment downtown. We had 12-foot ceilings, French doors and were located close to all the hot spots. We were making great money and playing the game we loved for a living. Life couldn't have been any better.

One of the differences I noticed right away when I first lived in Belgrade was that clothes dryers weren't common. In fact, I never saw one. As nice as our apartment was, we didn't have a washer, either. When it came time to wash our clothes, which we would delay until the last possible moment and stuff them all into a hockey bag. We would heave it over our shoulders and embark on a 30-minute walk to the rink.

While we practiced, Mladan, the team trainer would wash our clothes in the washer at the rink. After practice, we would pile the soaking wet heap of clothes into the bag and then lug it back home to hang up to dry in the apartment. The worst part was that the walk to the rink was all downhill and the walk home was uphill. So we would have the lighter load with the dry, dirty clothes walking downhill to the rink and then the soaked, heavy bag of clothes walking uphill on the way back home.

On laundry day, our apartment took on quite the transformation. Every chair, table, dresser, window shade and pot handle took on the form of a drying rack. We had to move my underwear and Scotty's socks out of the way to watch "Meerkat Mansion" on the only English TV channel we had. Scotty even tried to get crafty and use the oven as a quicker drying option until we nearly burned down a building that had survived two world wars and 78 days of NATO bombing.

I'm still not quite sure why there weren't any dryers. Maybe it was because hanging your clothes to dry, rather than putting them in the dryer, helped to maintain the quality of the clothes. Maybe it was a good way to conserve energy. Whatever the reason was, I developed a new appreciation for a clothing routine. Never again did I wear a T-shirt for the morning then throw it in the dirty clothes to put on a different shirt for the afternoon and evening. Whatever I put on in the morning stayed on for the rest of the day. I think I increased my shoulder strength, too, from lugging those wet sacks around downtown Belgrade.

Lost in Translation

Heading to play over in Europe was definitely going to be an eye-opener. It was a new opportunity in a foreign land and it was a chance to step outside of my comfort zone and learn about a new culture.

The first obstacle I knew I would have to tackle playing in Belgrade was the communication barrier. I didn't know one word of the language when I stepped off the plane and figured I would have to rely heavily on non-verbal cues.

Much to my delight, I discovered that nearly everyone I crossed paths with in Serbia spoke at least enough English to get by. Some of my teammates were completely fluent in English. In fact, most people that I came across spoke several languages and I'm not just talking languages of similar dialect and structure. One of my teammates, Beki Jankovic, spoke Serbian, English, French and German fluently among several other languages in which he could carry on a conversation.

The toughest part about communicating in my first year playing for HK Partizan was the fact that our coach, Vadim Musatov, who played 10 years in the Russian Superleague (known now as the Kontinental Hockey League) spoke only Russian. Vadim would explain a drill to us in Russian and then the assistant coach, Bera Nikola, would translate what he said into Serbian.

My roommate, Scott Wright, and I would be standing there looking at everyone as if they had six heads waiting for someone to translate it all into English. By this point, everyone was breaking off to begin the drill and finally one of the guys would say to us: "Ya, coach just said to go into the corner and pull down your pants and sing the Canadian National Anthem." To make matters worse, the guys would make Scotty and me go first and laugh as we bumbled our way through the drill.

The next time my domestic teammates decided to play a language-barrier trick on me was when we went out for a few beers on a day off. At the time, I was single and I wanted to learn a couple of catch phrases that I could say to a girl if I decided to approach one.

One time, I asked the guys how to say "Hi, my name is Jamie. Can I buy you a drink?" They all looked at each other and smiled, which should have been my first clue that something ridiculous was about to happen. I remember our captain, Bogdan Jankovic, nodding and then turning to me and saying: "No problem Jamer. Here is what you need to say..." He told me some words in Serbian and I rehearsed with him until I got the phrase down pat.

Bogdan nodded and said: "You're ready my friend. Go and dazzle the chicks." I was brimming with confidence, rehearsing the line over and over in my mind and I went up to a girl and dropped the line flawlessly. As soon as the last words left my mouth, she looked at me as if I just drop-kicked her dog right in front of her. She snorted like a bull and stormed away.

I turned back to a group of guys who were falling over each other in hysterics. Shaking my head, I walked back to the group and said: "OK you morons what did I just say?"

Bogdan, barely able to speak because he was out of breath from laughing so hard, said: "Jamer, you just said that your name is Jamie and that you want to wear her underwear as a hat." At this, I had to join in the laughter. It was actually pretty funny, considering I said it in such a polite, sweet voice.

After that, I never asked any of those knuckleheads for language advice, although they were always willing to offer it up. The rest of the season, that encounter at the bar became a running joke. One day one of the guys even came out for practice with a pair of underwear over his helmet. Lesson learned here? Trust your teammates not to embarrass you on the ice, but never in a bar.

Partizan Payday

One of the biggest nightmares you hear about playing in Europe is the odd story about players not getting paid on time or, in rare cases, at all. In my first season in Europe, I signed a contract to play in Belgrade for HK Partizan. The deal was arranged through a friend's agent and included a salary to be paid monthly, team-based performance bonuses, an apartment in downtown Belgrade, a two-way (return) flight from North America, equipment and sticks, a cell phone, and two four-course meals in a nice downtown restaurant per day. All in all, this was a hell of a deal for a league below the elite level in Europe.

The best part of the deal was that we were paid in Euros, in harmony with competitive import salary wages of leagues such as the French Magnus league, German Oberliga and the Dutch league. Since Serbia was not a part of the European Union and lagged behind economically, the salary we were making was huge when taking into consideration the cost of living in Belgrade and currency rates. To put it into perspective, we were making over twice as much as a doctor in Serbia.

We were paid once a month, and since the currency in Serbia wasn't euros, but rather dinars, our owner gave us a choice to either be paid in euros or dinars. We decided dinars would be best, that way we wouldn't have to go through the trouble of exchanging the cash later.

Initially, we didn't consider this, but one euro was equivalent to about 80 dinars, at the time. So when we went in to get paid, instead of leaving with a small wad of cash that could fit in your wallet, we left with four big stacks of bills.

Since we were only there for seven months or so, there really was no point in opening a bank account. The money we were paid was tax free, so we just took our money back to the apartment, where we had a wall safe, and just loaded the stacks of cash in there.

That season, we lived like kings and spared no expense. Since our room and board was covered, our only expenses were recreation. We lived life to the fullest and were still able to come back home with a nice sum of money saved up. On paydays, I felt like I was a mobster of some kind walking out of the rink with a paper bag full of money stacks. It's blind luck that nobody jumped me in the street and made off with my monthly salary.

My roommate and I hated the coach who took over mid-season, Frantisek Vorlicek (A Czech version of Gargamel from "The Smurfs." More on him in a later story), so much that we seriously considered dressing up in ski masks one payday and robbing him on his way home. We sat in a pub one day and played out the entire attack. I was going to spring out from behind a bush and tackle him and Scotty was going to swoop in and grab the bag of money. From beer No. 3 to beer No. six, it was a great idea. After beer No. 7, we lost motivation.

Wet Gear in Belgrade

In hockey, even more so than any other sport, players are obsessively particular about their equipment. Whether it is skates, sticks or goalie pads, hockey players are one odd group of anal-retentive doorknobs. It may be due to superstitious reasons or just plain comfort, but players will spend hours on end shaving, cutting, sewing and blow-torching pieces of their equipment in order to achieve some sort of harmony and contentment.

Sticks might just be the worst when it comes to obsessing and tinkering. I once played with a guy who used to work on his sticks like he was performing open-heart surgery. To start with, he would cut nearly two inches off the toe of his stick blade. After that, he'd be filing, shaving and blow- torching the thing to shape it to what, in his crazy mind, he felt was the perfect instrument to score goals, zip passes and apply the odd slash.

Another guy I played with used to use four different sticks per game, each one cut down to a different length than the others. He explained to me that studies showed that the more fatigued you got during the game, the more you bent over. Each stick was cut shorter so that he could use shorter sticks as the game went on. He had a stick for the first, second and third periods, respectively, and a fourth one in case we went into overtime.

Some guys like to use wax on the blade and others used baby powder. These techniques are used to help keep moisture off the blade and increase the grip on the puck. Some guys like to have sticky shafts and apply the "Beater", which is a cut off stick knob with tape wrapped around it in reverse to make a sticky surface to rub along the shaft of the stick. Others will wrap tape around the shaft of the stick in a candy cane fashion.

Preferences for sticks will also vary in shaft flex, curve of the blade, lie of the blade, knob construction, and paddle shape. Some guys prefer lighter sticks while others like a traditional heavy stick and shy away from the newer composite one-piece sticks. Each player's preference is unique and often different in one or more ways than the next. It's nearly impossible to find two players on a team who use the same configuration.

Skates are a whole other topic when it comes to preference. Some guys go barefoot, like me, while others wear sometimes up to three different types of socks. Some want a forward tilt in their boot, while others want a tilt more suited for a defenceman, who spends more time skating backwards. Players will get different profiles when it comes to skate sharpening, which has become extremely specific and an art form in itself. Some use wax laces to keep a tight fit while others tie their skates up loosely to allow for more flexion and movement in the boot.

When it came to skate sharpening, when I was young I used to get my skates sharpened almost every time I played. When I turned pro, I changed my preference and went almost completely to the other extreme. In a 72-game pro season, I might have sharpened my skates eight times. I would go sometimes over a month between sharpening. By that time in my career, I felt that I had more speed and glide when I didn't sharpen them as often.

When it came to the topic of equipment, apart from sticks and skates, there were too many intricacies to even get into, but one thing seemed to be consistent. Nearly all players agree upon the fact that they hate playing in soaking wet gear. Wet gear is extremely heavy and makes everything more tiring when you're on the ice. The one thing you always made sure to do when you got to a new destination on the road was to hang up your gear so it would dry out effectively. Most teams pack industrial fans to help speed up the process.

When I went to play in Belgrade, the one thing that bothered me was that I could never get my gear to dry out after practices and games. Our dressing room was in a belly of an old arena that was built in the early '70s. The dressing room was a dungeon and had a lot of character, but the one thing it had that I didn't care for was poor air circulation. There were vents, but there never seemed to be air coming out of them. We had makeshift hangers set up all over the ceiling of that room, but it didn't matter. Our gear was always soaked.

After chatting with some of my friends on another team in our league, HK Vojvodina, I soon discovered that they were experiencing the same problems as we were. They were constantly playing in soaking wet gear, too. It was like an Eastern European epidemic. Attack of the Soggies!

Any player can tell you that their biggest pet peeve in hockey is when you have to squish your feet into a soggy pair of skates and then slap drenched, cold shin pads on. You see, when your skates are constantly wet, the material on the inside of the tongue begins to rub on your feet. With the laces cutting through wet material, you end up getting an extremely painful and nagging injury called "lace bite". Lace bite mainly affects the skin but can also cause damage to the tendons and muscles in your lower shin and ankle.

Towards the end of the season, the boys in Vojvodina said enough is enough and they were able to finagle an industrial hot air dryer for their dressing room. It was time to put an end to the wet gear issue once and for all. The problem with this was that about a week later, while the dryer was on overnight, either an electrical short or a piece of material too close to the heat caused a fire in the dressing room, damaging all of the contents.

In the end, guys started packing up some of their gear and lugging it home after practices and games to dry out. I gave up on this quickly as I found trekking half an hour uphill after practice each day with 25 extra pounds of wet gear was probably going to give me a back injury. After a couple of those arduous trips, lace bite didn't seem too bad.

Gypsies

Until I went to play in Belgrade, Serbia, I had no idea what a Gypsy really was. I figured Gypsies wore long robes, travelled in caravans and read people's fortunes. I didn't realize that the Gypsy way of life was deep-rooted, principled and rich in tradition.

My first real introduction to the Gypsy way of life came on a cab ride from the airport into Belgrade. As we passed over the bridge into Belgrade, I looked out and saw a vast area filled with makeshift homes made of tin, cardboard and scraps. It was sad yet remarkable. I asked the cabbie what it was and he said that it was "Gypsyland". He said it was the area of the city where the Gypsies were given sanctuary.

Apparently, since Gypsyland was considered an eyesore, the government had offered up an old, vacated communist community housing building to the Gypsies, free of charge. The Gypsies declined the gesture, preferring to maintain their age-old way of life, crafting their homes, vehicles and wares from scraps found while foraging through the landfills and city garbage receptacles.

The Gypsies in Belgrade were really quite crafty and resourceful. One day, my roommate and I saw a Gypsy driving a makeshift vehicle through the busy city streets, towing a trailer behind it carrying his find for the day. It was a small motor, something similar to a lawnmower, with a singular tire in the front and two tires in the back. It had an old classroom chair for a seat and a long, pivoting bar with handlebars attached to the wheel as the steering mechanism. Since my roommate and I were considering buying a Yugo for 150 euros, we offered the Gypsy 100 euros for his contraption. He scoffed at us and declined our offer, blowing a big, black cloud of smoke up into our faces as he sped away in his Gypsymobile.

As resourceful and proud as the Gypsies in Belgrade were, I couldn't help but feel sorry for them as they walked around in severely weathered clothes with poor hygiene. Quite often you would see Gypsy kids as young as seven or eight years old walking around bars begging for change, before being shooed away by wait staff.

There was a saying in Belgrade when I was playing there: "Sleep with a Gypsy and benefit from seven years of good luck." This line used to get thrown around a lot when we were in scoring slumps or on losing streaks. We could be losing 6 - 0 and I could be minus-6 and one of the guys would lean over and say: "Relax, Brate. You just need to go out and bang a Gypsy tonight. Tomorrow you'll score a hat trick."

In a country that had experienced extreme heartache in the not-so-distant past, the plight and suffering of the Gypsies didn't seem all that important. For me, it was just another example of heart, courage and perseverance in a part of the world rife with inspiration. Playing in eastern Europe put everything into perspective for me. No longer did I feel sorry for myself for not reaching my dream of playing in the NHL. To lace 'em up every day with guys who had experienced real terror, yet were able to keep their head up and push forward, was truly inspiring.

That's Why They Call It The Cage, Baby!

In the NCAA, athletes are spoiled. They play and train in state-of-the-art facilities and travel, eat and sleep in style. In college, when hit the road, we stayed in hotels like the Westin or Marriott and ate at the Macaroni Grill or the Olive Garden. We played teams like the University of Wisconsin, which plays in the Kohl Centre in front of 14,000 fans and we had a staff of equipment managers that unpacked our gear for us.

At home, we were trained by a team of specialists that also trained the Ottawa Senators and used high- tech equipment to monitor our VO2 Max and lactate levels during exertion. We had elite workout equipment and a staff of trainers to mend every scratch, bump and bruise. We really lived like kings, and after four years, you got accustomed to it and really took things for granted.

My first year out of the NCAA, I ended up in Belgrade and was about to have my eyes opened in a big way. The crowds went from thousands to hundreds and the high-tech workout facility was transformed into "The Cage".

The Cage was a long stretch of concourse at the top of our home arena, the "Hala Pioner," that was enclosed by an iron cage. The weights and equipment in this makeshift gym looked like they were stolen from Popeye's garage. It was totally old school and we loved it. Every time we had workouts in there, we'd act like we were chimpanzees in a zoo and climb all over the inside of the cage making monkey noises and shaking the bars.

Our coach, Vadim Musatov, used to run the workouts and he'd have us doing circuit training that was straight out a of a ratty, dog-eared Soviet Union National Team binder he was given back in the '80s. We were doing some pretty funny exercises, such as working in pairs and jumping up into the arms of your partner who would toss you to the left or the right. It was old school stuff that would make a modern strength and conditioning coach wince, but we thought it was funny and played along enthusiastically.

That old gym had unbelievable character and made you feel like you were from another era, one when you really earned everything by the sweat of your brow and instincts were animalistic. The Cage gave us an identity to attach ourselves to. When we were in the cage, we were wild animals. When we came out of it, we carried that persona everywhere we went. We used to rip off a set squats, jump up on the side of the cage and scream out: "That's why they call it 'The Cage', baby!"

Shake and Bake

The last thing I thought I was going to inherit when I signed a contract to play in Europe was a pair of hamsters, but you know what they say: "When in Rome...," or in my case, Belgrade. One day after practice, my roommate, Scott Wright, and I were leaving the rink when one of the ladies who worked in the IIHF office popped her head out and asked us if we wanted to adopt two hamsters. Scotty and I just looked at each other, shrugged and said, "Sure, I guess."

So later that night, a cage with two hamsters was dropped off at our apartment. We decided to name the hamsters "Shake" and "Bake", and a season-long series of experiments began. At first, we spoiled the buggers with toys and balls that they could play with and we often brought carrots, tomatoes and lettuce home from the restaurant for the hamsters to snack on. We never could tell what sex they were and we used to joke and debate about if they were male or female. Shake was really aggressive and loved to mix it up and Bake was really docile and just wanted to eat all day. So, initially we'd crack jokes about Shake being the male and Bake being the female.

One thing the hamsters had in common was that they spent most of their time trying to figure out how to get out of the cage. We'd hear them constantly at night, gnawing on the bars, so eventually we put them in the kitchen, which was the only room in the apartment that was separated by the foyer. We felt bad for them being cooped up all day, so we brought home one of those big balls that they could run around the apartment in. That thing turned out to be better than TV. We'd sit there and laugh, watching them run around in that thing and bonk into walls and tables. Sometimes we'd put them both in there and watch them duke it out in the "Ball of Death".

One night, we didn't hear the ball rolling around anymore. When I went to investigate, I found the thing cracked open and Shake was nowhere to be found. We lived in an old Victorian-style building, so there were a lot of places Shake could have scurried off to. After a couple of days with no Shake, we conceded that he must have found a new home. All of a sudden, about four days after he ran off, he appeared in the middle of the living room while we were watching "Myth Busters" on the only English TV station we could get.

While Shake was away on his or her adventure, Bake was completely stressed out. He or she packed on about three ounces! That's when we decided that from then on, Shake was going to be a male and Bake was going to be a female, whether they liked it or not. After Shake returned from the mini brothels and hole-in-the-wall haunts, he laid a pretty good beating on Bake. I guess all the nagging and reprimanding was too much for him to take.

When the end of the season came, we duped another one of our teammates into taking the pair of rodents off our hands. Growing up I had dogs and cats but never any hamsters or gerbils. It was a fun experience having those two meatballs living with us and it gave us one more quirk to a season that was chock-full of head tilters.

My Key Won't Work

My first season in Belgrade, my roommate Scott Wright and I lived in an old apartment building right downtown. The building was a pretty nice building with a big, swirling staircase in the lobby that spun its way up to the second and third floors. The doors to all of the apartments were big thick redwood-type suckers with keyholes that required the long, old school "Tales from the Crypt" keys. The apartment itself was big with 12- foot ceilings, crown molding, and French doors leading into the bedrooms. There was a separate kitchen and a foyer area and the large windows in each room opened up to the street. All in all, we ended up with a pretty sweet setup.

Being young and living in downtown Belgrade, Scotty and I decided we were going to live it up to the fullest. We would often have teammates over for a few pops before we went out to a bar and hosted the odd poker night. We lived above a convenience store, so we would just pop up and down to grab more beer and snacks. We never really saw our neighbors from the building too often and they never complained about noise, so we assumed everything was hunky-dory.

One day, after we had a little poker game the night before, we were heading back from practice and for some reason I couldn't get my key into the lock to open the door to our apartment. I tried over and over and then looked inside and it appeared that our keyhole had been sealed up with cement. I said to Scotty: "I think someone has been screwing with our lock. Check it out." Scotty looked at it and agreed. Someone had jammed our lock with cement.

While we were fumbling around with the lock, the neighbors who lived above us started peeking over the railing. I caught them watching and asked them if they knew what happened to our lock. The man was timid and tried to scurry away, but the wife, who clearly wore the pants in the household, calmly said: "You guys were loud last night so we put cement in your lock."

I shook my head in bewilderment and replied: "You put cement in our lock? That's how you thought you would be able to solve a noise problem? Cement!? Why didn't you come down and ask us to quiet down? We would have gladly obliged."

She avoided reason and simply replied with more sternness to her voice, "You were too loud!"

That's about the time I started getting angry. I started walking into the opening of the staircase so I could address her more directly and stated: "You are just a common criminal. That's what you are. A criminal!"

At this she became incensed. She barked at me, "I certainly am not!" I said: "Yes you are! You committed the crime of vandalism. What crime did we commit? If you had called the police, they would have issued us a noise complaint warning, but if I call the police now, they will charge you with vandalism."

After this, she became very defensive and her voice

became louder and louder, spewing Serbian insults at me until I finally said to her: "I'll give you two options. Either I call the police and you defend yourself against a vandalism charge or you tell me which car is yours out back and I'll go out and kick in all the windows." After this, the husband came down to meet me, apologizing and pleading with me, saying that they would pay for the charge to replace the lock.

In the end, we ended up calling the owner, who put us up in a hotel for the night until a locksmith could come in the next day. Being stubborn, revenge-seeking hockey players, my roommate and I threw bigger, louder parties for the rest of the season and the neighbors never once ventured out to mess with our apartment again. As stubborn as I may be, my sense of compassion and reason is very strong and wide spread, but when backed into a corner, my wrath is mightier than hellfire.

First-Line Treatment

Most of my playing career, I never knew what it was like to be a first-line player. In minor hockey, I was always the smallest kid on the team who served as the "Grocery Stick" (Player who sits in the middle of the bench, between the forwards and defencemen, staring at the water bottles). In junior, it wasn't until my last year that I got a taste of what being a first-line player was all about. In college, I had to learn how to play all over again and went through a lot of adversity as my game transformed completely. As a pro, even though I had gotten it by that point, I was a depth guy who contributed primarily on the secondary special teams units.

The only true time in my career that I was "the go-to guy" was in my first year playing for HK Partizan. That season, I exploded offensively and played over 30 minutes a game getting ample time on both of the first special teams units. For the first time in a long time, I really felt that my performance could make or break the outcome of a game on a nightly basis. I felt confident in my abilities and I was playing with swagger.

In Europe, the style of play is quite different than that of the North American pro game. Playing on an Olympic-sized ice surface drastically changes the way the game is played and the overall system design. Since there is more room to maneuver on the big ice, your breakouts, fore-checks and power-play setup revolves heavily around puck possession, transition and speed. There is no such thing as dump and chase and you rarely run out of your way to make a big hit because you don't want to open up lanes for the opposition to generate speed.

Another interesting difference between the North American pro game and the European pro game was that forwards and defensemen worked in five-man units instead of the three-man forward units and two-man defensemen units operating separately. This meant that as a defenceman, I would always be playing with the same forward unit. I personally thought this made a lot of sense because it allowed you to harvest chemistry in a more complete and consistent manner and opened up the possibility of multiple strategies when it came to line matching.

Another intricacy of playing in Europe was that they truly held their first-line players in high regard. For example, in countries such as Sweden and Finland, the top scorer on the team wears a gold helmet. In many countries, they select a player of the game who is presented in a ceremony at center ice with a large basket containing booze, food and gifts. I assume the adulation showered upon first line players is set up to motivate other players to strive for greatness and to reward excellence.

I remember one day during my first season playing for HK Partizan, I showed up to the rink for practice and the first- and second-line players were all milling around the coaches office while the third- and fourth- line players were gearing up. I asked one of our players why they weren't getting ready. He responded: "The first two lines aren't practicing today. We're going to the owner's house for spa treatments and relaxation." I was stunned. I had never seen anything like that in all my years playing hockey.

The next thing I know, I'm at our owner's gated compound in the basement, where he had an indoor pool, sauna and massage tables. We lounged around all day, getting drinks and food served to us while we got massages, soaked in the pool and decompressed in the sauna. All the while, the third and fourth lines were on the ice getting put through the paces. This was definitely the royal treatment.

I remember that I couldn't fully enjoy it because I wasn't used to this type of treatment and because I didn't feel right doing it without everyone being involved. I'm not a big fan of celebrating statistical successes in sports because I believe it diminishes the importance and value of non-statistical contributions.

Hockey is a sport that is won and lost in so many areas that don't show up on a score sheet. Finishing checks, blocking shots, winning face-offs and playing strong defensively are all important things that help you win games.

I knew what it was like to be an unheralded, blue-collar soldier. I broke bones blocking shots and grinded it out in the corners and in front of the net to do whatever I could to get the two points. I knew what it was like to be a guy who never got his name in the paper or went for the three-star twirl at the end of the game. Lounging poolside, with a cold drink in my hand, I felt sleazy. I felt like I was betraying my roots and what I felt was important to winning.

Winning teams are composed of a full roster of players, all as equally important as the next. Everyone has a job and a time to shine at what they specialize in. If you score goals, block shots, kill penalties or shut down the opposing team's top line, the game will provide opportunities where your skill set is invaluable. That's the beauty of hockey. There are so many situations that arise that require a special role to be filled. If you don't build your team to handle all situations, you are set up for failure. When all players contribute in their own way, you have a powerful force.

One of the best team guys I ever played with was a guy from my junior days, Mike Laughlin. He used to have a saying: "We're a family! We're a fist!" If you don't find ways to motivate and make each player feel valued, your once-strong fist becomes an open hand.

Egypt or Snowboarding

Playing in Europe comes with a lot of perks that you don't get playing pro hockey in North America. For starters, you don't play as many games in Europe, so immediately your body is saying "Thank you!" Also, practices are not quite as intense as in North America and you typically aren't going to get banged around as much on the big Olympic ice surface as you would on the 200 by 85 North American sheets. Since many of the players in Europe play for their country's national teams, you also encounter mini-breaks throughout a season, like a break during the world junior championships.

In 2006-07, I was playing in Belgrade and we were told that we'd be getting a 10-day break right around Christmas to allow some of the younger players to take leave from their respective teams and compete in the world junior championships. This was a stressful time for my roommate Scott Wright and me because we had a major dilemma on our hands. We had to decide if we were going to vacation for a week in Egypt, where we could tour the pyramids and learn about King Tut and the Pharaohs, or we could head south to the Serbian resort town Kopaonik for a week of snowboarding and fun in the snowy mountains.

A few friends of ours who were Canadian imports for our rival, HK Vojvodina—Marc-Andre Fournier, Daniel Jacob, Jonathan Gauthier and Fred Perowne—were heading to Egypt and were trying to convince us to join them. In the end, we decided that the allure of a week of snowboarding and carefree fun was too hard to pass up and we packed up our snowsuits and headed south. Scotty had originally found a deal through a nearby travel agency that included a bus to and from the resort, lift passes for the week, rentals, and accommodation on the mountain, all for around 250 euros apiece. You couldn't beat that with a stick! All we had to cover was food, which we packed because our accommodation suite had a kitchen, and beer money.

So Monday morning we hopped on the bus and winded south through the picturesque villages of Serbia and up the narrow, snow-covered roads of the Kopaonik mountain ranges. We were teetering on two wheels around an icy corner, staring sure death in the face when Scotty and I started second guessing our decision not to go to Egypt. Eventually we pulled into the resort and were greeted with a spectacular sight that put our minds at ease. The resort looked like it was copied and pasted out of a Swiss Alps ski brochure. It was definitely a European hidden gem that, as we soon discovered, was a hot spot for travelers from the U.K. and France.

Initially, we thought we should rent skis and stay in our

comfort zone, but after chirping one another, we decided that we'd both give snowboarding a shot. The first run down, we spent most of the time on our backs and stomachs, but eventually we began to get the hang of it. By the end of the day, we could zip down the mountain without a single fall. I remember we decided to pack it in at about 4 p.m., and have a couple of beers and it was as if we'd both been in a car accident. We had more bumps and bruises than we'd ever accumulated in a hockey game.

As the week went on, we settled in to a pretty good routine. We'd get up in the morning and hit the slopes by 8 or 9 a.m. At noon, we'd stop for lunch at a tavern about halfway down the mountain. We'd typically have a pleskavica (Essentially a pork hamburger with loads of great veggies and sauces wrapped in a pita bun) and a beer tower, which was four liters of goodness for the equivalent of about 10 bucks.

After lunch, we'd put in another shift on the mountain and packed it in for the day around 4 or 5 p.m., depending on how beat up we were. We'd then soak in the pool and hot tub and grab dinner before we'd tour the resort bars for the evening.

After living like Sean White for a week, minus being wicked awesome, we were ready to head back to Belgrade to get the second half of the season underway. About a week or so later, Scotty and I took a couple of days during the week and went up to Novi Sad to visit our import friends who played for Vojvodina. They took us out to a few local cafes for homemade Rakia as we all recounted our respective world junior break trips.

After hearing the horror stories experienced by our friends, we were happy with the decision we made not to go to Egypt. Marc, Dan, Joe and Fred told us stories of how overpopulated and poverty-stricken Cairo was and about the scams the locals would work on tourists. They talked about how local guides were tricking tourists into putting down deposits and then not showing up at the meeting spots. They explained that the tours were over-hyped and that there wasn't the extensive access to the tombs and pyramids as depicted on TV ads and documentaries. All in all, they said they were glad they experienced it but were disappointed because they had built it up in their minds going into the trip.

Stressing over leisurely vacation decisions was just one of the struggles of playing in Europe. Others included which cafe patio to sit on to enjoy a fresh cup of European blend coffee or which museum, art gallery or medieval fortress to peruse from day to day. Making good money to play two games a week and practice without contact every day for an hour was a tough grind, but someone had to do it.

Motorcade and Armed Escort in Zagreb

Playing hockey in Eastern Europe was one of the best experiences of my life. I learned more about life living in Belgrade than anywhere else in the world. The lifelong friends I made there and the culture taught me the real meaning of honor and pride and about standing up for what is most important to you. I really learned to appreciate the people in life that are there for you no matter what and to live in the moment rather than stressing about the future or the past.

The lifestyle and priorities over in Eastern Europe were night and day when compared to what we experience on a day-to-day basis in North America. For starters, these people have recently experienced the devastation of war in their own backyard and have stared fear and uncertainty square in the face. They have suffered extreme economic collapse, only to build themselves back up through a strong sense of faith, culture and tradition.

Through tainted views of North American corporately owned news outlets, we really only see a western perspective of what has happened in the former Yugoslavia. There is a great documentary about the friendship of two basketball players, Vlade Divac and Drazen Petrovic, who grew up as best friends in Yugoslavia only to be torn apart later in life due to the struggles between their home countries of Serbia and Croatia.

The documentary, an ESPN "30 for 30" production entitled "Once Brothers", looks closely at the development of the war between the two countries and the effect it had on a once prosperous and beautiful region. These two elite athletes had never once fought between themselves, but their allegiance to their people was so strong that they could not continue a friendship because it would betray an undying oath of nationalism.

In 2006 when I first played in Belgrade, it was clear that deep-rooted animosity and anger was present between Serbians and Croatians. Walking in downtown Belgrade, one building still remained levelled from the 1999 NATO bombings—a grotesque reminder of a period in time when everything changed and, in a strange but inspiring sense, a reminder that pride and unity would prevail in the face of adversity.

Serbian teammates told me tales of the 76-day ordeal, recounting that bands of Serbian civilians lining the rooftops and streets, chanting and singing national hymns to show support and unity. Before all of the war and carnage, Serbians and Croatians used to be the best of friends, united by the Yugoslavian flag and living side by side as brothers. Since the earlier days of peace, so much turmoil has happened that it seems unlikely that a once iron-clad friendship between Serbia and Croatia will ever be mended.

In 2009, when I returned to play for HK Partizan, the team had been promoted to a new league and would be playing against teams in Austria, Slovenia and Croatia. Even when we weren't playing against a team from Croatia, we would have to trek through the country in order to reach Slovenia and Austria. So no matter what, all roads led through Croatia, and when you're riding on a team bus from Belgrade, you're essentially treading on enemy territory.

The first road trip we had that season was to Bled, Slovenia. Crossing into Croatia, we ended up getting stalled for quite some time at the border. I remember leaning over to a teammate and asking why we were being detained for so long. He simply replied, "Motorcade." We were waiting for vehicles driven by armed guards to accompany our bus through Croatia.

A couple of weeks later we played in Zagreb, Croatia, and once again awaited the arrival of an armed escort at the border to accompany us to the capital city. When we pulled into the arena in Zagreb, four armed guards, brandishing high-powered, semi-automatic rifles, emerged from the cars and escorted our group wherever we went. I can remember stretching and warming up in the back parking lot with these guys outlining our perimeter. It almost made you feel like you were royalty or something.

During our travels, I never once saw any hostility, but apparently it wasn't uncommon for a few fans to slam back a few too many pivos and Rakias and decide to take the war into their own hands. Pride in Eastern Europe, similar to what you see in England, is deeply connected and channeled through sports. Citizens view national sporting competitions as an extension of war and an exhibition of national pride.

This connection wasn't exclusive to national sporting teams. Eastern European citizens also connected themselves to professional club teams. Just like in Glasgow, Scotland, where the Celtic and the Rangers are bitter rivals and their clashes on the pitch often result in citywide riots, Belgrade is famous for its rivalry between club teams Cerena Zvezda (Red Star) and Partizan.

The two franchises own professional teams in soccer, basketball and hockey. To make things even more complicated, Cerena Zvezda and Partizan share a training complex and play home games in the same arena. During basketball games between the two rivals, it is a sellout beyond capacity and 1,000 members of Belgrade riot police are employed to keep hooligans in check. Talk about passion. This rivalry was the fiercest I've ever seen between two teams in my life. During the games, fans would deploy smoke bombs that were smuggled in and throw anything they could find in their pockets on the court.

Every year, we would receive team apparel such as, workout clothes, jackets, track suits, toques and hats. There was only one rule: don't ever wear any of this stuff in public. If you were to wear any of this walking the streets of Belgrade, there was a fairly good chance that you would take a good beating at the hands of some Cerena Zvczda fans. These fans were so passionate that they often sported one or several tattoos depicting their allegiance to their team and even were members of fan clubs that met on a weekly basis.

Choke the Czech

As mentioned earlier, Vadim Musatov was our coach when I first went to play in Europe. Vadim was a really interesting guy. He was a longtime Russian national team mainstay on the back end and played in the infamous "Punchup in Piestany" game in which Canada and Russia duked it out at the 1987 world junior championships. He used to carry around a DVD of the fight and pop it in for the boys and point to himself and say, through a translator: "I won my fight. I did my job!"

I liked Vadim and felt that he had a wealth of knowledge and a great understanding for the game. It was a tough season for Vadim because he had to leave behind his family in Russia to come and coach in Belgrade for the season and he seemed to be under a lot of pressure. The issue that eventually led to Vadim being dismissed had to do with his tactics in overplaying the top two lines. Vadim didn't use his depth lines and this prevented a lot of good young domestic players from gaining experience and getting a chance to develop.

About midway through the season, Vadim was fired and replaced by a man I absolutely loathed. His name was Frantisek Vorlicek and he was a former Czech Republic Extraliga coach who also coached Czech Republic teams at the national level. His style was the polar opposite to Vadim's. Vadim was a defenceman who played at a high level and felt that defensemen should be mobile and contribute offensively when the time was right. He was a big believer in the Russian mindset that teams should play as 5-man units. Frantisek was old school and, in my mind, was still living in the '60s. He felt that defensemen should be big and slow and never, under any circumstance, join the rush.

Right off the bat I knew I wasn't going to like this guy one bit. He had one of those outdoor voices, a real drill sergeant-type tone. He grew up in the height of communism and it was clear that he had a hard time moving on.

In his first practice after taking over as coach, he blew down a drill and started barking at me in Czech. I didn't know what he was saying but I could tell from his tone it was condescending. The guys told me that he was mad that I carried the puck past our blue line and that defensemen must pass to the forwards in our own end and then stay back until the other team started attacking. I just muttered to myself, "Here we go."

After that, he would blast his whistle and scream "bekovi" and point back to our end of the ice with a wooden stick that looked like it had just been cut from a neighboring tree. Bekovi was the Serbian word for "Defenseman".

At first, I would just nod and act like a good little boy, and then just do whatever I wanted anyway. I was having a great season and had just come off a game in which I had scored a hat trick and we won 7-0. Things were going well and I wasn't about to change my game for Captain Communist.

The rest of the season we locked horns and I started to get brasher. The next game, I scored a nice coast-to-coast goal and went by the bench after and smiled and winked at him. He turned beet red and stomped his feet like a four-year-old who just had a cookie taken away from him. After that, he tried to stick it to me by pulling me off the first power-play unit. That didn't bother me in the least because I would run and gun in every situation.

Eventually, the ownership decided that we should sit down together and hash out our differences. So Captain

Communist and I sat down and grunted and snarled and frustrated our translator to the point that I ended up just laughing at him and walking out of the meeting.

We weren't the first player and coach to feud with one another in sports and we weren't going to be the last. Players and coaches don't always have to get along and agree, and this situation wasn't going to go away by sitting down two stubborn people and hoping for a compromise.

The rest of the season continued on in much in the same manner as our first few weeks together did. We butted heads, I did what I wanted and, in the end, we still won games. Finally, we were in the league championship series against HK Vojvodina and we were up two games to one in the best-of-five series. We were one game away from ending the season on top and one game away from me never having to deal with Frantisek again.

All was going well, we were up 4 – 2 and time was winding down in the third period. I actually was playing very safe and conservatively that game, ensuring that we kept the lead and sealed the win. Late in the game, a seam opened up and I took off with the puck on an offensive rush. The rush ended in a save with a scrum in front and a faceoff to the left of the goalie. After the whistle, I could hear Frantisek screaming from the bench and then I felt a tap on my shin pad. It was one of our defensemen and he was nervously saying that coach wanted me off.

I didn't shake my head. I just headed to the bench and acted appropriately, even though I was fuming on the inside. I didn't want my emotions to show out of respect for the other team and for my teammates. We had a big crowd on hand in Novi Sad and we were minutes away from becoming league champs.

All of a sudden, as I came off the ice, Frantisek began stomping down the bench, screaming and pointing at me and making a spectacle. At this, I immediately felt like he was showing me up in front of everyone and embarrassing our team, considering we had the game in hand, so I lost it. I leapt at him and tried to grab his throat. I just missed and was immediately scooped up and held back by two teammates.

I still remember the look in Frantisek's eyes as my hands just missed his neck. It was a look of pure fear. He couldn't believe that someone would challenge him. All his life he had held a position of power, and in the Eastern European culture, no one ever challenges authority the way I had that season. He didn't know how to handle me and I wasn't about to stand by and take that. I am stubborn and proud and quite often this has hindered rather than helped me in life.

The game ended and we celebrated amid fireworks, cigars, confetti and champagne. It was a sweet win and even sweeter knowing that my tenure under Frantisek was over. After the final horn blew, he went his stubborn way and I went mine—in the opposite direction. The last time we ever looked at each other was when our eyes met after I nearly choked him, fear firmly affixed in his gaze and fire and rage in mine.

Euro-Style

I always fancied myself a pretty stylish dude. I try to keep up on the recent trends and even though I'm a bit cheap when buying clothes (I tend to stick to places like H&M and TJ Max), I think I am at least close to the cutting edge. As a North American, as stylish as you may think you are, when you hit up Europe, you are in for a rude awakening when it comes to style.

Getting off the plane in Europe as a North American is like going to your first day of high school wearing your dad's Wranglers and a Sunday cardigan. Europe is the headquarters for cutting edge. We're talking fashion centers Milan, Prague and Cannes. Before clothing, hairstyles or music get close to reaching American mainstream, they are market-tested in Europe. So when you hear a new song on the radio, chances are it has already been playing in European nightclubs for up to two years or more.

Prime example: When I was playing over in Europe in 2009, a song by Romanian musician Edward Maya called "Stereo Love" was a staple at the nightclubs. When I came back to North America, I had the song on my playlist and it came on one time when my girlfriend and I were driving. When she heard the song, she said: "This must be another one of your Euro bebop songs."

I replied: "Don't joke about it. I guarantee this will be a big hit in a year or so when it finally makes its way over here." She just rolled her eyes. Fast-forward to over a year later, "Stereo Love" debuted on the U.S. top 40 charts, where it remained for 17 straight weeks.

Cruising around Belgrade, which has a lively population of three million, I began to notice that everyone was dressed like they just walked off of a billboard. The clothes were trendy and it seemed that fashion was a major priority for the Eastern European culture. At first, I stayed conservative and rocked my TJ Max T-shirt and jeans with confidence and bravado. Soon, the boys started razzing me about my wardrobe and told me I was in serious need of a makeover. They were calling me "Jay-Z", saying that my jeans were too baggy, and I was wearing boot-cuts that aren't really baggy at all. Finally, I said: "Alright, boys, it's time to go shopping."

So one sunny afternoon, a few of the guys took me to

some shops along the main drags in the city square and I tried on some new duds. I remember it took me an agonizing five minutes to jam my junk into a skin-tight pair of jeans that looked like they had been shredded and stone dried. All the guys were cheering and saying: "Yes! You've got some style now Jay-Z!" Since I couldn't breathe or speak for fear of never being able to have kids, I was just shaking my head and waving my finger.

The other big difference that was immediately obvious was the wild hairstyles. Women's hair was so complex I couldn't even describe it, with different shapes, colors and streaks. One thing seemed to be a consistent theme with women's hair, there were a lot of blondes for a culture of basically all dark-featured citizens. I don't know if it was just a trend of the time, but all the women were dying their hair all kinds of different shades of blonde.

The male hairstyle of the time was the morph of half-mullet and half-Mohawk. It would start out with a faded, short-cut Mohawk in the front and blend into a neatly cropped mullet in the back. It was the good old "business in the front and party in the back", with a twist of rebellion. It seemed everyone was rocking this style. Even my roommate, Scott Wright, who was normally pretty conservative, ended up getting the euro crop.

In the end, I downloaded some euro-beats that were playing at all the clubs and cafes and picked up a few conductor-style caps. I even bought a couple of pairs of tight jeans that weren't as hard on the future kids and a couple of shirts you could only wear if you hadn't eaten in six days. I wasn't going to let my European experience slide by without inheriting a bit of the style to take back home with me.

The Day I Was a Jerk to Novak Djokovic

During the playoffs in my senior year at Clarkson, I got nailed with a dirty hit during our first-round series against Princeton. I felt a snap in my wrist as it bent back, but when I went for X-rays after the game, they said it was just a bad sprain. So I taped it up and played the rest of the playoffs.

In the offseason, the wrist would constantly nag me and I'd feel sharp pains after lifting weights and handling pucks during on-ice workouts. I had heard that wrist sprains could take a long time to heal, being in an area of overuse, so I chalked it up to usual wear and tear and trudged on through my off-season training. Once the season began and I was back into full contact, I noticed a significant jump in inflammation in the wrist and sharp pains were becoming more frequent. It wasn't to the point where I was considering going on the shelf, but it was nagging and would periodically lock up.

At about the mid-point of the season, I was involved in a two-on-two drill in practice. I went into the corner to pin a forward and I felt a distinctive pop in my wrist as I made contact. A few minutes later, coach blew the whistle for a water break. I skated over to the bench, removed my glove and went to grab a water bottle and ended up knocking it over. I tried to grab another one and came up with the same result. When I looked down at my left hand, the thumb was locked in an inward position. I tried to move the thumb and was unable to. Immediately it freaked me out because I had never experienced anything where I couldn't move something on my body before.

The next day, I got it examined and the results

showed that I had a displaced fracture of the scaphoid bone in my wrist. They said the injury was an old one that hadn't healed and that a piece of the bone had broken off and severed the tendon that attached my thumb. I told them about the injury I sustained in the playoffs against Princeton the year before and they said that I had been misdiagnosed with a sprain when in fact it was a fracture.

Apparently, when you break that bone, you are supposed to wait until the swelling subsides before getting an X-ray because at the time of injury, the joint swells up and the bones are compacted. When there is that much pressure in the joint, it becomes very hard to read the break on the X-ray.

At that time, the doctor said I would require surgery to reattach the tendon and the recovery period would be roughly six months. I asked if I could put off the surgery until after the season. I was told that I could but that I'd have to wear a playing cast and undergo regular treatments. That sounded good to me so we put off the surgery and I began weekly treatments.

The treatments were pretty frustrating because I was doing exercises to help increase mobility in the wrist and thumb, but because of the missing tendon, I was unable to get my thumb to perform what my mind wanted it to do. I had lost a great deal of range of motion in my wrist since I originally injured it, so the doctor wanted to try to break up any scar tissue that had accumulated. I always hated these treatments because my wrist always felt worse after the sessions than it did before they began.

At the sessions, there were other athletes getting their knees or shoulders or whatever worked on. There were always lots of basketball, soccer, tennis and water polo (which is a major sport in Eastern Europe) players getting treatments for various ailments. The facility was a highly-regarded rehab center that employed doctors that handled all of the professional teams in Belgrade.

During my third session, I was getting my wrist and thumb reefed on and the doctor introduced me to one of the other athletes who was receiving treatments on his knee. He didn't look like much and I wasn't as cordial as I could have been. At the time, I was grumpy because my wrist was hurting after getting more scar tissue broken up and I half-heartedly shook the guy's hand and basically arrogantly blew him off, giving him a snarly acknowledgement.

I remember him being a skinny, non-distinct guy and after I was rude to him, my roommate, who was having his back worked on, just shook his head while chuckling and said, "You're such a dick."

I snapped back: "What!? This isn't social hour. I hate being here getting yanked and cranked on as it is. I don't need to be meeting new friends."

Fast-forward to the end of the season after I returned home. We had just won the league championship, I had a really enjoyable season abroad and it was finally time to see the doctor again. When I went to the doctor back home, he examined my injury and said: "OK, we can do one of two things here. We can perform the surgery where we'll have to graft a new tendon from your hamstring and reconstruct the wrist and thumb and you'll be out six months or we can just leave it as is and you'll have decreased grip strength and limited mobility in the thumb but you won't have to miss any time." I looked down at my thumb and made the quick and easy decision to decline the surgery and play on.

The way I saw it, if I got the surgery, my career was probably over because I didn't have a contract yet and teams wouldn't be eager to sign a guy who was going to start the season on injured reserve. Since it was my bottom hand on the stick, I could still play without much hindrance. When we won the championship that season, we received a trophy and medals but no ring or anything to wear around to remind us of that success. To me, the dangly thumb was my ring. It was my constant reminder that I was a champion that season.

A couple of months into the off-season, a friend of mine invited me over to watch the Rogers Cup, which is a big professional tennis tournament held in Canada. We were sitting on his couch, getting ready to watch the final match between Roger Federer and a young up-and-comer named Novak Djokovic. After I heard the announcer talking about Djokovic's game, I turned to my friend and asked, "Who the hell is this Djokovic guy? I've never heard of him."

My friend said: "He's a new phenom from Serbia. I'm surprised you haven't heard of him, you just came from there."

All of a sudden, Djokovic is flashed on the TV screen and I'm in shock. Djokovic was the tennis player introduced to me during my wrist treatments whom I snubbed and acted like a jerk towards.

Here I was being an arrogant prick to this guy and he was about to become the new face of tennis. In hindsight, I can just imagine what his thoughts were at the time I was rude to him. He was probably thinking: "Hockey player? I didn't even know we played hockey in Serbia." Or: "I thought hockey players were supposed to be bigger."

The Brothers Jankovic

My biggest thrill playing overseas in Belgrade was having the chance to meet the Jankovic brothers: Bogdan, Bojan and Beki. These three brothers combined passion, perseverance and loyalty and taught me a great deal about life, pride and priority. All three are born leaders who put their heart and soul into everything they do and exhibit a great deal of compassion and respect for their community and country.

Bogdan is the oldest brother and was the captain of HK Partizan. He was also a well-respected leader in the national team program for Serbia. Bogdan was the first team member I met when I arrived in Belgrade. He had an ear-to-ear smile and a warm handshake. Right off the bat he was very friendly and welcoming. It didn't take long for Bogdan and me to develop a strong friendship. He was smart, had a great outlook on life and had experienced more in a short period than most do in a lifetime. He had lived through a major war that took place in his own backyard and, despite the terror he had witnessed first-hand, he was always able to find a positive slant to every situation.

Bogdan was enrolled in law school and helped out with youth hockey as well as using his salary as a hockey player to help support his mother and brothers. The three brothers lived in a two-bedroom apartment with their mother in downtown Belgrade, and judging by their constant exuberance, you would have thought they lived on a 50-acre ranch. Bojan and Beki shared one of the bedrooms and Bogdan, even though he was the oldest, slept on a couch in the living room. Quite often I would stop by to visit the brothers and we'd sit around telling stories, laughing and drinking Coca-Cola.

Bojan was the most athletically gifted of the brothers and played the game with reckless abandon and pure desire. The brothers were all big and strong, but Bojan was a pure ox. Bojan and I became best friends on the team nearly instantly as we shared the same sense of humor, stubbornness and passion for the game of hockey. Bojan and I joked constantly about movies, chirped teammates and partook in the odd pivo at nearby patios and pubs.

Beki was the youngest brother and easily the most worldly and philosophical. He spoke several languages fluently and enjoyed travelling to Switzerland in the summers to stay with their uncle. He was interested in different cultures and had a strong sense of who he was and where he wanted to go in life.

At an early time in their life, the brothers lost their father. It was a major tragedy for the tight-knit family. Since their father's death, the brothers have worked as a team with their mother to create a wonderful life based on love and loyalty and, much like their beloved country, they were able to rebuild and prosper despite enduring the pain of tragedy and loss.

The brothers weren't only my close friends, they were my cultural guides and teachers. I was constantly asking them questions and trying to learn about what life is and has been like for Eastern Europeans. They were always more than happy to share their experiences and historical information about the area. Talking with the brothers reminded me of times spent with my grandfather. They spoke eloquently about topics and always displayed a calm and welcoming demeanor.

We used to sit in our wet gear after practice every day, drinking raspberry tea out of grungy plastic cups until our trainer, Mladan, would kick us out of the room because he had to lock up and go home. We'd sit around and talk about hockey and anything under the sun with no real desire to let up. I really admired the brothers for their pride, confidence and the maturity they all possessed at a young age. I guess losing your father when you are young and living through NATO bombings and a war during your youth will do that to you.

The three of them loved hockey and truly loved it for all the right reasons. They didn't grow up in a country where hockey was what kids aspired to do when they grew up. It would be like growing up in Canada and wanting to spend your whole life playing racquetball. They started playing hockey because they loved it. In Serbia, there wasn't an opportunity to become a millionaire playing hockey. For a domestic Serbian player, the brothers had reached the pinnacle. They were professional players who also represented their country on the world stage numerous times, but they still weren't going to be able to make a living for the rest of their lives off these successes. Hockey to them was a passion.

At the end of my first season in Belgrade, I was happy to be going home to see my friends and family, but I was torn because it meant that I was leaving my new family and friends. Bogdan drove me to the airport when I was heading back after the season and I saw him shed a tear as he waved goodbye. There was a good possibility that this would be the last time I might see my friend.

A few years later, after playing in the ECHL and CHL, I was at a crossroads. I had surgery to reconstruct my right knee and knew that I wasn't going to be progressing any further in my hockey career. I could play a few more years and drag out the inevitable or I could close the book on my playing days and join the workforce.

At the conclusion of the 2008-09 season, I decided I was going to retire. That spring I spent a couple of months going to job fairs in Toronto and going on interviews with the prospect of finding a new career.

The market was tough and most of the jobs I was offered were on straight commission. After some long, hard soul-searching, I decided I would play one last season, and with the help of my long lost Serbian brothers, I was able to negotiate a contract to return to Belgrade where my professional career had begun.

I was excited to finish out my career where it had all started and to get a chance to help grow the game of hockey in a country where basketball, soccer and tennis reigned supreme. I had just completed my certification to become a personal trainer and worked out a deal that, in addition to playing, would see me take on the duties of strength and conditioning coach. All was looking good and I was excited to get back to Belgrade and reunite with my Serbian family. Upon arrival, I was met with some souring news.

The Jankovic brothers, who had played their entire careers for the Partizan organization, were being forced to accept pay reductions if they wanted to play. The team was moving into a higher division and the owner was scaling back some of the salaries for domestic players. For an import who is already making a lot of money, it wouldn't be a big deal to be scaled back, but for players who relied on every bit of their salaries to support a family, it was a slap in the face. Especially considering the fact that the brothers had refused more lucrative offers from opposing teams in the past to remain loyal to the franchise.

The brothers were one of the main reasons I had decided to play another season and now I was watching their heart being ripped out of their chest by a spiteful owner. I didn't like the situation one bit, and less than a month into the season, I packed up my bags and left. I tried to talk reason to team officials leading up to my departure, but this was something the owner wasn't willing to budge on. He was being stubborn and I figured the only way I could strike back and show my support and loyalty was to leave the team in the middle of the season.

The owner, angry at my decision, decided to stick it to me one last time by stiffing me for my previously agreed upon flight home, but I didn't care. I went home with my pride in check and I finally was able to retire on my terms and be content knowing that, in my mind, I did the right thing. I couldn't stand by and watch the Jankovic family, who defined why hockey is such a great sport and represented the face of hockey in Serbia, be treated in such a lowly manner. Despite staying in touch over social media, I haven't seen Bogdan, Bojan or Beki since I left Belgrade in the fall of 2009. I vow that someday I will return to visit my brothers, but I will have to wait a few years until my daughter is old enough to appreciate a trip overseas. I want her to be able to see where daddy once lived and to meet his brothers from another land.

Sleepless in Frankfurt

There were two important lessons I learned from playing hockey abroad. One was to read your contract closely, and the second was to make sure you get to select your flights before the team books them. There is nothing worse than a flight overseas that has three or four connections with long, agonizing layovers.

One return trip I was on that was particularly awful was the flight back from Serbia in my first tour over there for the 2006-07 season. My flight out of Belgrade left at 5 a.m., and we decided to stay up all night and have a going away party before I left. I ended up boarding the first flight drunk and almost wasn't allowed to leave because my work visa wasn't stamped when I first arrived in the country, back in the fall. Eventually, they let me through customs and I had a 30-minute nap on the flight to Frankfurt, Germany.

Once in Frankfurt, I was suddenly awakened when a flight attendant shook my shoulder to tell me that we were landing and that the terminal at which we were supposed to be deplaning was out of service. We were going to be taking shuttles from the runway to the main airport. At this point, my hangover was in full effect and, as luck would have it, there was only one shuttle bus and it only held about 20 people per trip. Since I needed the fresh air anyways, I decided to walk the 15 minutes to the main airport. Everything was going well and I was enjoying the breeze on the stroll across the tarmac when all of a sudden the skies opened up and it began to pour rain.

When I finally reached the Frankfurt Airport, looking like a wet rat, I scanned the monitor for my next flight and saw that it had been delayed by about four hours. Instead of boarding my next flight to Toronto in an hour, I was going to have to hang out in Frankfurt airport for the next five hours, soaked to the bone. By this point, I was cranky and dead tired. To make matters worse, the airport was jammed full with travelers and there wasn't a seat open in the entire building. I scanned the gate area for an open piece of carpet and plopped myself down, tucked my corduroy jacket beneath my head and settled in for a little cat nap.

As mentioned in a previous story, I was able to save up some cash after the season, approximately 4,500 euros, despite living like a rock star for the whole season. This sum was tucked in an envelope inside the left-hand breast pocket of my jacket. So throughout my restless time on the hard floor amid thousands of travelers speaking 20 different languages, I split my time between worrying about my money being stolen, worrying about sleeping through my next flight and trying to find a position where my whole body didn't ache.

Once I finally boarded the flight to Toronto, I was able to get some long-awaited sleep. When we landed at Pearson International Airport, I was never so happy to be back on Canadian soil. A part of us always feels a strong connection to where we were born, but after a couple of weeks I began to miss my new-found brothers back in Serbia. There still isn't a day that goes by that I don't think back to those days playing in Belgrade and about the personal connections I made and life lessons I learned.

The World of a Pro Goalie

Goalies have a world-renowned reputation of being quirky and odd. Being a goalie, you are pretty much isolated and in your own world. You have one job to do and that is to stop pucks. If you win, you were supposed to; if you lose, you are the goat. There is so much pressure being a goalie. To top it off, you have to stand in front of 90 m.p.h. shots all night.

Being a goalie is a tough career choice in hockey because there is only room for one true starter on every team. That means that only 30 goalies can be NHL starting goalies. If you have a team like the New Jersey Devils with Martin Brodeur, then you've got one guy starting for 20 straight years.

In an NHL team's system, there is only room for six goalies: Two at the NHL level, two in the AHL and two in the ECHL. That's roughly only 180 spots for goalies in all of pro hockey. To put that into perspective, there are approximately around 1,000 forward spots and 600 defensemen spots in North American pro hockey.

When I was in college, David McKee was the cat's meow when it came to goalies. In his junior year, he was a Hobey Baker Award finalist and signed a three-year entry deal with Anaheim Ducks. When you sign a player out of college before the season ends, you have to keep him on the NHL roster. So Dave got to spend two months in Anaheim, and once they were beat out, he was named to the U.S. roster for the world championships as the third-string goalie.

Two years later, Dave and I were teammates in Augusta, GA., which was Anaheim's ECHL affiliate. The previous year, David played in Portland in the AHL and was recently bumped down with the emergence of Jonas Hiller and a trade that brought Gerald Coleman, who had played two games in NHL the year before, over from the Tampa Bay Lightning.

That season, Anaheim had J.S. Giguere and Ilya Bryzgalov in the NHL, Hiller and Coleman in the AHL and J.P. Levasseur, Nathan Marsters, David McKee and Bobby Goepfert fighting for spots in the ECHL. In total, this was eight top flight goalies fighting for six spots in a deep system.

To put it in perspective, Marsters had played two seasons already in the AHL and was a very good goalie who had attended NHL camps in Los Angeles and Anaheim. Levasseur was an Anaheim pick who was fresh out of the QMJHL and was under contract with the big club. He was tabbed to be the eventual successor to incumbent Giguere. Goepfert just signed with Anaheim out of college and was the goalie that played for the U.S. and beat the Canadians at the world junior championships that were hosted in Halifax. Then there was McKee. These were some pretty impressive resumes battling for spots in the ECHL.

Eventually, it became a numbers game and the higher-ups decided to trade McKee and Marsters to keep Levasseur and Goepfert in the system. It was sad to see outstanding talents like Marsters and McKee go. These were guys with extended AHL experience and dominant college hockey resumes. Watching them leave also created a lot of pressure for the two rookies, Levasseur and Goepfert, to step up and perform. With all that pressure and competition, no wonder goalies are always a bit off. Thinking about that always made me glad I was a defenceman.

A Real Pisser of a Goalie

Goalies, more than another other position player, are notorious for having some wild and crazy superstitions. Patrick Roy used to talk to his goal posts during the game and treated them as if they were a living being. His view was that if he treated his posts well, they would be there when he needed them most.

On one team I played on we had a goalie, I'll call him "Vinny". Vinny was a bit eccentric, to say the least, but a very hard-working and dedicated netminder. Vinny came to our team to fill in the backup role. In fact, he was essentially brought in to be the back-up to the back-up. By the end of the season, Vinny not only became our starter, but he became the best goalie in the league, winning a major award and leading us to a championship.

Vinny was also one of the funniest guys I have ever played with. He was always the class clown of the team and was always there to lighten up the mood. He was also very quirky when it came to superstitions and preparing for games.

He was similar in his quirkiness to most goalies in that he had his on-ice routines and put his equipment on a certain way but he had one particular quirk that set him apart from anyone I'd ever come across. The thing that gave Vinny legendary quirkiness status was that he used to pee his pants every game. Every single game he played in, he would piss in his goalie pants! Imagine!

Apparently, it originated from his younger days when he had to pee so bad during a game that he just let it go because he couldn't leave the ice during the game. He ended up standing on his head that game and produced a shutout in the process. From then on, Vinny pissed his pants in every game as a way to drum up some good luck. Needless to say, when we'd hit the road, Vinny had tons of room to himself to prepare for games.

The Goepf-Man Strikes Again

One of the funniest guys I've ever had the pleasure of playing with was goaltender Bobby Goepfert, the self-proclaimed "Goepf-Man," when I was in Augusta of the ECHL. He was always up for a good joke or prank. He used to love drawing pictures making fun of teammates on the white boards at the rink. Every day when you'd show up for practice, there would be some new artwork taking a pot-shot at one of our teammates.

At Christmas time, our owner threw a big, ritzy party at his house with an open bar and lots of great hors d'ouvres. I can remember that our coach, Bob Ferguson, was a little annoyed because he knew we had an important stretch of games coming up and didn't want us getting too tilted. On the other hand, he used to play the game and understood the importance of keeping morale high, especially around Christmas time when most guys didn't get to see their family.

He allowed us to tip back a few, but said we were going to have a morning practice the next day and we'd better not be horseshit. Needless to say, we indulged a bit more than we should have and everyone had a pretty good glow on when the night came to an end.

The next morning we all showed up early at the practice rink and it was like watching "Return of the Living Dead" with all the zombies walking in. We were laughing about how awful we felt and how brutal this practice was going to be. All of a sudden, in teeters Goepfert, the team's resident jester, and he looks like death warmed over. We're throwing tape at him and he's telling us: "If anyone shoots high I'm gonna puke all over them."

We were enjoying our last moments prior to what was to be a definite bagger of a practice. We were so caught up in the joking that we didn't realize that Bobby forgot to change into his under-gear before putting on his equipment. He hadn't realized it, either, until he was fully dressed. By that time, he didn't have time to change or he would have been late and you didn't want to be late for Fergie's practices, especially when he gave you the green light the night before.

So here was the Goepf-Man in full gear on top of his jeans and button-down bar shirt with his wallet, keys and cell phone in his pockets, about to hit the ice for an hour practice. Fergie knew when we hit the ice it was going to be sloppy. All the guys were trying really hard not to look hung over, but it was a lost cause. We were skating around, warming up, and all the while the Goepf-Man was saying stuff like: "Don't shoot low. Put everything in my gloves because I can't go down in my jeans."

Later, in a drill, one of the guys shot one just inside the post and Bobby made a reactionary stretch and went down. He was moaning that he had landed on his keys. When Fergie asked what was going on with the Goepf- Man, we had to let him in on it. After we told him, he just laughed out loud and skated away. After about 20 minutes of a sloppy practice, Fergie let everyone go home.

Sometimes if your team is in a slump, it's beneficial to let the boys cut loose and get into some mischief. That can boost morale and bring the team closer together. I keep in touch with a lot of my team mates from my playing days and we still look back and laugh about that Christmas party and the Goepf-Man falling on his keys in practice the next day.

Masterful Experience

The greatest perk, without a doubt, about playing hockey in Augusta, GA, was being able to witness golf's greatest annual tournament, The Masters. When I was playing in Augusta, we lived in a gated housing complex on Berckmans Road, which backed onto Augusta National right behind the trees looming over Amen Corner. We lived in the best spot in the city.

The thing a lot of people don't know about Augusta National is that it is closed to the public and is only open to its exclusive list of members four months of the year. The rest of the time, teams of groundskeepers meticulously comb the course, fixing every imperfection so that come Masters Week, the course sparkles. It took Bill Gates 10 years on a waiting list before they would let him become a member of the prestigious course.

The year I played in Augusta, I had no idea what to

expect when it came to Masters Week. I didn't think there was a chance in hell that I was going to get a shot to see a round. During Masters Week, the entire city of Augusta transforms to host the sacred event. Hooters restaurant transforms its parking lot into a circus event and fly in the best-looking "Hooter Girls" from all over the country. All of the hotels within a 100-mile radius are booked solid a year in advance and half of the streets are blocked off for special events.

John Daly, who wasn't even in the Masters field that year, had his million-dollar RV parked out back of the Hooters. One of the booster club members, who lets Big John shack up at his place every year during Masters Week, had us come down one day and enjoy a few pops with Daly at Hooters. It was such a zoo with people coming up to him for autographs that we didn't stay for very long. I remember thinking that if I were John Daly, I would rather be having a drink in a hole in the wall somewhere with some privacy than being mauled like that.

As we were leaving the Hooters, I can remember looking at the pictures on the wall of all of the celebrities who had passed through over the years. I saw one particular picture of Tiger Woods, surrounded by about six buxom beauties. I nudged my buddy beside me and said: "I bet ol' Tiger there has a bit of a wild side. I bet he likes to cut loose with the ladies a bit, eh?" This was back in 2008 when he was still nerdy and squeaky clean, well before the skeletons started pouring out of the closet.

Tickets are a wild subject when it comes to Masters Week. You see, you can't just simply go online and buy tickets to the Masters like you can for other events. Masters tickets are distributed through members and donated to charities and various causes. Through these channels, tickets become available for auction or sale and the prices of these tickets become astronomical. The Masters isn't like other golf tournaments. The number of people in the course at any given time is small compared to other major golf events.

Tickets for the Masters are also only good for each individual day, for the most part. It isn't uncommon to walk along Washington Road in Augusta and see a man selling Tuesday practice round day passes for $1,000 a pop. People come in for the week from all over the world and won't even blink an eye as they rip out their wallets and shell out thousands of dollars for tickets. It is really quite an amazing thing to see.

The road that runs alongside Augusta National, Berckmans Road, has been a topic of much debate over the past decade or so. Augusta National has been buying up properties along the road—many of the small bungalow variety—for the purpose of closing the road altogether and developing the land for parking and extra par-3 course holes. The problem is there are a few homeowners on Berckmans who have been there for years and years and aren't budging. I spoke to one gentleman who owned a two-bedroom bungalow. He said he was offered $5 million to sell his house that year. Two years before that, the offer was $3 million. He said he was going to hold out until it reaches $10 million and retire.

Another big seller during Masters Week in Augusta is the opportunity to rent a nearby house for the week. Out-of-town hot shots will sometimes pay up to $35,000 to rent a house for the week. One of the stipulations that were clearly written into our contracts when I played in Augusta was that we were strictly prohibited from subletting our houses for Masters Week. Back in July when I signed my contract, I thought that was a ridiculous rule, but come April, I was wishing that wasn't a clause. I would have gladly slept in my car for a week to rake in $35,000.

When it came to tickets, I really lucked out. I was able to come across two free tickets for the practice round on Monday. Two players naively paid $250 per ticket for the same passes, even though several of the veterans on the team kept saying to hold off. What the vets were hinting at was that we had practice at 9 a.m. every morning and wouldn't be able to head to the course until about noon. All the older folks would head in at 6 a.m. to watch Tiger and Phil Mickelson get their rounds in and then head home at noon after putting in a six-hour shift in the sun. Since the tickets were only good for each day and they weren't coming back, we simply waited until they came out and politely asked if we could use their passes. Some would decline, but most were quite happy to oblige.

One piece of information that the vets enjoyed holding back on Day 1 was that beers were only $2 on the grounds. Here we were, slugging back pint after pint before we headed in so that we wouldn't be shelling out for $10 beers like at every other sporting event. These beers came in a commemorative plastic keeper cup and were only $2. Top-shelf turkey sandwiches were only $1.50. Augusta National has so much money that it doesn't need special ad contracts. It has such a large endowment that it takes Masters Week and treats its guests.

Masters Week Parking Fiasco

Masters Week in Augusta, GA, was really something amazing to experience. Many local businesses and proprietors made the bulk of their year's profits in one week as the electricity and mystique of golf's greatest and most prestigious tournament bled through the community.

Founded by the late, great Bobby Jones and built on 365 acres of prime property, Augusta National Golf Club is the Mecca for hackers and whackers from around the globe. From scratch golfers to weekend warriors, hordes flock each year to pay homage to golf's greatest weekend event.

Living on the backside of the course in a gated community on Berckman's Road came with a lot of perks. I got to brag to all my golf buddies back home about where I was living and I even got to lace a few drives into the sacred grasses of the pristine course. As much as I'd like to leave out the full details, I have to admit that the inconsistent golf shots came from my backyard and over the fence of Augusta National's property during the off-season and not from within the hallowed grounds. No one outside of golf professionals and the exclusive membership list and their guests, is allowed to play the immaculate course.

During Masters Week, parking became somewhat of a circus around the city of Augusta. People, along with renting out their houses, would sell parking space on their property. It wasn't uncommon to drive along any given Augusta street and see cars packed on lawns and backyards. Homeowners, with wads of cash in hand, were selling parking space for $35 a day.

The gated community in which we lived was operated by a local property management company. The community was maintained by the company, and during Masters Week, the company would sell parking space to pad its bank account. In order to not disturb the tenants of the community, the company gave each resident an orange pylon and a set of rules for parking during Masters Week. The pylon was to be placed in our specified tenant parking spot when we were away from home, to show Masters parkers that the spot was reserved for residents and off limits. Simple enough, right?

As the week progressed and droves began to flood the city for the event, parking became scarce. Amidst panic, people began to get creative. Cars could be found on the sides of hills and in any open space they could find where there wasn't a "No Parking" sign. Once these spots were filled, creativity quickly turned to ignorance and all civility went out the window.

Every day, we would practice from 9 to 10 a.m. and would be away from our houses from 8 to 11 a.m. Like good little soldiers, we would follow the rules and place our pylon, to be seen clearly in the middle of our resident parking spot. When we returned home, it was like flipping a coin to see whether someone had ignored the pylon and parked in your spot.

Now everyone has had, at one time or another, someone park in their spot before. Quite often, it was just a matter of walking into the building and having the person come out and move their vehicle. The problem in this situation was that the parking culprit was amidst tens of thousands of people on a ranging golf course.

You would literally have to wait possibly seven or eight hours for the person to return to their car. Eventually, my teammates and I were fed up with the ignorance. We had tried to complain to the property management company to no avail. We tried to have a car towed once and were basically laughed at. The time had come when we had to take matters into our own hands if we wanted to get results, or at least get even. Being born pranksters, the task at hand was going to be both satisfying and downright fun.

The next day, we returned home from practice and the reserved parking space of one of my team-mates, Adrian Veideman, "Veids", was violated by a red Ford

Expedition.

It was on!

Veids called us over and we decided it would be a perfect day to clean out his fridge. It had been quite some time since Veids had done so and I am certain there were some new scientific discoveries being harvested behind the one-month-past-due milk. Since we didn't want to waste a garbage bag, what better home for the repugnant food waste than our new-found friend, Mr. Red Ford Expedition.

We had a blast smashing rotten eggs, green oranges and furry vegetables on the hood and roof of the Expedition. The smeared peanut butter and Cheez Whiz was the perfect complement to the deep red exterior, and the rotten milk trickled nicely into the vents.

An hour later, another teammate, Larry, returned home from grocery shopping to find his pylon smashed beneath a black BMW.

Round 2!

After tiring ourselves out with the Expedition, we decided to take a simpler approach to revenge in this case. It was a nice, sunny day, so we decided to park Larry's truck behind the BMW, blocking his retreat, and enjoy a few beers in the nice warm sun. After about three hours, the owner of the BMW emerged from the course, ready to retrieve his vehicle.

After assessing the situation, the BMW owner barked out: "Some idiot parked behind me! Do you guys know whose truck this is?"

Larry calmly replied: "That's my truck and you're the idiot who parked in my spot."

Bobby BMW retorted: "There was no cone there so it's a free spot", to which Larry stated: "Actually, the cone is smashed under your front left tire."

Embarrassed but not ready to either apologize or

admit fault, Bobby BMW barked: "Well move your truck so I can get out."

At this request, we all erupted in laughter. I chimed in: "Hey Larry, you better not get behind the wheel. I think you've had a few too many. Can anyone else move Larry's truck for this douchebag?"

My roommate, B.J. Crum, jumped in: "I've had too many, Jamer, what about you, Goepfert? Can you move the truck for this dipshit?"

This continued on, until the guy threw a hissy fit and tried calling a tow truck but was met with the same conclusion we had reached earlier. Next up, he called the police, who were much too busy with other issues to deal with a petty parking squabble. Eventually, we just moved the truck because we were tired of listening to the jackass moan and complain.

He must have found out the number for the property management company and complained, because after that incident, we didn't have any trouble with people parking in our spots. The company didn't dare say a word to us because we represented the bulk of the community's inhabitants and we had already lodged complaints about the parking mess up to that point. Sometimes, vigilante justice is still the best form of vengeance.

Wet Jeans

My first season in Augusta we had a great group of guys and we were really close-knit. We played hard together on and off the ice. We were young and enjoyed the odd night out to blow off some steam.

That season, our coach, Bob Ferguson, gave us some rope but warned us not to hang ourselves with it. He would always say: "I'm not here to be your babysitter. You are grown men. You can make your own decisions. If you want to go out and have a beer, then go out and have a beer. If it starts affecting your performance on the ice, the choice is simple for me." That was a pretty reasonable and honest spiel, but all we ever really took out of that was, "...go out and have a beer..."

One Tuesday night, a bunch of us decided to go out and have a few pops at the local cowboy bar called "The Country Club." We didn't play again until Friday and figured this was as good a time as any for a "go night." I was living with Nick Toneys and J.P. Levasseur at the time. J.P. was on a call-up to the Portland Pirates in the AHL and Toneys wasn't much for going out during the week, so in my household I was the only one going out. Before we headed out to The Country Club, a bunch of us had a few casual beers at Eric Lundberg and Jason Kostadine's place, played darts, argued over baseball and made fun of each other. All was good in the world and things were rolling along nicely.

Fast forward to 2 a.m.

After shoveling a late-night snack of greasy pizza down the hatch and walking back from the bar, I said goodnight to Lundy and Kossy and reached into my pocket to get my keys. They weren't there. No problem, I always left the patio door unlocked. I scurried around back, climbed over the fence and went to open the patio door, only to find that it was also locked. "Fuckin' Toneys," I muttered to myself.

Since I was locked out of my house, I decided to head back over to Lundy and Kossy's place and crash on the couch. We practiced the next day at 9 a.m., so I would just get up at 8, go back to my place, grab a quick shower, change and then head down to the rink with Toneys. So I set my phone alarm for 7:45 a.m. and drifted off to sleep.

The next morning, I woke up with a little bit of a hangover, but not too bad. I drank lots of water the night before and took an aspirin and a fish oil gel tablet (the unofficial hangover prevention recipe of the ECHL). For some reason, however, my jeans were soaked. I couldn't figure out why I was wet until I realized that I pissed myself in the middle of the night. I got up shaking my head, chuckling a little to myself and headed outside to make the 20-metre walk to my place.

When I got to my place, the door was locked and Toneys' car was gone. "Fuckin' Toneys," I muttered to myself. I walked back to Lundy and Kossy's and told them that I'd be needing a ride. I didn't tell them that I pissed myself because I was afraid Kossy wouldn't let me ride in his car in my piss-soaked jeans. It was one thing to practice hung over and stink up the place, but it was a totally different animal if you were hung over and missed practice altogether. That would basically be a precursor to a plane ticket home.

When we got to the rink, I quickly ran in and entered our dressing room through the back way, to not draw attention to myself. When I got into the changing area, I wriggled out of my wet jeans and quickly jumped in the shower. It was just blind luck that Fergie or one of the training staff didn't walk in as I was trying to hide the fact that I never made it home the night before and was hurrying out of my piss-soaked bar clothes.

After showering and brushing my teeth, I walked over to Lundy and blew in his face and asked, "Do I smell that bad?"

He made a face and said: "It's not great. You should probably hang in the back of the lines today."

The first lesson about practicing hung over is to get into the room and get ready for practice without drawing attention to yourself. I had accomplished the first stage, now for stage 2, which was the hard part: being crisp and efficient in drills. The one thing about playing hung over was that you played guilty, meaning that you really focused hard on what you were doing and gave it your all. You were never just going through the motions.

That practice I went out and had one of the best practices of the year. My passes were crisp, I was moving my feet and I was winning all my battles. I had accomplished the undetected hangover practice! Or so I thought.

After practice, I was walking out of the dressing room in my surprisingly dry jeans and a spare T-shirt I always kept in my stall, so I wouldn't have to wear my bar shirt from the night before and give myself away after all that hard work. I was confident and proud. All of a sudden, Fergie came out of his office and passed by me. He smiled at me and shook his head.

He knew!

You could never pull one over on Fergie. Somehow he always knew.

Giving Back and Getting Back

One of your main duties off the ice as a professional hockey player, whether you play in the NHL or the SPHL, is to make public appearances to help promote the team and to give back to the community. These events ranged from appearances at a local car dealership to talking to kids at an elementary school. One day you might be at a hospital talking to sick kids and handing out memorabilia, and the next day you might be in a school gym, talking to a room full of kids about the importance of working hard in the classroom.

At the start of the season, the team community relations coordinator would schedule events and then set up a rotation so that everyone on the team got involved in the community. As the season progresses, guys get injured and have to go to treatment appointments or have to take their kids to the dentist, so the schedule kind of goes out the window and players basically volunteer. Some guys would even pay other players to sub in for their appearances.

I never minded doing the appearances because it helped pass the time and I enjoyed going and talking with the kids and fans. I can remember going to community events as a kid that were attended by our local OHL team. I really looked up to those players back then and it meant the world to me to get to meet guys like Chris Gratton and Brett Lindros and spend a bit of time with them. In small towns, minor pros or major junior players are role models and public figures. Giving back and helping out in the community goes a long way to making people feel connected to something special.

When I played in Augusta, my good buddy and teammate Jason Platt and I would always volunteer to do community appearances together. Platter was a draft pick of the Edmonton Oilers and played for a number of years in the AHL. He was a great player from whom I learned extensively about playing in my own end and making myself more valuable to a team. Platter's dad was a former football player at Michigan State, where his roommate was Bubba Smith, who played "Hightower" in the "Police Academy" movies! Hanging out with Platter and teaming up to do the community events provided me with ample opportunity to pick his brain about being a pro.

On top of the satisfaction of giving back, we used to love to do it because you always got a free lunch out of it. In an attempt to entice more players to step up, the community relations coordinator would give us gift certificates to local restaurants. We'd go and do the event and then chow down after at T.G.I. Fridays or the Heavenly Ham, which was a great deli shop. It was a great setup for us!

Being from a relatively small city in Canada, which is a mosaic of culture, I wasn't used to the unofficial segregation that there was in Augusta. Once you crossed the bridge into the part of the city where our rink, the James Brown Arena, was located, it was a predominantly all-black community. Part of our outreach, with regards to getting out and connecting with the community, was to try to connect with the black community in Augusta and get them interested in the game of hockey. Hockey wasn't something kids, black or white, played growing up in those parts, so it was a big challenge to try to sell a game that wasn't really accessible. Kids weren't quick to embrace a sport that they couldn't relate to.

Quite often, Platter and I would go to a predominantly all-black elementary school and go from class to class talking to the kids about hockey and about learning. It was really enjoyable because these kids, even though they hadn't experienced hockey, really took a shining to what we were presenting. We'd get sticks and pucks out and have the kids shooting on us as we played goalie for them in the gym. We'd bring a bunch of gear down and have them try it all on. We basically got to be kids for the day and horse around, so it was a blast for us. We were probably having more fun than the kids.

The toughest assignment I ever had in all the places I played was also in Augusta. One day, about five of us went to the local sick kids hospital to hand out teddy bears and help bring some cheer. We were told in advance that these were kids who were on the mend from an injury or maybe had an illness and had to stay in hospital for a few days to recover. We were supposed to go in and give out the teddy bears and bring cheer to everyone.

When we got there, we found out that the kids we were visiting were terminally ill. The staff read out some strict instructions, telling us words and phrases to avoid such as "I hope you get better soon" or "Hang in there, buddy, things will get better." These kids were dying and there was nothing anyone could do about it.

I remember walking into the rooms and you would see the parents sitting there just completely drained. The kids looked so weak and sad, it was just awful. You just wanted to start crying and hug them. I felt bad each time we walked into a room because some of the kids were so young that they wouldn't even know who we were or why we were there. Maybe the parents and the kids didn't want us in there. It was a tough situation in every way because these families were dealing with inconceivable pain and anguish and in all likelihood didn't want strangers coming in.

The ride back to the rink that day, all five of us sat in that car completely silent. It was a harsh and unfair reality that really made you think about life and your priorities. I was mad at the team for not telling us what we were heading into, not for selfish reasons but for the families we were possibly infringing upon. After that, I shied away from the hospital events.

Over the years, whether it was in junior, college or pro, I met a lot of great people through community-related events. I learned a great deal about life talking with fans, and about what each team represented to the community.

Sometimes it was hard to get my head around because, in my mind, we were just a bunch of meatheads who were lucky enough to get a chance to play a sport for small paycheques. But for kids, we represented something bigger. To some young fans, we were role models to try to emulate and strive to become.

The Dreaded Green Jacket

Every team has a post-game ritual or ceremony when it comes to singling out members of the team. When I was at Clarkson, we had a yellow hardhat that one of our teammates, Chris Brekelmans, whose family owned an excavation company, supplied and was given to the game's hardest worker. I've been on teams where we had a beaten-up old lunch pail that was handed out to the player of the game as selected by the previous player of the game. No matter what it might be, the ritual of a prop that is passed around each game to a deserving recipient is a pretty common practice and helps to promote excellence and camaraderie.

When I played in Augusta, there was a truly creative and unique post-game ritual that had been passed down, year to year. After each game, the players would congregate in a large room, which was a spruced-up loading dock at the end of the arena, playfully called the "Lynx Den." The Lynx Den was a place where fans could mingle with the players and share stories, food and drink, and get pictures and autographs. It was basically like an indoor post-game tailgate. Usually there was a microphone and the coach and/or some of the players might give some post-game speeches. This was also the place where jersey auctions would take place after specialty nights.

The post-game ritual for the Augusta Lynx each game was that the player who currently had the worst plus/minus on the team would have to wear a green jacket while spending time mingling with fans in the Lynx Den. Everyone knew the significance of the jacket, it was supposed to create a bit of playful embarrassment for the player so he would compete harder to raise his plus/minus. The jacket was old and dusty and would always be returned to a hanger in the corner of the dressing room after each booster club meeting.

Donning the green jacket was ironic because in Augusta, where the Masters is held each spring, the green jacket represents something magical and majestic. Winning the Masters and getting to sport the green jacket is the most difficult feat in professional golf, making Augusta one of the most significant cities in the entire world when it comes to a single golfing event. To win a green jacket as a golfer is to say that your name will be immortalized. For golfers around the world, the chance to put on the green jacket was a chance to become a legend.

For us, the green jacket was repugnant. We didn't want that thing anywhere near us. In golf it is the objective to have a minus in front of your numbered score. It's a sport in which a minus represents a positive. In hockey, it is the complete opposite. So we decided that playing in the city that brought greatness to the green jacket, we'd turn the tradition on its head and apply it to our sport. Thus became the legend of "The Dreaded Green Jacket" in Augusta.

Amarillo by Morning

A month into my second year playing for Augusta in the ECHL, the team came upon financial hardship and the franchise ended up folding. This left 23 players scrambling to find teams. That season alone, six teams went belly up in the ECHL, making competition for jobs in pro hockey fierce. As soon as news broke, everyone started calling their agents and former teammates trying to find a place to catch on. I didn't have an agent at the time, so my strategy was to go through my phone book and call all my buddies who were playing pro and hopefully find a team that needed a defenceman.

As luck would have it, the first guy I called, Austin Sutter—whom I roomed with during a brief stay in Shreveport—said that they just had a couple of defensemen go down to injury. Suttsy was playing for the Amarillo Gorillas in the CHL, where he was an all-star and an assistant captain. He said he would call his coach to find out if they were in the market for a defenseman and get back to me. As this was taking place, I was out with a bunch of the guys having a last- hurrah dustup. We were barbecuing and getting into some cold ones and had plans to hit up the local country bar.

About 15 minutes after I got off the phone with Suttsy, Amarillo's head coach, Tom Coolen, called me and we had a nice little chat. After the usual get-to-know-you stuff, Tom said: "Alright Jamie, we'd like to bring you on board."

I said: "Great! Where do we go from here?"

He replied: "Well we leave for a week-long road trip Thursday morning. Can you get here by then?"

Excited and ignorant to the journey on which I was about to embark, I said: "No problem, I'll be there ASAP!"

So after whooping it up for one last night with the boys, I woke up at 8 a.m. with a nice little hangover and started packing up my car. Just before I headed out, I quickly punched my journey into MapQuest. The result popped up as over 2,000 kms and 22 hours. All of a sudden, my hangover got worse. Twenty-two hours! How was I going to pull this one off? I was hitting the road at 9 a.m. on Wednesday and the bus left Amarillo for the road trip on Thursday at 11 a.m. I had to cover that distance with only a few hours to spare and no chance to stop to sleep.

So I said my goodbyes and hopped in my 2000 Chrysler Concorde, which was like a pontoon boat on wheels, and began the long journey. The first few hours flew by as I crossed into Alabama and passed Talladega Speedway where I met some wild locals when I stopped for gas. They were befuddled by the fact that I was a Canadian. It wouldn't have been any stranger had I said I was from the planet Krypton.

By dinner time, I was thinking, "This isn't so bad, I'm not even tired. I'll make it no problem." At about 7 p.m., I was able to pick up the Kansas City Royals game on the radio. Life couldn't get much better. When the game ended, I found a station and listened to Steve Spurrier talk about the SEC and then heard the debut of Beyonce's "Put a Ring on It."

At about 2 a.m., after being on the road for the past 18 hours, including two 40-minute stops for food, I started to drift off at the wheel. I could feel myself nodding off, so I threw in some gum and cranked up the radio. This helped for a little while, but soon the road signs became a blur and I could feel myself drifting again. I had to try to tough it out for another half-hour or so because there wasn't anywhere to pull off and the exit I had to take was coming up shortly.

After another 10 minutes, I succumbed to exhaustion and fell asleep behind the wheel. What seemed like a split second later, I was woken by the rumble strips as I drifted to the shoulder of the Interstate. I started to panic, for a lot of obvious reasons, but the main reason I was panicking was that I didn't want to miss the turnoff. Luckily, I woke up with about five miles to go before the exit, which meant that I was asleep at the wheel for the past 7 or more miles! I needed to get to the turnoff and find a coffee shop fast.

After another quick stop for high-test coffee and gas, which may or may not have been poured from the same jug, I was back behind the wheel, alert and ready. The rest of the trip to Amarillo went off without any more hitches as I plowed through Oklahoma and into Texas.

I arrived in Amarillo at my buddy Suttsy's house, where we caught up quickly and then headed over to the rink. We pulled into the rink at about 10:15 a.m. and I signed my contract, grabbed some gear and piled onto the bus. Since I had played enough games at the pro level, I was lucky enough to be able to bump someone out of a bunk and immediately crashed for the remainder of the trip to Odessa, Texas, where I would play my first game as a Gorilla.

When I woke up, we were unloading the bus and, since we took a wrong turn along the way, we were way behind schedule. Warm up was at 6:30 p.m. and it was already 5:55. I groggily scrambled off the bus, grabbed my gear and headed for the dressing room amid the stampede of rushing Gorilla teammates, who I still hadn't had a chance to meet. Amid the chaos in the dressing room, I shook hands and got names from most of the guys. To make matters worse, the helmet I was given was way too big and the sticks had the worst possible curves. Our trainer was able to swap out the helmet with one from the other team, but I'd have to make do with the sticks.

Half of us made it out on time for warm up and I remember being so exhausted that I felt like it was all just a dream. My legs felt funny and I couldn't get my hands to function in the stiff new gloves. I felt like I was playing a foreign sport and that I had never been on skates before. These guys were going to release me right after the game for sure. They were probably thinking, "Where the hell did this guy come from?"

Luckily I was able to score on the power play on my third shift of the game and we cruised to an early lead and a big win. With both teams coming off a busy couple of weeks, the pace of the game slowed down after the early onslaught, which was a godsend for me. The rest of the game I was able to play conservatively and go through the motions.

That night, I got probably the best sleep of my life, which was pretty special considering how tough it can be to sleep in a bunk on a bus. The next morning, we arrived in Corpus Christi, Texas, which was the next stop on our road trip. After Corpus, we shot up to Oklahoma City for a game before winding up the trip in Fort Worth and heading back home to Amarillo.

Such is the life for a minor pro hockey player. No. 1 lesson learned from this whole ordeal? Always check MapQuest before telling a coach you will be there in time for a road trip.

No Luck in Lubbock

One of the major issues for team officials of professional teams in the southern U.S. is trying to juggle scheduling around rodeo season. When I played in Augusta and Amarillo, there were always big rodeo shows coming in and out of town. All the barrel racing and bull-riding shows were held at the rink. Management knew in advance about these dates and would try to set it up that we'd be on the road for a week or so while the rodeo was taking place back home.

One time, shortly after I joined the team in Amarillo, a major rodeo was taking place at our rink that would be going on for two weeks. We were gone for about 9 or 10 days on a road trip and would have a rare four-day break between games once we returned. It was nice to have the break, but the problem was we didn't have a place to practice. Since our rink was the only sheet of ice in Amarillo, we had to book ice and commute to Lubbock, Texas, which was two hours away.

So after a day of rest, we piled into cars with our stinky gear and made the trip to Lubbock to practice for an hour. I remember four of us were jammed into our buddy's Honda Civic, sweating in the scorching sun, cruising down the Interstate to Lubbock and thinking to ourselves: "What the hell are we doing with our lives?"

Lubbock used to have a team in the CHL called the "Cotton Kings," but they folded a couple of years back and it looked as though the rink hadn't been touched or maintained since then. The rink was dusty and musty and we couldn't wait to get the practice over with and head back home.

When it comes to practice, some guys like to get out early and snap a few pucks around and get their hands and feet ready before coach comes out and formalizes everything. So a bunch of us were out just before practice started, firing pucks and dangling around when one of the guys shattered the glass right behind the net. This isn't something that is really all that uncommon, but when you're down in Texas at a rink that is barely used with one rink worker sleeping in the back, you've really got an issue on your hands.

After the slovenly rink attendant emerged from his slumber, he examined the mess and said that we'd have to stay off the ice until he fixed the glass. We thought that was reasonable and asked, "How long will that take?"

He hemmed and hawed and then said: "I'll probably have the new one put in by tomorrow afternoon."

We should have known just by looking at the guy that he wasn't going to go above and beyond on anything. So after three minutes on the ice, we called it a day and showered and packed everything back up for the two-hour trip back to Amarillo. About a third of the team didn't even set foot on the ice before the glass shattered and we were told we'd have to cancel our practice. Imagine how excited we were about the whole thing. Drive four hours for three minutes of practice. After that mess, we didn't bother trying to get ice for the next three days, which is an eternity for a professional hockey player.

After the rodeo packed up and left town, we settled back into our digs at the Amarillo Civic Center. For the next week, that place reeked of horseshit and hay. The next time we took the ice was for a warm up against Rocky Mountain and it felt like we were skating in cement boots.

Scariest Night in My Hockey Career

The scariest night in my hockey career is easily a night during the 2008-09 season when I was playing for the Amarillo Gorillas. We played at home that night and information had been leaked earlier in the day that the infamously violent MS-13 gang was initiating new members that night in Amarillo. The leak stated that three women were to be murdered as part of the initiation. The Amarillo police department had the city on high alert that night, but for some reason it was decided to not cancel our game in light of the threat.

That season, the majority of our team was either married or had girlfriends, so it was organized that all of the wives, children and girlfriends would carpool out of town to a safe house in order to avoid the potentially deadly situation. There was speculation going around that it was all just a big hoax to create panic, but this was a situation that no one was about to put to chance. It was serious enough that the Amarillo police department issued a statement telling people to stay indoors after dark and to lock all doors and windows.

That night, our attendance was expectedly low and everyone was on edge. The night came and went and in the morning it was announced that no incidents had taken place. It was never verified for sure if it was a hoax or if the initiation was just held off due to the leak. Either way, the mere threat of innocent casualties, especially to mothers, daughters or wives, was enough to put an entire city at a standstill.

Pick on Someone Your Own Size!

During the 2008-09 season in Amarillo, we were on a road trip that ended with three games in Prescott Valley, Ariz., against the Arizona Sundogs. It was the last game of the set and we were leading 3–0 early in the third period. Arizona was struggling and you could tell the players were getting frustrated. They were looking to stir things up and find a way to spark their way back into the game.

Arizona had a big winger that year named Joel Irving. Irving was a former Montreal Canadiens pick who was built like a brick shithouse at 6-4, 245 pounds. He played for a number of years for Montreal's AHL affiliate and in the ECHL and had the unique combination of size, toughness and soft hands. During the three-game set, we had held Irving, one of their top scorers, at bay and he was really starting to get unnerved.

As time ticked away, Irving began running around and taking liberties on our smaller players. I remember he ran Jonathan Ornelas, one of our diminutive, skilled forwards, right in front of our bench and I leapt up and started barking at him: "You're real tough Irving, picking on our small guys, you gutless prick! Why don't you try it on someone your own size."

He quickly snapped back: "Next shift we're going and you're dead."

Moments later, we were whistled for a penalty and I hopped on to start the penalty kill. I lined up for the draw and Irving cruised in beside me, leaned over and said: "As soon as this PP is over, I'm gonna cave your face in." There was no turning back now. I had called him out when I barked at him from the bench. Since he was one of their top scorers and always parked his huge frame in front of our net on the PP, I decided not to waste any time and try to take him off the ice right away.

The puck dropped and I cross-checked him and said: "Forget waiting, let's do it now!" He obliged and we backed off, removed our helmets and began circling, sizing each other up. Since I was giving up four inches and about 50 pounds, I knew I had to try to get inside his right shoulder in order to shorten up his punches. I waited and waited for the right moment and then lunged in with my eyes set on a spot just above his right bicep. Irving, having been in a lot of pro fights, read my intention and reeled his right shoulder back. My left hand, missing my target, grabbed his jersey in the middle of the chest.

At that point, I knew I was going to be taking an array of right bombs as I had allowed him to use his reach and leverage. He began slamming anvil-sized rights into my left temple and forehead. To counter, I began timing my rights in between his throws without much success as he had used his left arm to string me out, taking away any power I could muster on my punches. I turned my head away to give him the top of my head to pound away on and tried to re-adjust my left hand grip to get under is right arm. As I finally was able to work my grip into an effective spot, Irving crashed a right uppercut under my left eye. My head snapped back and I heard a collective "Ohhhhh" from the 4,500 or so in attendance at the Toyota Centre.

There is something about getting tagged hard in a fight. It almost wakes you up and triggers an extra gear. At the beginning of fights, the combatants usually look to pick spots and there is a lot of jockeying for position. There is a fear, not of getting hurt but rather a fear of losing and getting embarrassed. Once you get drilled, you have nothing left to lose, so you can cut loose and risk getting drilled again. You can take more chances once you've been hit hard because you need to get offensive if you want to make up ground in the fight.

So, as my head recoiled from the massive Irving uppercut, the switch went off in my mind that I should forget about defending and just go on the attack. After that shot, I began throwing wild rights. I was finally able to connect with one and our momentum took us down to the ice before we were separated.

After the fight, I was disappointed in myself because I hadn't executed my game plan. I wasn't able to limit his reach and leverage, and in the end I lost decisively. Although I lost, I had done my job and stopped Irving from running around and taking liberties. I also had taken one of their better players off the ice for five minutes, hindering their chances of a comeback. From Irving's perspective, he had also done his job. The momentum from the scrap might have helped spark some energy into the Arizona bench and give them the jump they needed to get back in the game.

After our five-minute majors expired and I skated back to our bench, I was met with taps from my teammates and our coach, Brian Pellerin, came down and gave me a pat on the back. He was half laughing because he knew that I had bitten off more than I could chew. I wasn't a fighter by any means, but I stepped up when a job needed to be done. Knowing that helped ease the pain of being embarrassed in front of 4,500 fans.

The next day at practice, I had to adjust my helmet size to fit over my head. The hard rights that Irving had slammed into my temple and forehead had swelled up into big knots. I couldn't get my helmet on because there were about six knots that had swelled to the size of peanut shells.

Two weeks later, we played Arizona at home and Irving lined up next to me on the draw. I leaned over and said, loud enough that everyone at the draw could hear: "Hey Irv, a couple of weeks ago when I told you to pick on someone your own size, I meant him," and pointed to my defense partner, Neil Smith, who was our tough guy that year. Irving started laughing hysterically.

Fighting in hockey, although emotionally charged and heated, is not usually personal. It's part of a job and a means to an end. You do what it takes to keep a job and to help the team win. All that matters is that "W".

Jonny No-Elbows

When I played in Amarillo in the CHL, I played with an old rival from my college days, Jonathan Ornelas, who played at RPI. Jonny was a good little forward who could skate like the wind and wasn't afraid to grind it out in the corners. He would take a hit and spin off guys in the corner and, with his speed, he was an offensive threat every time he was on the ice.

One day, I was looking to create a bit of mischief before practice and was trying to set up a prank in Jonny's stall. I can't remember exactly what the prank was. I think it was either the shaving cream in the gloves or the cup of water under the helmet trick. Either way, I realized that Jonny didn't have any elbow pads in his stall. I turned and asked his old college team mate, Jake Morissette, what the deal was and he said that Jonny never wore elbow pads.

I couldn't believe it. Of all the equipment that I wouldn't want to forget, elbow pads were near the top of the list. Even with elbow pads, it's murder when you crash down and land on your elbow. Especially crazy was the fact that Jonny was so good in the corners. When you're digging in the pits, you always have your arms up on the glass to shield yourself.

At first, I thought they were messing with me, but then I saw Jonny go out for our next game with no elbow pads. He must have had steel plates in his arms. Here I was thinking I was picky about my equipment.

I once had no shoes and complained, until I met a man who had no elbow pads.

Credit Card Roulette

Going out for dinner with the boys was always a great way to decompress and unwind. Most of the time, once you were settled into a routine, you would split on groceries with your roommate and take turns making meals. But, sometimes it was nice to just get out of the house and relax at a restaurant.

One of the things most teams did for the players was negotiate sponsorship deals with local restaurants that would allow players to get discounts off their meals. The team might also work out deals with golf courses, gyms, and even dental offices. When I played in Augusta in the ECHL, we had a 50% discount at T.G.I. Fridays, free greens fees at both Jones Creek Golf & Country Club and The River Golf Club, free eye exams and a free pair of glasses at 1-Hour Optical, and free cleanings, X-rays and fillings for you and your family at Augusta Smiling. These were a few perks that went a long way to help players feel more valued, since the contracts weren't going to set you up for anything beyond the season.

When you get a bunch of athletes together, everything becomes a competition. When you hit the road and the per diem is distributed, the cards come out and the gambling begins. Some guys like to play poker, euchre or "Shnarples". Shnarples was a unique game that I have never seen played outside of hockey circles. It was a bit of a cross between euchre and gin rummy. Although it wasn't for big money, cash was always involved in these games. Since pride is what is most important to hockey players, compounded with the fact that nobody likes to lose, there were always arguments over scorekeeping and cheating.

When you had leisure time during home stretches and decided to get a few boys together after practice and hit the golf course, the wallets would come out and games would be devised to make the round more interesting. You might break into two teams and play a buck-a-hole, or each hole would be given a value and a skins match would be set up. There would usually be a pot collected for a winner-take-all "longest drive" hole and "closest to the pin". Basically everything came with a wager.

When you would go out to a bar, the competition became about picking up women. Guys would scan a bar and pick out girls and challenge each other to see if they could pick them up. It might be something like: "Hey Stewy, I bet you 20 bucks you can't get that blonde over there to give you her number," or, "Hey Stewy, if you can get that brunette to go home with you, I'll pick up your tab." It seems insensitive and barbaric, and it totally was, but that was just the way it was when everything was about winning.

Even when you went out to eat, you couldn't just relax. Quite often, if a bunch of us went out to dinner somewhere, we'd play a game we called "Credit Card Roulette." Credit card roulette was simple, everyone would order what they wanted to eat for dinner and then at the end of the meal, everyone would put their credit card into a hat or a basket and they would be shuffled around. When the bill came, a card would be pulled from the hat and whomever the card belonged to would pick up the tab for the group.

Since we played in the minors and didn't make huge salaries, we usually instituted the rule that only food would be included in the game. All the beers and other drinks had to be on separate bills. Even with just meals on a tab, if you had 10 guys going out to the Outback Steakhouse, bills would be in the $250 to $300 range.

Athletes at high levels need to have a deep-rooted, competitive nature. It's what makes good players that much better. Because a strong compete level is what drives athletes, it nearly always spills over into other aspects of their lives. Whether it's golf, badminton, eating, drinking or Monopoly, a driven athlete is going to do whatever he can to win and then he's going to pout like a three-year-old if he loses.

Professional Tourist/Hockey Player

One of the biggest bonuses about playing pro hockey is getting to travel and see different parts of the world. It's like a paid vacation, in a way. Travelling around, playing in different cities or different countries, you get to see things and experience things that most people need to book trips and spend money to do.

Although we did a lot of travelling, it wasn't like we had a lot of time on the road to sightsee. Most of the time, you are stashed away in some bunk on a nearly windowless bus or at a rink or hotel, but every once in a while, there are opportunities to wander and take some time for yourself.

One of the things that allowed me to experience a bit more when we'd head out on the road was the fact that I never took pre-game naps. Most guys I played with would shut it down for two or three hours every gameday afternoon as part of their pre-game ritual. I tried to nap earlier in my career, but I found it made me feel sluggish and grumpy. It would take me until the third period to get the cobwebs out of my head. So instead of napping, I would go for walks around whatever city we were playing in.

My ritual of going for pre-game walks started back in college. We'd be playing teams like: Yale, Harvard, Dartmouth, Princeton and Cornell. All of these schools had immaculate campuses filled with rich history. I used to take my camera on my tours and take pictures of the architecture on the campuses and the neat plaques and statues.

Playing in the ECHL and CHL, most of the excitement of travel was being able to touch soil in so many famous U.S. states and cities. Being a kid from Canada, the only other way I would have been able to experience what I did playing hockey would have been to save up money and embark on an extensive and expensive road trip. At the time I played in the league, the ECHL spanned from Alaska down to Fort Myers, Fla., and west to Bakersfield, CA. When you combined it with the CHL, which recently added its first Canadian franchise in Brampton, Ont., you had two leagues that held teams in nearly every state in the U.S.

During my days living on the bus while playing for Amarillo, Texas, in the CHL, we might play a game Friday night in snow-covered Fort Collins, CO., or Rapid City, S.D., and then we'd play a Saturday night game down in tropical McAllen, Texas. If you went on a road trip for a week, you'd have to pack for both the snow and the beach. The vastness in geography of the leagues and the variety of climates made for some pretty interesting road trips.

Since the U.S. is rich in history, each minor league city had something to offer when it came to uniqueness and culture. Whether it was a famous landmark or a renowned restaurant, each city had something neat to check out. For example, on a trip down to play in Pensacola, Fla., we ate a post-game meal in a restaurant called McGuire's Irish Pub, which is famous for having a tradition where patrons can write their name on a dollar bill and have it stapled to the ceiling. The tradition started back in the late '70s when Molly McGuire received a dollar as a tip and stapled it to the wall behind the bar for good luck. The tradition caught on quickly and McGuire's now has more than $750,000 in singles stapled all over the restaurant. Since there is so much money tacked to the walls and ceiling, the restaurant has to keep track of it and include it as part of its net worth for tax purposes.

Playing in Amarillo, I had access to some amazing history and culture right in my own backyard. For starters, several of us lived in Canyon, Texas, on the campus of West Texas A&M University. The biggest draw in the appropriately named town of Canyon is the second-largest canyon in the U.S.—the Palo Duro Canyon.

On the outskirts of Amarillo sits The Big Texan steakhouse which is famous for being the home of the original 72-ounce steak challenge. In order to eat for free and have yourself immortalized with your picture on the wall, you have to complete the challenge of eating a 72-ounce steak, including all the sides and fixings, in an hour or less.

Also adding to the allure of Amarillo is the renowned Cadillac Ranch, which is a part of the landmark series speckled along the legendary former Route 66. The Cadillac Ranch is essentially a series of Cadillacs in numerical order according to make and model half-buried, nose-first in the ground in a line. Although it is a small landmark, the Cadillac Ranch has been honored in songs by Bruce Springstein and the Nitty Gritty Band, as well as being the setting for music videos and television show snippets.

Playing in Augusta, Ga., I had the privilege of living in a gated housing complex on the backside of Augusta National Golf Club, home of The Masters golf tournament. During the 2008 Masters tournament, when Trevor Immelman captured his first green jacket, I had the luxury of walking the hallowed grounds for three rounds. While traipsing the immaculate course in complete awe, I even had the fluke chance to meet and shake hands with golf legend Gary Player.

On a southern swing down to Biloxi, Miss., I was able to witness the after-effects of the devastating hurricane Katrina. While walking the debris-littered beaches along the Gulf of Mexico, you could almost see the exuberance that once made the city a highly coveted tourist destination. All that remained of a once-flourishing industry was the Hard Rock Cafe and Casino, which looked to be an oasis amid the ravaged landscape.

On a southern Texas stop in Corpus Christi, I was able to take time to walk the coastline of the "Sparkling City by the Sea". During some down time in Corpus, I was fortunate enough to take in a bit of U.S. military history by checking out the USS Lexington, a famous retired aircraft carrier-turned-floating-museum that was active during the Second World War and served as part of the set for the filming of the movie "Pearl Harbor."

On a less-spectacular trip to Odessa, Texas, driving along the dusty roads past oilfields, lined by derricks as far as the eye can see, I was able to experience the setting for the popular book-turned-movie-and-television-series, "Friday Night Lights" by H.G. Bissinger. Ratliff Field, home of the Permian High School Panthers, sat conveniently across the road from the Ector County Coliseum, where we played against the hometown Odessa Jackalopes. We actually walked across the road and used the famous field to warm up and prep for our game.

The fringe benefits of a pro hockey career aren't fully appreciated until it's all said and done. While you're playing, it's all about reaching the dream and you become consumed with the pressures of reaching the next level. When you get a chance to step back and really examine the journey, you begin to realize the underlying benefits of following through on that dream. While the paycheques may not be colossal, the experiences and lessons learned along the way are priceless.

The Mike Sgroi Experience

Every now and then, a player comes through hockey whose name sends chills down your spine. For my era while playing in the minors it was Mike Sgroi. Sgroi was a six-foot-five, 235-pound winger from Toronto who was as tough as he was unpredictable. A YouTube sensation, hundreds of Sgroi's fights can be found online, including some off-ice fights where he moonlighted as a mixed martial arts Muay Thai fighter in the cage circuits during the off-season.

Sgroi began his pro career in the minors in 2000 and had played for 28 teams through the 2012-13 season. Over that span, Sgroi had some epic bouts with NHL heavyweights such as, Derek Boogaard, Matt Carkner, Paul Bissonnette, Shawn Thornton and George Parros, among many others. Sgroi also competed in the infamous "Battle of the Hockey Enforcers" in 2005, an event that was postponed and relocated several times before finally being sanctioned in Prince George, B.C. Sgroi reached the final and lost a close match to Dean Mayrand.

The thing that made Sgroi so intriguing was his pure love for fighting. He absolutely lived for it. The reason he was so dangerous was that he never knew when to turn the switch off and he had the size and strength to inflict a lot of damage. It wasn't uncommon for Sgroi to continue pounding downed opponents after the refs had stepped in to break it up. With his size and hand speed, he was a devastating force and that unpredictability put him in an exclusive class of psycho.

The first year I played against Sgroi was in the ECHL during the 2007-08 season when he was playing for the Pensacola Ice Pilots. That season, Pensacola was a basement-dweller team and Sgroi found himself in a new, unfamiliar role. Between Pensacola and Johnstown that season, Sgroi racked up 47 points, including 25 goals, in 53 games on top of his more consistent stat of 257 penalty minutes. You might look at those stats and say, "Wow, Mike Sgroi can do it all!" In reality, his point totals that season were more likely inflated due to the fact that no one wanted to go within 25 feet of him.

That season, he basically skated around untouched because everyone knew that he might literally bite your nose off if you were standing too close to him. Sgroi constantly had a wild-eyed look to him. He was in a perpetual state of vibration. His head snapped around like a bird as he combed the ice searching for willing and unwilling combatants, alike.

One night in Pensacola, my defense partner, Jason Platt, who was a great open-ice hitter, absolutely steamrolled Sgroi at center ice. Sgroi popped up like he was shot out of a cannon and went bananas, jumping Platt and swinging at everyone who came within arm's length to break it up, including the linesmen. He was an absolute lunatic on the ice and had everyone walking on egg shells because you never knew when he would just flip the switch and go haywire.

In the movie "Slapshot", there is a character named Ogie Oglethorp and all the players talk about him like he is the plague. Guys get nervous when they think Oglethorp is in the lineup, knowing he could just lose it and rip your head off your body at any moment. Mike Sgroi, while I was playing in the minors, was the real-life Ogie Oglethorp. You dreaded when you had to line up against him and sighed with relief when you found out he was injured, suspended or had been traded or called up.

The next season, one of my teammates, Justin Coutu, ended up rooming with Sgroi in Johnstown, PA. and said that he was actually a really nice guy. That is usually the case when it comes to enforcers. They have the toughest job in hockey and spend so much time playing the role of bully, when in fact they are usually the nicest guys on the team.

When you have a guy like that on your team, it's like going to the playground with your big brother. You know you can just be yourself and have fun and nobody is going to mess with you.

Off-Season Blues

Off-seasons for a minor leaguer are bittersweet. Part of you is happy for it to be over because you just spent the past eight months destroying your body, putting it through the ringer and, unless you won it all, you are probably bummed out and disappointed about the result of your season. As a result of the grind, I used to lose 15 pounds every season. I would go into camp at 200 or 205 and come out of it looking like a wet rat at 185.

The other part of you is sad because you know what is awaiting you. For the past eight months, you have been able to play a sport that you love and the best part was you were getting paid to do it. While all of your friends had been grinding away at a desk or in a crawl space on a job site for eight hours a day, you were working on your one-timers and one-on-ones for an hour a day in the morning and then working on your short game with a 12-pack of Bud Light in the back of your golf cart in the afternoons. As much as you were burnt out from the 72-game season plus playoffs and thousands of miles travelled going from town to town, you didn't really have much to complain about.

It doesn't take long for the disappointment and exhaustion of the season to wear off. Maybe a couple of weeks went by and then you are back on the phone with your agent trying to find a place to play for next season. Another year in the Coast, trying to get a call-up to the American league? Maybe go and make some extra dough under the table in the CHL? Or maybe it's time to head over to Europe and make some real money and see the world?

You quickly forget about the aches and pains and mental anguish of underachieving in the playoffs and that pure love for hockey takes hold of you, making you yearn for the start of a new season. For me, it was all of that, and of course the less-glamorous, inevitable prospect of going back to my old job of tending bar and living in my grandmother's basement for the summer.

The sadness that came along with being a minor leaguer was that you couldn't cruise on what you raked in during the season. Making between $500 to $750 a week wasn't enough to justify going unemployed during the summer. In the summers, I used to return to Kingston, Ont., and sling pints for weddings and regulars at a couple of bars in town. Bartending was appropriate because it kept me on the healthy side of the countertop during peak hours. The flexibility of the job allowed me to train during the days, work at nights, and then take a few weeks off here and there if I wanted to go work a hockey school down in Lake Placid or up in Ottawa.

The flip side to having a sporadic schedule that might see you here one week and gone the next was that I couldn't really find a place to rent for such a short period of time. Luckily, my Nana lived in Kingston and just happened to have some room for me to shack up and come and go as I pleased.

From my perspective, it was a pretty sweet deal. I lived rent-free, had a flexible job and was able to train during the day. From an outsider's perspective, it was pretty embarrassing. Here was a 26-year-old professional hockey player, living in his grandmother's basement, having to work two jobs. Weren't pro hockey players were supposed to make good money? Grow up, Peter Pan!

Living with Nana was a treat! I just spent the last season living with two other guys in a house where it was always a struggle to see who was going to grab groceries, take out the garbage or pick up all the empty beer cans. Nana had cleaning ladies that came by, so everything was always clean. When I'd head to work, Nana would insist on doing my laundry. In return, I just had to help out with a few errands here and there.

One of my duties was to take dear old Nana grocery shopping. In her early nineties, Nana had a lot of hop in her step, but she still needed someone to drive her around and lug the load.

It was priceless when we'd hit up Loblaws for a grocery run. Nana was completely old school. She would sit down at the kitchen table before we left and write down everything she needed on a notepad as things popped into her head. Once in the grocery store, we'd scoot around starting at the top of the list and slowly work our way down. The problem with this method was that Nana's brain didn't work in the same way the grocery store was laid out. At the kitchen table, while making out her list, she would write down: milk, cucumbers, cheese, tomatoes, butter, apples… She insisted on following the order of the list, so we would be going from one end of the store to the other and back again until all of the items were crossed off.

After about 1.5 km and seven items, I would say: "Come on, Nana, let me see the list and I'll go run and grab a bunch of things and meet you in the spice aisle."

She would promptly swat my hand away and say: "Don't you worry about my list! I've got things under control."

Oh Mylanta!

So after hiking around Loblaws for nearly three hours, covered in a solid coat of sweat, we would pull into the checkout line. The usual routine would ensue:

> Nana: Hi Bernice! How are things?
>
> Bernice: Oh hello Irene! Things are going well.
>
> Nana: How did it go at the doctor's the other day? Did he sort out that foot problem?
>
> Bernice: Well he said that I might have to go see a pedophilist or pediatricianist or whatever they call them to give it a look-see. Who is this you have with you today?
>
> Nana: Oh Bernice, aren't I just the luckiest. This is my grandson Jamie. Isn't he just a handsome hunk of a lad?
>
> Bernice: Oh yes!

Meanwhile, I'd be squirming because there would be a line forming behind us wrapping around the store and poor old Nana would be fumbling around her gargantuan purse looking for the bank card my dad activated for her since Loblaws no longer takes personal cheques. Corporate bastards!

Now the concept of a debit card to my Nana was like putting Abraham Lincoln in a Ferrari Testarossa. Finally, Nana would pull out her debit card and begin tapping upwards of 13 digits on the keypad. This is swiftly followed by an error buzzer.

> Me: "Nana what's going on? Don't you know your PIN number?"
>
> Nana: "Ya I just put it in and it came up wrong. The machine must be broken."
>
> Me: "Well you just punched in like 20 numbers. Those PINs are only supposed to be four to eight digits."
>
> Nana: "Well it's MELBA." (Melba was the name of my Nana's deceased dog. Thanks for letting everyone in the store know what your PIN number is. Add another stop to the errand list to stop at the bank to change Nana's PIN on the way home.)
>
> Me: "Nana, that word is only five digits long. Why do you put in so many digits?"
>
> Nana: "Well, 'M' is the 13th letter in the alphabet, so I put in '13' and then 'E' is the fifth letter so I enter '05'…" (My headache starts to intensify.)
>
> Me: "Ooooooookay, how about I just put it in and I'll explain it to you in the car, away

from the angry mob grumbling behind us looking for a rafter to string us up by."

All in all, living with Nana was great. It was entertaining and fun to hear all the stories about how much of a bonehead my dad was growing up or what it was like growing up when life was more about working to put food on the table. We're talking about a woman who lived through two world wars and the Great Depression.

It also helped to keep me on the straight and narrow during the off-season, when it was always easy to get into trouble. It wasn't like I could stumble through the door at 3:30 a.m. after a Friday night out, slobbering all over some floozy I picked up at the after-hours pizza joint. It gave me a nice balance and allowed me to focus on what was important to get ready for next season.

One of the bars that I worked in the off-season was a little hole in the wall, tucked in the backside of Kingston's Portsmouth Olympic Harbour. The bar was called, "The Snack Bar". The Snack Bar was located beside the Kingston Penitentiary, then home to Canada's most notorious criminals, including Paul Bernardo, Clifford Olson and Mohammad Shafia. The bar was a regular haunt for several active and retired pen guards as well as a slew of neighborhood regulars.

I used to dread these shifts for two main reasons. First reason was I didn't want to sit and listen to stories from the retired guards about people hanging themselves in their cells or stabbing other inmates to death in the lunch line. Take your PTSD down to the mental health clinic, boys. The second reason was that everyone would find out I played hockey and either tell me a story of how they got screwed over and should have played in the NHL or would spew pure ignorance about the game of hockey as if it were gospel.

I would get remarks like: "I heard you play hockey down in like Georgia or Texas or something. What do you want to do? Are you thinking that maybe you can work your way up and play for the Kingston Frontenacs someday?" Here I was playing in the ECHL, a professional hockey league with NHL affiliations, and this guy was asking me if I wanted to try to work my way up to playing for a team in the OHL, a junior hockey league. Some people just have no clue, but won't admit that maybe they don't know much about the game of hockey.

Other times, I would get comments like: "They should cut the NHL back down to six teams. Every team now has maybe two or three good players, but the rest of them are bums." So here he is saying that 85% of NHL hockey players are awful. Meanwhile, I'm scratching and clawing from two leagues below the NHL, trying to find my way. If these multimillionaire NHL players are so brutal, what does that make me? Maybe I should just go out back and shoot myself.

My favorites were the guys who would come in and tell me about how they played 1,000 games in the NHL and scored a million goals. It didn't take a scan through hockeydb.com to figure out they were completely full of shit. That they were 5-4 and weighed 115 pounds between smokes was enough to make you roll your eyes.

One guy said he played in the OHL for the Toronto Marlies and he was on a line with Brian "Spinner" Spencer. He said he and Spinner used to pile in four goals a game apiece and then go drive 20 pints of Budweiser down the hatch. Funny, because Brian Spencer was from out west and never played for the Marlies or any team in the OHL.

I never did call any of their bluffs because I figured

if they had to make up grandiose stories about imaginary glory days, maybe it was best to let them pretend it was true. Most of these guys had obviously seen some rough times and probably didn't have the best of luck over the years. Who knows, maybe someday I might be one of those guys, cranking on Nevada tickets, drinking stale Molson Export.

By the end of the summer, as the days leading up to training camp grew nearer, you would get a telling feeling in the pit of your stomach. You were itching to get the season started and thinking about all the fun you knew you were going to have. The start of every new season was like a fresh start. A clean slate to try to prove you belonged and deserved to get promoted. The muscle was back on, the injuries were healed. You felt you were faster and stronger than you have ever been going into camp. You were ready to make this the season that everything would all come together. This year was going to be different. This year, you were going to make it.

The Hierarchy of Professional Hockey

There is a certain mental picture that pops up when people think of professional athletes. Most people immediately think of fancy cars and flashy jewelry draped upon an egotistical jerk, flocked by bodacious bimbos. At least that's what I pictured when I made it my dream to become one.

In reality, being a professional athlete can mean a variety of things. At the top of the sports world, there is the superstar athlete who signs the multimillion-dollar deal and hangs out with Jay-Z and Rhianna. This type of professional athlete represents a tiny portion of the professional athlete population. These guys are royalty. But like any monarchy, the riches tend to remain locked securely in the palace while the peons fight for scraps at the foothills.

Below the kings of sport are divisions of subordinates who make up the rest of the professional sports kingdom. There are athletes who play two to 10 years at the major levels and make a good living at it. Then there are the guys who get a couple of cups of coffee at the prime-time level, playing stints in different cities spread across a few years. Below that, there are the minor leaguers who actually make up the largest portion of professional athletes in the world. These are the guys who, despite popular assumptions about the general finances of professional athletes, make barely enough money to take care of themselves, much less a family.

In hockey, like all professional sports, the annual salary structure is extremely top heavy. The NHL minimum salary is $500,000 with players making an average annual salary of $2.4 million. Top paid talents rake in upwards of $10 million per year.

In the past five years, the Kontinental Hockey League (KHL) has begun to rival the NHL, competing for players and from a max-salary standpoint offer compensation that is congruent with NHL standards. Buoyed by the fact that KHL contracts are tax-free, the monetary allure has been enough to see star NHL players flee for multi-year pacts overseas. Most notably, Jaromir Jagr, who in 2008 was reeled in by a rumored three-year, $21-million deal to play for Omsk Avangard. The tax-free deal would have been the equivalent of signing a three-year, $33-million contract, which at the time was the richest contract in the world.

Dropping down a level on the global hockey scale, financially speaking, is European Elite hockey. In top

European leagues, such as the SM Liga (Finland), SEL (Sweden), DEL (Germany), and the Swiss A League, top players fetch anywhere between $60,000 and $500,000 per season, tax-free. These leagues are riddled with former NHL players who are either at the end of their careers or are unable to secure full-time NHL positions. Financially speaking, it makes sense for a player in his late 20s or early 30s who has fewer than 100 NHL games under his belt to spend the last few years in Europe, collecting a nice, fat paycheque.

At the American Hockey League (AHL) level, the top affiliate league to the NHL, players rake in anywhere between $39,000 and $300,000 annually. The odd exception is when a player at the NHL level, with a big contract, is put through waivers in order to be sent down, thus shielding his gargantuan salary from the cap. This is evident when you see a player like Mike Komisarek making $5 million to play in the AHL. Most AHL players are signed to two-way NHL deals where they make "NHL money" when they are called up and "AHL money" when they are sent down. These are salaries that are prorated according to the amounts agreed upon at each level.

Once you drop below the AHL level, the salary amounts begin to free-fall at mach-10 rates. At the ECHL level, which is equivalent to baseball's Double-A, annual salaries range from $10,640 to $28,000 for the season. The only difference at this level is that your housing is covered by the team and doesn't come out of your salary. At higher levels, it is up to the player to locate accommodation and pay rent. The Double-A level is where contracts aren't guaranteed beyond a two-week severance package. This means that as long as a player is active, he can be released by the team without fear of having to honor the length of the contract. ECHL deals are signed on a year-to-year basis.

Dropping down even further to the Southern Professional Hockey League (SPHL), players earn between $4,200 and $14,000 per year, with most players receiving weekly paycheques in the $200 to $250 range.

You might look at the salaries in the ECHL and SPHL and ask yourself why would these people put their bodies on the line for such a small amount of money and no guarantees? The simple answer is that if you are being paid to play, then technically the dream is still alive and well. There are enough stories of long-shot glory out there to fill a library. Joel Ward spent four years at the University of Prince Edward Island (UPEI) in the CIS, often thought to be a graveyard of hockey dreams, before making the arduous climb up the ranks to make millions at the NHL level.

Then there is Tim Thomas, who couldn't get a sniff at the NHL level until he was 31 years old. Thomas spent a decade toiling in the minors and overseas before winning two Vezina Trophies and a Stanley Cup in a span of seven years in the NHL.

And lest we forget Dustin Penner, who played university club hockey at Minot State after he was cut three times from local junior teams. It was blind luck that landed Penner at the University of Maine after he was spotted by Black Bears assistant coach Grant Standbrook at a summer prospects tournament. Penner spent only one season at Maine before signing an NHL contract with the Anaheim Ducks in 2004.

At the conclusion of the 2012-13 season, more than 490 players who had played in the ECHL had gone on to play in the NHL. This long list includes players such as Thomas, Alex Burrows, Olaf Kolzig, Mark Streit, Michael Ryder, Andrew Brunette, Jonathan Quick, Jaroslav Halak, James Reimer, David Desharnais and

Francois Beauchemin, among many other players who went on to long, productive NHL careers. So many bona fide NHL stars had to earn their stripes in minor leagues such as the ECHL before they were able to prove their worth at higher levels. Knowing that there is a chance however unlikely it might be keeps minor leaguers in uniform.

The other aspect that keeps players motivated at the minor league level is the minuscule difference in individual skill levels from one level to the next. To put it into perspective, take a look at the skills competition results from 2011 for the NHL and ECHL levels. At the 2011 NHL All-Star Skills Competition, Michael Grabner of the New York Islanders took home the fastest skater event with a time of 14.238 seconds, holding off Edmonton's Taylor Hall, who clocked in at 14.715. At the 2011 ECHL All-Star skills competition, two levels below, Eric Lampe of the Elmira Jackels won the ECHL competition with a time of 14.445, edging Vyacheslav Trukhno of the Bakersfield Condors (14.712 seconds). In the same year, Zdeno Chara took home the NHL hardest shot competition with a new record of 105.9 mph, while Josh Godfrey won the hardest shot event at the ECHL level with a 102.7 mph blast.

The fact is, some players in the ECHL can shoot harder and skate faster than players at the NHL level. That reality keeps players striving because they know that sometimes it just takes a window of opportunity to open at the right time to change the course of a career. A hot streak at the right moment, in front of the right set of eyes, can be the difference between making $39,000 or $2 million.

Some players can have all the talent in the world, but don't process the game well enough to succeed at higher levels. It's the immeasurable and ever-important attribute called "hockey sense" that determines if you will make a good living in this game. Some players just don't have it and never will. The other immensely important intangibles are heart and character. Some players will go through walls and play through anything to win. If you have that kind of determination and desire, skill becomes less of a major priority. For every Steven Stamkos, there are four Darren McCartys.

The Ever-Changing Landscape of the Minor Leagues

Professional hockey, whether it is at the NHL or minor league level, is a bottom-line business. Players are commodities and teams are service providers. Without revenue, there is no spectacle; without a spectacle, there are no fans. Once a market is tapped, the carnival packs up its trucks and moves on to the next city to deliver its display of graceful aggression and wonderment.

Throughout the years, minor league teams have been born, folded, relocated and recreated. Even the leagues themselves go through transitions. Figuring out how the minor leagues originated and developed into what we see today is as confusing as Abbott and Costello's "Who's on First". The minor league hockey adaptation of the comedy shtick might go something like this:

> Abbott:
> "So the ECHL is the East Coast Hockey League?"

Costello:
"Yes, but it used to be the Eastern Professional Hockey League (EPHL), and has also absorbed teams from the former West Coast Hockey League (WCHL)."

Abbott:
"So you're telling me that the *EAST* Coast Hockey League has teams on the West Coast?"

Costello:
"Yes, the ECHL is a Double-A league and has California-based teams in Stockton, Ontario, Bakersfield and San Francisco, as well as teams in Las Vegas, Utah, Idaho, and even a team in Alaska."

Abbott:
"Alright, alright, I get it... Sort of. Now tell me, what is this Central Hockey League (CHL) and how did it come into being?"

Costello:
"The CHL, also a Double-A league, started out as the CHL but then became the Western Professional Hockey League (WPHL), before it went back to being the CHL again. In addition, a league known as the United Hockey League (UHL), which used to be the Colonial Hockey League (CoHL), and would later be known as the International Hockey League (IHL), was absorbed by today's CHL."

Abbott:
"Wait a minute, so you're saying that the IHL,

which used to be the UHL, after being the CoHL, is now a part of the CHL?"

Costello:
"Yes, but before the name 'IHL' was given to the old UHL, it was an entirely different league that was on par with the American Hockey League (AHL), which is designated at the Triple-A level. The AHL ended up absorbing the old IHL and then years later, the IHL name was re-branded to take the place of the UHL name."

Abbott:
"So let me get this straight, the IHL was like the AHL, and then became part of the AHL. Then years later, the IHL came back as the UHL and then became part of the CHL, which used to be the WPHL?

Costello:
"You got it. Oh ya, I forgot to mention the SPHL."

Abbott:
"What is the SPHL?"

Costello:
"The SPHL is the Southern Professional Hockey League. It's the hockey equivalent of baseball's Single-A. Before it was the SPHL, it was the SEHL and the WHA2. Also, a lot of the SPHL cities used to be ECHL cities. Places like Biloxi, Miss., and Huntsville, Ala., were awarded SPHL franchises after they folded in the ECHL."

Abbott:
"Sheesh, why don't they just make up their minds already?!"

The other confusing part about the structure of the minor leagues is the folding, renaming, re-affiliations and expansions of teams. For example, the Kalamazoo Wings went from the IHL, when it was on par with the AHL, to the UHL (which became the CHL), eventually winding up in the ECHL. Franchises are born, thrive, dive and then fold or relocate all within a matter of five to 10 years. It's not uncommon to see a thriving team, playing in front of packed houses, sputter and keel over a few short years later. It's the unpredictable nature and volatility of the minor leagues that makes it difficult for teams to survive. Any dip in the economy affects franchises ten-fold due to the shift in priorities of small-town hockey fans.

Another major component that affects the fate of minor league franchises is whether it has a business arrangement or affiliation with an NHL team. With backing from NHL franchises, minor league teams benefit from added financial security and organizational stockpiling of talent. This adds to the allure of the spectacle. People are more inclined to go to a game when they think they might have a chance to see the next NHL superstar on his way up the ladder. The problem is, most of these affiliation agreements are signed on a year-to-year basis, and when the affiliation is pulled, all of the financial stability and mystical allure goes along with it, leaving the minor league franchise scrambling to catch another ride.

Both of the teams for which I played, Augusta in the ECHL and Amarillo in the CHL, have since folded. Two other teams with which I was briefly associated with, the

Bossier-Shreveport Mudbugs and the Texas Brahmas of the CHL, have also since folded. During the 2008-09 season, I was part of the first ECHL franchise to fold mid-season, when the Augusta Lynx closed their doors in the fall of 2008. The 2008-09 season was a massacre of sorts, with teams based in Augusta, Dayton, Fresno, Mississippi and Phoenix closing up shop in the ECHL, along with the CHL franchises of New Mexico, Rocky Mountain and Oklahoma City. That season witnessed nine total closures at the Double-A level.

Some great minor league cities have hosted franchises and lost them, only to regain them years later. Lively southern U.S. cities such as New Orleans, Biloxi, Corpus Christi, Bossier-Shreveport, Albuquerque, Jacksonville, Lafayette and Augusta have seen teams come and go and will probably be prominent again in the world of minor pro hockey.

The minor leagues work in cycles. As the economy ebbs and flows, so, too, does the lifeblood of the minors. At peak times, arenas in small towns across the U.S. are bursting at the seams, hanging on every toe-drag, bodycheck and haymaker. When times are tough and money is tight, the arena lights are shut off until the dawn of better days. Once the tide reaches its peak again, lines will be painted, dust will be cleared and fresh new faces will fill programs, reminding fans that the NHL's next big ticket just might be getting his feet wet for the new team in town.

The Toughest Job in Pro Sports

He sits at a rickety desk in a converted storage room. The scattered towers of scouting reports, strategy schemes and transaction lists create shadows beneath the blinding industrial overhead lights. A laptop doubling as a video review system sits atop his desk amid the scattered papers. Coupled with a dinged-up BlackBerry, the laptop will serve as the major recruiting, system review and business tool at his disposal.

Faded pictures of past glory line the surrounding walls of the office. A trophy from a championship won too many years ago to remember, sits on a shelf in the corner, collecting dust. A jersey from his playing days is encased in a glass tomb on the wall behind his desk. These items are all hopeful reminders that past triumphs will breed future glory.

His face is scarred and weathered from years of navigating the rocky path of professional hockey. He took to the ice during the days when men were men and gas was 35 cents a gallon. Each scar tells a tale of honor and courage, reminding everyone that he has been there and knows what it takes. His hair is grey and thinner than the massive mane he once sported during his glory days. His eyes are sunken, yet piercing, filled with knowledge and passion about a game that has changed more times than Dennis Rodman's hair color. He is, by all measures and standards, a successful minor league coach, and he has, without a shred of doubt, the toughest job in pro sports.

Most of the coaches at the minor league level are hockey lifers who are either holding on to some shape or form of the dream, or simply don't know any other way to make ends meet. The lifestyle is somewhat of a graduated extension of that of the minor league players they coach. The pay is better, but in relation to the added responsibility and workload, not quite sufficient. In addition to coaching, most of these men will don multiple organizational hats, involving anything from working off-season NHL development camps to various administrative duties, such as soliciting corporate sponsorships or reconciling gate receipts.

Since team budgets in the minors are tight, coaches have to get creative and cut corners anywhere they can. There is no money to go towards recruiting, so they need to rely on connections to secure talent for each upcoming season. If they are lucky enough to have an NHL affiliation, recruiting becomes a lot easier as players are filtered down through the system. Having a big club affiliation also helps alleviate a great deal of financial burden.

The drawback to having an affiliation is that the decisions you make, from who to start in net, to who will quarterback your power play, are now most likely going to be decided from above. Since the NHL team is lending you its prospects and providing some financial relief, it has secured a major stake in your organization and, in turn, what you decide to do with it.

It's a tough predicament. On one hand, you're grateful to have the benefit of an NHL affiliation to alleviate the pressure to attract top talent and stay in the black, but on the other hand, you lose out on how much say you have in crucial decisions. Despite being relegated to a glorified passenger, the responsibility remains strongly secured upon your shoulders. You might get a crop of prospects sent down and discover that they are too raw and inexperienced to provide the impact you expect from your top-line guys. The better players might actually be ECHL-contracted guys who are proven at that level and have been through the wars but don't get the top minutes because the big club wants that ice to go to its younger investments. In turn, this does a number on morale, and if the losses start piling up, it's your head that will be on the chopping block.

The other inevitable fact for minor league coaches is that you will be fired, multiple times. In my second season in the ECHL, I re-signed early in the off-season with Augusta. I was one of the first players to re-sign with the team and was excited to play another season under ECHL coaching legend Bob Ferguson. Fergie gave me all kinds of praise and said he had a plan for me for the next season and that things were going to be great. One week later, Fergie left the team to become the assistant GM of the Iowa Chops, Anaheim's AHL affiliate. For the next month, I had no idea for whom I would be playing. Finally, in July, Augusta named John Marks as the new head coach of the Lynx.

Marks was no slouch when it came to coaching. He played 10 years for the Chicago Blackhawks, riding shotgun on a line with Stan Mikita for a bulk of those years. He was a former NHL all-star and, by the time I met him, had been coaching for nearly 30 years. Obviously, I was going to play for a highly decorated general.

Marksy was typical of most minor league coaches who have ridden it hard for a lot of years. He chewed tobacco furiously, had a gruff voice and liked the odd pop here and there. Over the course of a 30-year career behind the bench, through the 2012-13 season, Marks had coached 10 teams spread out across the U.S. He had won championships and finished dead last, often spending only one or two seasons in any given place.

Coaches, like players, ride the hard miles on the bus, often traversing from small town to small town in the middle of the night. They eat the same bowel-destroying meals on the road as the players do and sleep in the same coffin-sized bunks. The only difference is coaches can't go on the IR.

When you lose bad and the game finishes, coaches will say to players: "Let's put that one behind us and focus on the next game." As a player, that's the best advice going, but for a coach, it's just empty propaganda. After the game, the real pressure begins to mount. You question everything from line combinations to system play, and you're fielding calls from owners and management asking how you could lose a game so badly. There is nowhere to hide, and it's not like you can quit. Quitting means finding a new line of work and telling your family that the previous 10 years spent away from home were all for nothing.

The lucky few will have enough success that someone higher up the ranks will take notice and give them an opportunity. Unless you have a famous daddy who can open doors or have your name etched in stone at the Hockey Hall of Fame, you're probably going to have to settle for riding cramped buses from dusk till dawn and selling ad space to T.G.I. Fridays for $200 per square inch. As in any line of business, coaching is often about whom you know or being ridiculously successful to the point where people have no choice but to give you your dream shot.

Fergie-isms

One year, while playing in Augusta in the ECHL, we had a coach named Bob Ferguson. Fergie was the son of former NHL left winger Lorne Ferguson, who played several years for the Boston Bruins, Detroit Red Wings and Chicago Blackhawks. As a player, Fergie had been selected by the New York Islanders in the 1974 NHL Entry Draft. After bouncing around the minors and battling knee injuries, he settled into what has become a 30-years-plus coaching career.

Fergie was a classic, good ol' boy hockey coach. He was knowledgeable, competitive and had a terrific dry sense of humor. One of the things that made Fergie a gem was his classic one-liners that always had us in stitches. He would throw out lines like: "Hey, Donny Dangles! Those moves might have worked in Hayseedville, Alberta, or wherever the hell you came from, but you can stuff em' back in your bag."

Sometimes he'd blow the whistle in practice and start barking stuff like: "I don't want to see any more High School Harry shit! Dump the puck in like a man! Don't give me that one leg in the air, flip-shot bullshit!" You'd have to stifle your laughter because he'd drop one of his famous Fergie-isms and then glare around the room, completely straight-faced and angry, just waiting for some poor shmuck to giggle so he could rip them a new asshole.

Whenever we would have a bad period, Fergie would come into the dressing room like a tornado ripping through a trailer park in Kansas. He looked like Chris Farley in the "Saturday Night Live" skit "Down by the River", pulling on his belt and kicking over Gatorade jugs. His face would get so red you were always afraid he was going to have a heart attack. These were the times when the one-liners would be flowing like lava.

He'd be yelling stuff like: "Somebody better tell Hammerstein that we're in a hockey rink and not the Gaslight Lounge! He's too busy looking at Holly Hotpants in the third row to figure out we're down 4 - 1!"

Fergie was also good at making sure nobody got too high or too low. I can remember one time when we won three big games in a row. We had a terrible start in the fourth game, down 3 – 1 against a weaker team. Fergie came into the room after the first period and let us have it. He put our laughter-stifling skills to the test with this doozy: "Well la de da! We won three in a row and you guys are walking around like you're Studly Hungwell. Get real."

My all-time favorite Fergie-ism happened at a booster club party that followed a really bad stretch of games in the middle of the season. Usually at the booster functions, the boys would cut loose and enjoy a few pops. But, when you're in the middle of a bad skid, everyone walks around on eggshells. You don't want to give the coach a reason to single you out.

At this particular function, one of the guys made the mistake of appearing to have too much fun. He was carrying on, having a few beers and laughing loudly at jokes. You could tell Fergie was getting annoyed. He walked right over to the player and said: "Hey, you know what AHL team called for you today?"

The player got really excited, eagerly replying, "Who?"

With a straight face, Fergie replied: "Nobody!"

It was almost as if someone had punched the player in the stomach. His face went white as a ghost as Fergie turned his back and walked away.

Fergie had some of the best advice I had ever received in my career. He told us to clean up our act when it came to the bar scene. He said: "You want to know how to enjoy a long, successful career in hockey? Rule No. 1: always leave the bar before last call. Line up your gal early on in the night, put in your time and then skip out before 2 a.m. Nothing good ever happens after the ugly lights comes on." It was always funny hearing lines like that come from a grumpy-looking man with a dead serious expression.

Fergie had the right combination of dry humor and sternness to coach at the minor pro level. He knew when to push and when to keep things light. You weren't always happy with Fergie, but you respected him. That was what kept players from crossing the line.

24 Hours in the Life of a Minor Leaguer

Playing in the minor leagues comes with the prestige of being deemed a professional athlete. That prestige ends with the title. Once the contract is signed, you become a soldier at the bottom rung of the ladder. My dreams of flying first-class charters and staying in five-star hotels were quickly dashed when I boarded a musty, laminate-walled sleeper bus with faulty shocks, heading 12 hours south to Nowheresville, Texas. I became a tad giddy when the trainer handed me an envelope containing $37, a day's worth of per diem, until one of the vets in the back scoffed that NHLers receive $100 a day on road trips, despite making millions.

It's the first road trip of my professional career. Up until now, my previous road trips had consisted of two to seven-hour bus rides the night before a game and checking into an upscale hotel. We would eat three-course meals at nice restaurants. Our trainer would prep our dressing room overnight while we slumbered on down-filled pillows, dreaming dreams of all the great things we would do in our hockey careers once our college days ended. We would play two games at some Ivy League university, built in the 1800s, before heading back home. Surely, this five-game road trip would no different.

I made my way through the bus, ducking, turning sideways and stepping over coolers of Gatorade and boxes of expired beef jerky until I met one of the vets loading his pillows into a bunk. "Which bunk is available?" I asked. The grizzled vet turned to me and laughed.

"Since you're a rookie and we only have 15 bunks for 20 guys, you're standing on it," he said, pointing to the floor.

"What hotel are we staying at tonight?" I asked him.

He turned to me, as if I was from Mars, waved his hand in a circle and said: "You're looking at it, kid."

The bus finally pulled out of the rink at 10:30 p.m. We were scheduled to arrive at our next destination at 10 a.m., just in time to unload and be on the ice for an 11 a.m. pregame skate. I tried to stay up, playing a card game called "shnarples," to avoid making my bed in the high-traffic aisle. I'd never heard of shnarples, but I got the feeling that the vet teaching me how to play was taking advantage of me, rather than helping me. Within two hours, all my per diem was gone.

At about 2:30 a.m., I found myself slipping in and out of consciousness at the card table. I bundled up some foam given to me by one of the vets, who said "this stuff will save your career," and constructed a makeshift bed in the aisle between the rows of bunks. I laid down sideways, the only way I could comfortably fit in the narrow aisle, and quickly fell asleep, despite my orthopedically dysfunctional position.

As I dozed off, I felt a heavy thud on the outside of my right thigh that jerked me out of my slumber. "Sorry, Rook," came a voice amid the darkness, one the vets trying to make his way to the washroom along the cramped aisle. I quickly fell back asleep, only to be woken up shortly afterwards by another heavy heel, this time awkwardly placed on my shoulder.

"Fuck, Rook, I didn't even see ya there! Sorry, pal," an unidentifiable player said.

This parade of missteps continued for the next three hours, until the bus came shuddering to an abrupt halt. The overhead lights blasted on, followed by a chorus of groans and expletives.

"What the fuck is going on now, for fuck sakes," barked one of the captains.

Another player snapped: "Fuck, Bussy, you back on the Quaaludes again?"

Slowly, everyone got out of their bunks and moved to the front of the bus, like a swarm of zombies, to determine what the issue was. As I stepped off the bus, I saw that we'd hit a deer, a big one at that. The deer, or what looked like the upper half of a deer, was a bloody mess. The antlers were jammed into what was left of the grill of the bus, and our bus driver and trainer were yanking on the antlers and arguing in Spanish.

One of the players, an avid hunter, was gleefully jumping around shouting: "That's a 15-pointer! Open up the side compartments! Someone grab me the saw. I'm gonna mount those antlers on the front of the bus!"

After a half-hour delay, we were back on the road with a new color scheme on the front of the bus. At about 8 a.m., we pulled off the road again to stop at one of the most popular haunts of minor pro teams across the southern U.S., the Waffle House. The coach gave us the option of staying in bed or going in to grab some breakfast. Wired from our run-in with Bambi, combined with the fear of being trampled by a mob of hungry lead-foots, I decided to join the breakfast club.

Disheveled and decked out in team tracksuits, we lumbered into the establishment and piled into booths. I flipped through a menu of artery-clogging dishes and settled on the standard Waffle House two- egg special. Since I lost my per diem playing shnarples, I paid for the nutritional feast with some of the money I earned bartending in the summer.

After marveling at the old jukebox selection, watching an interestingly colored spider devour a fly, slurping back four coffees and slopping down a ketchup-smothered grease plate, I headed back onto the bus to round out the last couple hours of the trip playing euchre with three other wide- eyed rookies.

We finally arrived at (insert American conglomerate of choice) Arena at 10:15 a.m., and lugged the load of trunks and bags up the loading dock ramp and into the visitors dressing room hallway. One of the vets offered me 10 bucks if I would carry his bag in and hang up his gear, which I snatched quickly from his hand, all too eager to prostitute myself out for petty cash. The pregame skate was optional and this particular 13-year vet was taking the option to spend the next two hours sleeping in his bunk.

After breaking my skate blade trying to pick up an errant pass four minutes into pregame skate, I was forced to call it a morning. The trainer informed me that he had to trade with the other team for a replacement blade, since he didn't have my size in the trunk.

After showering, I took a stroll around the concourse of the arena, looking for a pocket of space where I could get service on my pay-as-you-go Verizon cellphone. Finally, I found a hot spot between the "Whataburger" stand and "Section 22."

I punched my parents' home phone digits into my phone and after two rings, my dad answered, "Hello?"

"Hey dad," I replied. "How's it going?" he asked.

I tilted my head to ensure I stayed in the airtime hot zone. "Not much. Just got off the ice from pregame skate. I broke my skate blade so I had to get off early."

He started into an old school sermon. "Oh ya? Are you wearing those ugly silver skates? Those things are ugly. You should get a pair of all black skates. They look much better."

"Ya, ya dad, the tube skates went out of style with the leather helmets. I'm wearing Vapor XXXs. They're the best ones now," I replied while rolling my eyes."

"Ya, well they look stupid," he said.

I looked to change the subject. "What's mom up He let out a delayed sigh. "I don't know. I think she went to get groceries."

I continued down the laundry list of family members. "How's Nana doing?"

"She's good. What time is your game tonight?" He asked, clearly wanting to change the subject from the boring, formal drib drab.

"It's at seven o'clock central time, so it'll be eight your time," I replied.

"Well make sure to go with it. Don't just throw it off the glass," he said, trying to add in some fatherly advice.

"Dad, I gotta do what the situation offers me," I whined.

He eases off with one last piece of advice. "I'm just saying you should go with it more. Take more chances."

The airtime pocket began to close in on me as my dad's voice cut in and out. I wrapped up the conversation quickly, "Dad, you're cutting out. I gotta go anyways. Later."

I made my way back around to the loading dock and hopped back on the bus. Once the rest of the players who opted to skate filed on, we headed to a hotel. We pulled into what was actually a pretty nice hotel, considering some of the dumps we later stayed at. Since we were going to be playing the same team for the next two nights, we checked in on the first day and would be grabbing a late checkout the next day, before playing the second game. After the second game, we'd be back on the oversized hearse on wheels, complete with 15 coffins.

At the hotel, our coach passed out rooming assignments. When he got to my name, he announced that three of us would be bunking together instead of the usual two per room. Since owners don't want to shell out for an extra room for one guy, they will jam three to a room and order a cot to save some cash. The three of us looked awkwardly at each other, trying to figure out who was going to be the weak link that got relegated to the creaky military cot.

After dropping off our stuff in the room, we headed down to the lobby restaurant for a pre-ordered pregame meal of overcooked pasta, rubberized processed chicken and runny tomato sauce. The meal wasn't nearly the best I'd ever had. In college, we used to eat pregame meals at the Macaroni Grill or Olive Garden. At this point, given what I subjected my poor stomach to that morning, a free meal that isn't from the Waffle House or Chick-Fil-A sounded great to me.

Clique by clique the players started to head back up to their rooms after the meal to grab a two-to-three hour nap. Most players nap in order to be fully rested and energized to hit the ice and give it their all. I tried to nap in the past, but always found that I woke up cranky and lethargic and came crawling out of the gates, unable to find my stride until the later stages of the third period. By that time, I had probably been burned more times than Cajun chicken and been reamed out and benched.

Instead of napping, I just laid in my bed looking at a

sliver of light shining in from the corner of the blackout curtains. I started thinking about my life, my career and about how I got to that point. Back when I was in college, everyone's dream was to have a big year and sign an NHL deal. I had stopped Phil Kessel on a one-on-one and laid out Matt Moulson, so why shouldn't I think I had a chance.

Back in college, we looked down upon leagues like the ECHL and CHL, thinking that if we ever did have to play at a level that low, we'd just be there on a conditioning stint or for a week or two to start a season. Even when my college days ended and I signed in the CHL, I always figured I'd light it up and get called up before I knew it. Yet, there I was, in the middle of a dusty town, just hoping that I played well enough to last another week.

Somewhere in the midst of self-pity, I ended up dozing off. My journey into dreamland was cut short by the sharp ring of a rotary phone on the bedside table. I panicked, knocking over one of my roommates' chew spitters, sending revolting black goo all over the carpet as I reached for the phone. It ended up being the wakeup call we ordered. I was pissed off at myself for falling asleep because I felt like complete ass. I moaned and groaned and reluctantly splashed water on my face and hair, trying to look presentable. After putting on my suit, I headed down to the lobby, where most of the team had gathered. We then filed onto the bus. Already I was getting sick of that thing.

After a short, five-minute drive, we pulled up to the rink to get ready for the game. For the next two hours, everyone dispersed and partook in their pregame rituals. Some guys spent the next hour pampering their sticks while others rode stationary bikes, ran stairs and went through a series of stretching techniques. Some guys sat in the stands, looking out over the calm, misty ice and chewed tobacco while envisioning themselves scoring a hat trick. Others kicked a soccer ball around in a circle playing a game we affectionately called "Fuckball". Certain players, who were nursing an injury of some kind, got treatment and had appendages taped and prepped while others went over systems with veteran players and coaches. Players do whatever they need to do for an hour and a half before warmup in order to get ready, preparing themselves mentally and physically.

I performed the "Rookie Double-Check". I checked the bottom of my skates to make sure there was no clear tape on them. I then examined my jersey to ensure that there weren't any creative alterations. My gloves, shin pads and elbow pads turned up shaving cream-free, much to my delight, even after you clean that stuff out, it leaves a slimy film behind. The last and most commonly targeted piece of equipment for pranks, my helmet, was checked. I carefully lifted it straight up to discover a cup of Gatorade sitting underneath, which I cheerfully chugged. My discovery brought about groans from some nearby pranksters. Not going to get me with the Gatorade shower today, boys!

When we hit the ice for warmup, one of my favorite songs, "Kickstart My Heart" by Motley Crew, was pumping over the large overhead speakers in the arena. After a few twirls around the ice, I perched myself near the red-line to stretch and catch up with a former teammate from college who was playing for the other team.

"What the fuck is there to do in this dump of a town?" I asked him.

He replied with a hint of agony in his voice: "I knowwwww, it's almost as bad as Wheeling."

I shot him a shocking look. "That bad, eh?"

"We went to the bar the other night and I almost went

home with a three," he replied.

He sets me up perfectly, so I slam home the chirp. "Well that's not that bad. I remember you taking home a lot of twos in college."

He playfully speared me. "Fuck you, scumbag. I always went home with the prom queens."

Laughing, I replied: "Well the prom queen of Sausage Fest University doesn't exactly say much."

He nodded, conceding that there was some truth to my remark. "Whatever, they all look the same in the dark. Hey, I played against Vinny the other night." "Ya? How's he doing?" I asked.

"Same old. Apparently he's got some 40-year-old broad on the go with a built-in family. Her dad's some oil industry big shot."

I laughed while changing stretching positions. "Doesn't surprise me one bit."

We both stood up and tapped each other on the shin pads. "Good seeing you, pal, keep your head up," I chirped.

He shook his head and scoffed: "I'll just go hang out in the corners. Lord knows you won't be there."

After warmup, everyone got settled for a quick, cliché-filled pep talk from coach. "All right, fellas, we didn't drive 12 fuckin' hours into the middle of Buttfuck, Texas, to lose to these guys. Up and down the lineup we're bigger, faster and just downright better than these guys. It's going to come down to which team has more heart tonight. We're going to outwork 'em in every zone. I want quick shifts, everyone finishing checks, pushing the pace for 60 minutes tonight. Stubbsy, you're in nets, Moose and Whiskers on the point and Chuckie's line goin' up front. Let's pay the bills, fellas!"

It's basically the exact speech used by every coach in history, with different clichés substituted in, yet we always flew out of the room to hit the ice like we were about to cross the Rubicon to invade Rome.

Our opposition hit the ice to the crackle and flash of some entrance fireworks, accompanied by a cheesy theme song. After some taunting by a furry mascot on skates, the starting lineups stood on the blue-line for the national anthem, followed by a prayer. Yes, I just said prayer. In the South, where the bible belt is located, religion is a big part of everyday life. A prayer was often recited after the national anthems in a large number of arenas to ensure the safety of the players and the officials. It was ironic, because three minutes after the prayer ended, they'd be screaming to have the ref's head removed from his body.

The first 10 minutes of the game were intense, with lots of hits and chirping. As the period began to wind down, the pace slowed down considerably as the wear and tear of playing five games in seven nights began to take its toll on both teams. Skating on the ice at this point was like running on the beach. The puck was bouncing around the rut-filled surface like a tennis ball. Just before the close of the period, we scored a goal amid a furious scramble in front of their net.

In between periods, Chuckie got eight stitches above his lip to repair the after-effects of a high stick. Some guys retaped and waxed their sticks, swapped complaints about the refs and re-enacted plays that happened in the first period. Other guys took off half of their gear and sat back and put in a chew, while others got their skates sharpened and whined about how bad the ice was.

With about four minutes left on the intermission clock, coach came back in for another generic rant. "We're up by one on the scoreboard, but I have us losing that period. We got outworked, outshot and most of you are playing like your jobs are safe. I'm here to tell you, boys, that nobody's job is safe. You better start playing like you've got something to lose or I'll be on the wire tomorrow looking for guys who will!"

The second period was much of the same as the first, aside from a good scrap between the team heavyweights and a goal for each team. After two periods, we were leading 2-1 in our fifth game of the season, first on the road.

The rituals between the second and third periods were the same, and the speech from coach was a bit more uplifting. "That was a much better period. Good scrap by Clank. A couple clicks for Scribbles for netting his first pro goal. We've got some momentum here boys, but the key is not to get complacent. Let's keep the pedal to the metal and finish these pukes off!"

The third period started off bad as Chuckie took a slashing penalty and our opposition scored on the power play. They added another goal three minutes later to put us in a hole. Nucky tried to kill the momentum with a scrap after they took the lead, and the rest of the period was pretty even until the last minute, when we scored on another scramble with the goalie pulled. Overtime solved nothing and we ended up collecting an SOL (shootout loss) after losing in the seventh round of the shootout.

After the game, doors were slammed and Gatorade jugs were kicked. Guys hung their heads and F-bombs were hurled at no one in particular. Coach came in and reminded us that we had 67 more games to go and that we showed a lot of character coming back late in the period. He threw a not-so-anonymous dagger about taking bad penalties and reminded us that 45 minutes of hard work does not make a 60-minute game.

After showering up, we partook in a buffet that was

laid out by the home team's booster club in the lower concourse. There were silver pans of fried chicken, rice, scalloped potatoes, coleslaw, caesar salad and buns. The surprise spread was one of the many small perks of playing in the minor leagues. The fans were very loyal and accommodating of both the home and opposing teams. That meal saved me from dipping into my bartending money for a late-night run to Chick-Fil-A.

After the quick post-game meal, we hopped back on the bus to head to the hotel. Since we were playing the same team again the next night, we slept in nice, lush beds at the hotel instead of on the bus, teetering along to the next small town.

Coach addressed everyone when we got off the bus. "I'm not your babysitter and you are all grown men. If you want to go out and have a couple pops tonight, then so be it. I have two rules about when we're on the road. One, no drinking in the hotel lobby bar, and two, no bringing ditch pigs back to the hotel. You want to bury the sausage, you do it in the back of Bobby-Sue's Chevette. Just remember, we have another big game tomorrow and three more games after that before we head back home. Take care of your bodies and your bodies will take care of you."

Knowing that I probably wouldn't get another good night's sleep, I'd be sleeping in the aisle of the bus the rest of the road trip, I headed straight upstairs to pass out. Following tomorrow's game, we'd be spending the next four nights traipsing from small southern town to small southern town, chasing a dream. Each game and each day represented a tick on the clock. The clock is a countdown to the end of a dream and the end of a career. Too many ticks at this level signified another window of opportunity closing. Maybe in one of those sun-scorched towns there would be a set of eyes that would swing the tides in my favor.

Bus League Bad Habits

Playing in the minors is hard on the body and mind. Teams often play back-to-back nights while travelling hundreds of miles between games. The pay is low, the food is bad, and team priorities are geared towards thriftiness rather than comfort for the players. Playing in such conditions often breeds bad habits. Other bad habits picked up by minor leaguers are simply the result of acclimating to the culture of hockey.

Bad habits in the minors have a tendency to work like a string of dominos. One bad habit leads to another, which spawns another, and so forth. The first bad habit I will address, gambling, stems from an inner desire to win. As mentioned earlier, pro hockey players are competitive in everything they do. In order to get to that level, you have to have a desire to win and a healthy hatred of losing. Whether it's cards, golf, women or drinking, money is always involved in one form of wager or another.

The problem with the amount of gambling that occurs between minor leaguers is that most players don't make enough money to fund these wagers and still live within their means. Any money that is accumulated, per diem on road trips especially, is often used to ante in to card games and other mindless forms of betting.

When we'd receive our per diem for the day, and I was as guilty of this as the next guy, that money would go straight into a session of shnarples, poker, black jack or euchre. Once that cash was gone, the pleading and moaning would start from guys trying to talk their way back into the game. A cash-depleted player might say: "Let me back in the game, I'm good for it. Just mark me down for an IOU and I'll give you the cash tomorrow." The problem was, when it came time to collect, guys would deny owing anything or would delay the matter by ensuring, "I'll have it for you next roadie."

If you were bad at repaying debts, there was always a good dare to help clear the books. One time I swam five laps in a busy hotel pool, wearing a hoodie and jeans, to eliminate a $20 debt. Another time, we got one of the guys to drink a bottle of vinegar at a restaurant to clear up a $10 tab. Desperate times call for desperate measures.

Another bad habit that stems from being poor and gambling away all the peanuts that come across your table is a poor diet. During home stretches, you eat sensibly and mind what you're putting in your body. When you're on the road, it's often fast food stops after games, or filling up on the gift packs of granola bars and cookies that the booster club stocks on the bus for road trips.

Per diem at the Double-A level in 2007 amounted to $37 per day. You're probably thinking to yourself, "$37 isn't too bad. You should be able to eat healthy on $37 a day." This is true. Today, years removed from my playing days, I could easily eat healthy for a day on $37. When I was 25 or 26 years old, burning thousands of calories a day and weighing 200 pounds, I ate like a great white shark. If we were stopping at Subway, it was two foot-longs, cookies and a drink. We're talking about upwards of a $20 meal.

The odd time, you might get lucky and wind up at a hotel that had a grocery store close by. If that was the case, you could pop in and load up on produce and other items to put together a healthy meal. Most of the time, we'd be eating at a restaurant as a team. After you'd paid for an entrée, with taxes and tip in, you'd be walking away

$20 to $25 poorer.

After spending a couple of days on the toilet after a road trip, you would make a promise to yourself that you were going to organize and pre-pack meals into a cooler next time and eat healthy. Before you knew it, you were back on the road for a week-long road trip, stuffing Quaker Oats fat bars and ginger snaps down your gullet.

By far the most disgusting habit you see at the minor league level, and I'm ashamed to say I partook in this, was chewing tobacco. With long stretches on a bus, at a rink or sitting in your hotel room, throwing in a dip became a socially acceptable way to help pass the time and relax the nerves. Wherever there are people dipping, there are Gatorade bottles or beer cans with the tops cut off being used as "spitters".

The worst part about having guys around chewing was that there were always spitters lying around, many of them missing lids. Time after time, spitters were getting knocked over, oozing gooey filth over whatever was close by. The grossest thing I've ever seen, and this happened more times than I can recall, was when someone would accidentally drink from a beer can that was being used as a spitter. We'd be having a party and a guy would reach back to grab his beer and accidentally grab the spitter sitting next to it. You'd see some pretty wild faces on guys after they took a swig of someone else's saliva and discarded tobacco juice.

Once you got hooked on chewing, you became a celebrated member of the tobacco-using family. I played with a guy who quickly went from chewing to smoking cigarettes. We were playing in Europe and dip was extremely difficult to come by. If you wanted to get your hands on some, you had to order it in from Sweden or Denmark. It was expensive and a major hassle to have imported. Since he was hooked on the stuff, and because everyone smoked in Europe, he decided to make the switch to cigarettes. Before long, he was sucking back a pack per day.

One of the habits that just went along with the hockey culture was swearing like a sailor when you were around the boys. We were all extremely guilty of it, but there were always a few that took it to legendary levels. One of my teammates, let's call him "Marty" was in a league of his own when it came to this. He was like a walking tornado of F-bombs when he was at the rink. Every sentence he threw out had a minimum of four F-bombs in it. For example, he might be griping about someone on the other team in between periods: "Can you fucking believe that fucking number forty-fucking-four for fuck sakes? He fucking sticks me and I fucking give it right back and he fucking goes whining to the fucking ref. Like fuckkkkk me, eh?"

Marty had a great career and ended up getting a coaching gig in the NCAA coaching women's hockey after he hung up the blades. When we heard he accepted the position we all razzed him hard: "Marty! You can't coach women's hockey!"

"Fuck me, bud, those girls swear more than me, fuck," he replied. He was probably right. We used to share a hallway with the women's team when I played at Clarkson and you would have sworn Denis Leary was out there most days.

The last two bad habits, which are of the more serious variety, are drinking and painkillers. Frighteningly, these habits often go hand in hand. Drinking is something that is heavily engrained in hockey culture. Growing up, watching NHL games on TV, there was the "Molson Cup Three-Stars" at the conclusion of every game, and every other commercial was a beer commercial, linking Canada's game with alcohol. It was subliminal conditioning and it was extremely effective.

My dad played in the "Beer Leagues," as they were called, and I used to go to his games so I could run around the stands and collect wayward pucks. After the game, I'd sit in the musty dressing room with all the old boys as they slugged back a case of Labbatt's 50. In every rink there is a prominent sign in every room that says "Alcohol Prohibited," but everyone knows that any rink rat worth his salt isn't going to hold a group of men's leaguers accountable to that regulation.

Drinking beer and playing hockey is as much a match as movies and popcorn. In the beginning, it was something you did because it was fun, it was what people did at parties. If you were shy, it helped you hit on girls. As you rose higher in hockey, drinking became more than just a thing to do at parties. Booze was a cheap painkiller and it also helped you deal with issues that you wanted to keep hidden in the back of your mind. It was a stress reliever, painkiller, bad girlfriend-forgetter and mind eraser all wrapped up into one tall, frosty glass.

The problem with drinking was that it could only do so much for you. When you turned pro and the physicality and grind became more pressing on your body, booze wasn't enough to satisfy all of your needs. All of a sudden, you were playing 30 to 40 more games per season, and the hits, punches and sticks to the face were coming with more force and frequency. You needed something stronger to help you get through the grind, and that's when the wonderful white pills showed up to the party. Oxys, Percs, Vics and muscle relaxers became the new cure-all remedy. Can't sleep? Pop two Vics. Back hurts? Here's a few Percs. Knee's still fucked? A few of these Oxys will sort you right out.

Playing hockey in the minors is a lot like selling your house, cleaning out your bank account and heading to the casino. You play your cards right and hit a big hand at the right time, you can achieve riches beyond your wildest dreams. If you hang around too long, letting all the bad habits consume you, you run the risk of losing everything.

Minor League Cost-Savers

As mentioned in earlier tales, minor league hockey players aren't exactly raking in the big bucks. In order to come out of a season with any amount of savings, you need to be savvy and find ways to cut corners, financially speaking. Cost-cutting is just another one of the necessary skills required to survive and thrive in the minor leagues.

Although the salaries in the low minors resemble the income of the college kid who makes your Grande Americano at Starbucks, minor leaguers do experience some small, but beneficial, perks. For starters, housing is covered, which is a major bonus. There is nothing worse than having to search for an apartment in a strange town, knowing that you could be traded or demoted at any given time.

Another perk that goes a long way for minor leaguers is discount cards. Most teams negotiate advertising deals with local businesses and set up certain discounts for their players. When I played in Augusta, we had 50% off at T.G.I. Fridays, free teeth-cleaning and fillings at Augusta Smiling, free eye exams and glasses at an optical center, free golf memberships at two courses, and several other food-related discounts. Added up over the course of a season, all of these perks saved us a lot of money.

The more time you spent in the minors, picking the brains of the veterans, the more you learned about how to make your weekly pittance go further. Vets know all the ways to have fun, eat and live a comfortable life without having to empty your wallet. The key is not to sacrifice experience, but rather to experience all the great things the absence of money has to offer.

The one cost of living that is undoubtedly necessary, but open to many forms of thrifty maneuvering, is sustenance. You have to eat, especially when you are burning thousands of calories a day between practices, workouts and games. The key to saving money on your grocery bill is selection. In the minors, grocery shopping becomes an art form. You might go to the local "Save-A-Lot" to get your generic items such as soup, cereal, pasta, etc. The next stop might be at a local butcher, where you get a discount because the owner is a season ticket holder. Since hockey players require a lot of carbohydrates, pasta was always a common, cheap meal choice for dinner. A massive pot of spaghetti or penne was made and leftovers lasted for days.

I often opted to volunteer in the community, which in turn meant a free lunch on the team. As for breakfast, the meal that is said to be the most important of the day, and the one I often skipped, there were always bagels, peanut butter, bananas, apples, oranges and protein bars at the rink before morning practices and pre-game skates.

On the road, you were given a per diem on top of your regular salary to help offset the inflated costs of living on the go. The key to this was to stay out of the card games and use your per diem for what it was intended for. If you were lucky to get a hotel near a grocery store you could live sensibly on sandwiches and Chunky soup for the week.

The booster club was a huge help if you were

looking to save a few bucks. It often threw potluck parties where the spread was like something out of a Dr. Seuss book with never-ending tables of homemade scalloped potatoes, coleslaw and chicken gumbo. At the beginning of each season, the booster club provided each player with a welcome package, complete with gift cards, toiletries and many other necessities. It threw tailgate parties after games in the arena parking lot, grilling hamburgers, sausages and hotdogs.

When I played in Amarillo, Texas, I made good friends with a number of the booster club members. One booster family had us over every other Wednesday for steak dinner. Another booster club member had us over every Sunday for a full day of football, barbecue and beer. The booster clubs had a passion for the game of hockey, the team, and always went the extra mile for the boys.

One bonus, or drawback, to playing in the minors, depending on whether you are speaking financially or from a sanity standpoint, was the amount of free time on your hands. On days when we didn't play at home, which amounted to three to four days per week, we would practice at 9 a.m. and be out of the rink by 11. For the rest of the day you had to find ways to entertain yourself. Some guys took courses online. Others took long naps. There were guys that played golf and there were guys who played video games. The key was to find cheap ways to kill a day. When you lived in a southern town in Florida, Georgia or Louisiana, it was too easy and tempting to go for lunch on a patio somewhere and spend the day slugging back margaritas and Coronas.

For me, golf became my off-ice obsession. The season and a half I played in Augusta, I trimmed my handicap by eight strokes. I was golfing four times a week at two of the nicest courses I had ever seen. The best part was that it wasn't costing me anything, aside from a few balls that found their way into Alligator Bay. I was living the life of Riley.

Other random, cheap opportunities would pop up from time to time. You just had to be patient and wait. In Augusta, our owner had season tickets to the Atlanta Thrashers NHL games. Quite often he would inform us that he was unable to go and had four tickets available for whoever wanted them.

Even the greatest attraction of the year in Augusta, the Masters, could be experienced inexpensively. By being patient, we were able to attend three practice rounds for free, while others forked out thousands for the opportunity to walk the hallowed grounds of Augusta National Golf Club.

The first year I played pro, I signed with Bossier-Shreveport in the CHL and flew down. In the minors, you could book your flights and pay for them in advance and the team would reimburse your cost of travel. This included the plane ticket, any meals you had while in transit and, if need be, hotels. The issue with this form of travel was that teams often took their time to pay up after the receipts were submitted. After a struggle, you were always able to get what was owed to you. It was the trip home that always proved to be the biggest headache.

After a debacle of fighting with team front office administration to get paid for my travel and losing my golf clubs in transit, I decided that wherever I signed next season, I would drive down. One of the vets told me a good way to make some money off of your travels. So the next season I put the plan into action. The trick goes something like this. On your way down, take your time. Take the scenic highways and stay in decent hotels. Make sure to eat a breakfast, lunch and dinner each day and don't try to be cheap. Teams often take the total that you submit for the way down, duplicate it and give it to you in advance of your departure at the end of the season to avoid a hassle.

When you hit the road at the end of the year, you try to get home as quickly as possible. Take the fastest route. Leave early in the morning and make all your meals before you go and put them in a cooler. If you must stop to rest, don't stay in a hotel. Just pull off the side of the road at a rest station and sleep in your car. If you follow all these steps, you can easily make a few hundred extra bucks.

Another way to finagle some deals and save yourself some cash was to put your complimentary tickets for each home game to good use. One guy I played with used his two comp tickets to secure free oil changes and tire rotations. Another guy used his comp tickets to get free haircuts. When I played in Amarillo, I became addicted to playing the guitar. There was a guitar shop in town that I used to go to and I'd leave two tickets for the owner. In return, he gave me free guitar picks, straps, restringing services and he gave me a 50% discount on a Fender acoustic guitar and a free mini-amp for my electric guitar.

Saving money in the minors, when done with precision and tact, doesn't mean you have to sacrifice experiencing life. Saving a little bit here and there adds up and means you are able to return home with a little more cash stashed away. With an inflated bankroll heading into the summer, you can take a bit of time to decompress before slugging away at an off-season job. If giving my tickets away to a guy who looks like Axl Rose could buy me a couple weeks off before I had to go back to pouring lagers for ignorant know-it-alls, I was all for it.

Requiem for a Hockey Dream

Before money became involved in my hockey career, I never gave painkillers a thought or even really knew what they were or how powerful they could be. The first time I was introduced to them was during my sophomore year in college. I dislocated my SC joint, the area at the top of your chest where the sternum meets the collarbone. Since the injury was one of those hockey injuries that you gut out and play through, I was given a figure-eight brace to wear and some painkillers.

At the time when I was taking them, nearly half of our team was on one type of pain med or another. In order to play through separated shoulders, sprained knees or ankles, broken ribs, herniated discs and strained backs. Some guys were even getting cortisone shots. There was constant pressure to play through injuries. There is a stigma surrounding hockey players who go on the injured reserve (IR). Being on the IR means you are a "Band-Aid" (Someone who is always getting hurt) or soft, so you do whatever you can to make sure you never have to miss time due to injury.

A couple trips to the IR and coaches start to forget about you. If a team sees a history in a player of missing time due to injury, it will shy away from drafting him or signing him. If the player spends time on the IR, he is one of two things: He is either prone to injury and, in essence, a lemon; or he is soft and weak and doesn't have what it takes to compete at high levels.

In the minors, playing in leagues such as the AHL or ECHL, you are likely someone who can be easily replaced. If you suffer a major injury, such as tearing up a knee or sustaining a serious concussion, two things happen while you rot away on the IR. Firstly, you get a black mark on your record of durability as a player. People will now start to look at you as a pathetic cripple who may never bounce back and will surely be a shadow of his former self if he ever does. Secondly, someone has been called up to replace you and given a shot to take your spot for good. When you do return from the IR, you will have to compete with the player who is filling your shoes in order to regain your job. Keep in mind, you haven't been in a game situation in probably three months and this other player is in peak form.

In the minors, you're in a tough spot because contracts aren't guaranteed for the year. As long as you are medically cleared to play, you can be released at any time. When I was in the ECHL and CHL, we had the Professional Hockey Players Association (PHPA) to protect us. Union representatives would tell us never to play hurt. They would say: "Just tell your coach that you don't feel ready to play and we'll have your back if any issue arises." That sounded great in theory, but if you were to ever tell a coach you didn't feel like playing because your shoulder was sore, the reply would be: "OK, no problem. We'll put you on the 7-day IR." The next day, they would trade for another player, and when you would come off of the 7-day IR, you'd get the tap on the shoulder from the trainer to go see the coach in his office. Coach would be waiting to tell you that you've been put on waivers.

In my first year in the ECHL, we were working out at our practice facility that had soft, rut-filled ice. I got caught up in a rut in the corner and suffered a bad high-ankle sprain. I remember I felt a sharp pop above the boot of my skate and thought for sure that I had broken my fibula. An X-ray showed a significant separation in the bones and the doctor said I suffered a high-ankle sprain. A teammate of mine had suffered the same injury the year before and said that I would have been better off breaking my leg.

Since it was "only a sprain" and could be taped up, it was one of those injuries that you could technically play with. I ended up playing through the injury, but the pain was so bad that my entire leg went numb when I'd take a hard stride on the bad leg. To help get through the pain, I was prescribed with Vicodin and Tinanzidine. Ironically, at around the same time, two leagues above me, Sidney Crosby suffered the same injury and missed two months. The difference was, I was easily replaceable while Crosby was the face of hockey and the NHL's biggest asset.

When you're playing through an injury, one of the downsides is that you are putting yourself at risk for other injuries by overcompensating. When I had the high-ankle sprain, I struggled through five games until I ended up tearing my ACL, MCL and PCL in my right knee. I was taking pills for the pain and, with the ankle taped up, I wasn't skating the way I normally did. I had to alter my stride a bit because I couldn't flex my foot the way I normally did.

We were playing in Cincinnati and I pinched in at the blue-line to make a play on David Desharnais. My bad foot got wedged behind his leg and I felt a sharp, numb pain shoot up my leg, which was happening a lot with the banged up ankle. I went to quickly withdraw my foot and push off and when I did, my right leg collapsed under my body and I fell back. At that point the knee completely buckled underneath me.

Playing with that bad ankle left me open to other injuries and eventually it was my knee that paid the price. I ended up having reconstructive surgery and was slated to miss the rest of the season. I was pissed off at everyone, including myself, when I injured my knee. I knew I shouldn't have been playing, but I also knew that if I didn't, I wouldn't have had a job when I came back. I was mad at myself for getting hurt and mad at the team for putting me in that position. I ended up carrying that anger and resentment with me for a long time.

When you're out with a major injury, such as a torn ACL, you basically become an afterthought. All of a sudden you are in your own world, where your new teammates are the training staff and rehab team. You don't work out with your teammates anymore. You don't practice. When you finally get to go back on the ice, you're practicing by yourself before or after the team conducts its full practice. You don't go with the team on road trips, which is where the real team bonding and gelling occurs. You basically become an outcast. Half the time, your teammates don't want to be around you because you remind them that bad things can happen at any time. It's almost like you are a disease.

All of these feelings of loneliness and worthlessness combine with the pain of not being able to compete. It begins to eat away at you. You are filled with doubt. You don't know what the future will hold for you. Doctors tell you that the chances of making a full recovery are good, but there is always the chance that the ligament graft won't take, or that the knee can be re-injured. You used to laugh and joke with the coach and feel valued, and now he walks past you and nods while trying to avoid any type of conversation or contact. Literally everything in your world is turned on its head.

Right after surgery, you feel like you can do anything. You're still hopped up on the good meds from the hospital and the femoral nerve block in your leg is still in effect. The next morning, you feel as though you have been hit by a truck and backed over, for good measure.

For the next three days after the surgery, you feel as though every hangover in your life has come back at once to haunt you. These are the days when the five prescriptions the doctors gives you become more important than food. You look at the pill bottles, stacked like perfect, glistening silos on your bedside table, and you open each one. Vicodin, Oxycontin, Percocet, Tinanzidine, and Diazepam.

Pop…pop…pop…pop…pop.

All of a sudden you feel euphoric. The dull pain that feels like it's coming from the pit of your bones is gone. Your self-pity and constant state of post- injury depression fade away. You feel like a normal human being again, only better.

They tell you not to drink alcohol while you take these pills, but you do. Why? Because you did it before and nothing bad happened. Back when you didn't even know what it was you were taking. Besides, one of your teammates read an article that said professional athletes are bigger and stronger, and their bodies can absorb more than the average human being. So it's OK to have a few drinks and take your pills. Part of you also doesn't care anymore. You just want to do what you want to do.

You embrace the party more when you're injured, because it's the only time you feel like you're a valued member of the team. When it comes to parties, you're now the guy who has all the pills. Guys you barely hung out with before the injury become your best friends. It's always: "You're the best, man. I love you! By the way, do you have any of that Oxy I can grab from ya?" You're being used, and you know it. But in the emotional state you're in, you'll take whatever you can get to make you feel relevant again.

You start to ask yourself, "Why did they give me five prescriptions anyway?" It seems even stranger when you go to the doctor and every two weeks he's offering to refill your scripts. Even if you took them as prescribed every day, you wouldn't even be halfway through the bottles. Since everyone wants them, you go along with it. This is how the team cache is built. You question it again. Why so many pills? Then you remember that we live in a greed-driven society, and that pharmaceutical company fat cats pad their ridiculous bank accounts on the back of addiction and depression. They grease the palms of the medical service industry to push their product.

The rich get richer.

The rehab for the injury is worse than the injury itself. You get probed at the doctor's office and then head over to the rehab center, where they grind out your scar tissue and make you ride, step up and stride until your knee feels like it's going to explode. After that, it's ultrasound, ice baths and more treatment that makes you feel worse. In the back of your mind, you keep thinking this could all be for nothing. The game that you make your triumphant comeback, could be the game where you tear it all up again, putting you back to square one.

Once you've had a taste of what painkillers can do for you when you are at your lowest point, both emotionally and physically, you begin to make them a part of your daily regimen. With a 72-game regular season in the minors, the daily grind takes its toll on you. That 72-game season includes "hard" travel. What I mean by hard travel is that you are shuttling around the country on cramped buses, not flying charters like you would if you could only reach the fleeting dream you are constantly driving towards. To save money, owners set up schedules so that you will be sleeping overnight on the bus instead of at hotels. You crawl into a bunk, big enough that your shoulders touch on each side of the two-inch-thick, pleather-covered mattress pad, but small enough that you have to tuck your legs up a bit because your body is too long to lay flat.

Sleeping on the bus is hard. You get to a point where you're exasperated. You're sore because you've just played eight games in the past 10 days, and you haven't had a good night's sleep since the last time you played at home. Finally, you bitch about it to one of the guys and he hands you a couple of pills and says: "Take these and you'll wake up in Laredo and feel like you just slept for a week." You take them and he's right! You go out that night and play with more energy than you have in months. That's how it starts with pills on the road.

One of the most difficult aspects of the whole situation regarding painkillers in professional sports is the stigma surrounding it. Popular public perception is that taking pain pills is a choice that people make. When they get addicted, it is their own fault. The problem with the pills is that you either use them to make sure you can get out of bed each day and function on the ice, or you give up the dream you've been chasing your whole life and go find some other line of work. Also, it's not like these pills are that hard to get with physicians saying: "Only take these if you absolutely need them." They are literally shoved down athletes' throats. The pharmaceutical industry is big business, and professional athletes are a big part of their customer base.

In the minors, painkiller abuse was rampant and was definitely an issue that was grossly ignored. I can't speak for the NHL level, but I know that for minor leaguers, who make significantly less money, painkillers were just a part of everyday life. For a long-shot prospect in the minors, where guarantees are as good as the discount paper they are written on, if taking painkillers was a way to keep your job and keep the dream alive, then you were going to do it.

In hockey, pain medicine use isn't regulated and it's something that is essentially legal. As long as you have pain, you can be prescribed with the pills. Playing a sport like hockey, going head to head with six-foot-three, 215-pound athletes 72 times a year, you're going to experience a lot of pain. The human body isn't designed to take contact the way it does shift after shift in a hockey game. Since you aren't breaking any rules and it makes it easier for you to go out every night and perform, you don't feel like you are doing anything wrong. You put trust in the system, thinking that if this was something that was going to hurt you, they wouldn't be letting you do it. It never crosses your mind that these pills can consume your life and start tearing it apart. I've seen scarred-up minor pro lifers, who were once top prospects, have their life ripped apart from painkiller addiction. Guys who were stars in junior and drafted by NHL teams, some who even played in the NHL, needed the pills to keep the dream alive and didn't realize how badly they were addicted. They were paralyzed, watching everything crash down around them.

The pills hook you because pain and depression go hand in hand. When you take the pills, they make all that go away. But when you come off of those euphoric effects, it all comes back and punches you square in the face. So to feel good again, you take more. Since athletes are bigger and stronger, they tend to need bigger doses in order to satisfy the need. Dealing with bigger and bigger doses, your body starts to become accustomed. Now you're getting into levels that are extremely dangerous and potentially lethal.

The fact is, players unions and professional leagues alike are failing their athletes. By not addressing the painkiller issue, leagues like the NHL, AHL, ECHL and leagues all the way down are turning a blind eye to a serious issue that is ruining lives and putting people in perilous danger. The reason I say people, and not just players, is that a depressed, addicted athlete is unpredictable in what they might do. At their lowest point, it's not uncommon for addicts to harm others as well as themselves.

There needs to be regulation on these harmful drugs in professional sports, and more needs to be done to protect injured athletes and remove the stigma surrounding perceived weakness. Outsiders will say that these guys choose to live like this and if they don't like it, they should just get a job like everyone else. The point isn't whether it's a choice, it's that it all can be prevented and avoided.

On May 13, 2011, NHL winger Derek Boogaard died as a result of a lethal combination of oxycodone and alcohol. Boogaard had been sidelined with post-concussion syndrome and was experiencing extreme depression. His death, coupled with the eerily-similar, tragic deaths of NHL colleagues Rick Rypien and Wade Belak within the same year, sent a chill through the hockey world. Yet after the debates and public media banter fizzled out, the proverbial other cheek was turned and everything went back to business as usual. If anything, these deaths were chalked up to the fault of rising concussion rates, while the issue of painkillers was swept under the carpet.

In 2013, the Boogaard family filed a wrongful death suit against the NHL, alleging that the team physicians of the Minnesota Wild and New York Rangers carelessly prescribed Boogaard painkillers that led to his addiction. The lawsuit also alleged that the drug treatment programs arranged by the NHL failed to properly conduct treatment, knowing Boogaard's history with painkillers and the nature of his profession.

When I first heard of the lawsuit, I thought to myself, "It's about time." I am actually surprised that more athletes haven't come forward with these types of lawsuits. If more people come forward and make a stand, then change surrounding the issue of painkillers and the harmful effects on professional hockey might take place. The more the issue is ignored, the worse things are going to get.

Moustache Boy

In pro hockey, everything is about quantity. More games, more practices and more injuries. On days we didn't play, we practiced. On days we did play, we had a pre-game skate. When you are on the ice every day, practicing for eight months, you are bound to find quirky ways to entertain yourself.

After every practice or pre-game skate, there was anywhere from 10 to 30 minutes you could use to work on individual skills: one-timers, face offs, footwork and other constructive activities. Most of the time, we would play games like Rebound, 3-Puck or Moustache Boy. These were competitive little games that often involved embarrassing wagers. The losers of these games usually had to suffer public humiliation and other forms of playful shame.

Moustache Boy was especially fun because the loser had to grow a moustache for one month. Since it was such a common game to play amongst pro hockey teams, you could always tell who the monthly Moustache Boy loser on every team was.

Moustache Boy was similar in structure to Showdown,

where everyone goes in on breakaways until one winner remains. If you miss, you are done. In Moustache Boy, it's the opposite. If you score, you're done. If you miss, you keep going until there is one loser. The loser of Moustache Boy gets to rock a "duster" for the next 30 days. Since the loser had to wear the shameful caterpillar or push broom, depending on your hormonal makeup, the game could only be played once a month.

On days that we couldn't play Moustache Boy, we played Juice Boy instead. Juice Boy was exactly like Moustache Boy except the loser had to fill up Gatorade cups for everyone after practice and bring them, one-by-one, to each player and say, "Here you are, sir."

Another variation of Moustache Boy is Stick Boy. In this version of the game, when a player scores, he throws his stick and skates off the ice. The loser has to pick up all the sticks, which are now scattered all over the ice, and carry them all into the dressing room and carefully align them in order on the stick rack.

Little games like Moustache Boy were a fun way to break the monotony. Playing hockey for a living, just like another other job, is full of tedium and routines. Once things become stagnant, you need to figure out ways to spice things up.

American Guns

Americans, as a whole, are unique. They combine a strong blend of patriotism, pride and ambition. Like all countries, the U.S. has experienced a wide range of emotions and impactful experiences. Where there is success, there is struggle. Where there is elation, there is heartache. And where there is triumph, there is defeat.

One thing that sets the U.S. apart from any other nation, however, is an incomparable swagger. This swagger exudes in the iconic culture of the U.S. It doesn't get more American than Clint Eastwood and John Wayne, and one thing that these larger-than-life characters have in common is swagger and a gun.

When I was picked up by the Amarillo Gorillas a month into the 2008-09 season, I was embarking on a wave of unfamiliarity. I was going to a new team in a new league. I was going to have new roommates and live in a new city and state. I even started using a new stick curve. Moving to Texas was an exciting new experience.

You couldn't help but hear the theme to "The Lone Ranger" playing in your head as your drove along Route 66 past dusty cow pastures and rolling tumbleweeds. It was the Wild West, where men were men and two things were certain in life: Everyone kept their chin up and everyone carried a gun.

The first time I held a gun was in Amarillo that season. My roommate, Mike Handza, who was from Pittsburgh, had a sleek-looking handgun that he either kept in the apartment or in the glove compartment of his truck. "Handz" was a guy's guy who definitely had the American swagger in spades.

Handz was a great roommate and he and I got into lots of trouble. But one thing that was great about having Handz and his gun around was that it allowed me to walk around like I was 10 feet tall. I mean I felt like I was walking around town with "Wild Bill" Hickok. Nobody was going to mess with us.

For example, we had to drive 22 miles to and from the rink every day, and when we would leave for the rink in the morning, the interstate was packed with commuters. One day, while cruising to the rink on a busy morning, one particular driver tried to cut Handz off. Handz sped up, passed the guy and cut him off. This went back and forth for a bit until Handz asked me to open the glove box and hand him the gun. I handed it over to him and he held it up and tapped it on the window, motioning to the other driver. The outwardly aggressive driver suddenly shriveled in his seat and dropped back by about six cars. Nobody cut us off the rest of the commute.

Another time, we were having a party on an off day at our West Texas A&M on-campus apartment when things got a bit hairy. The West Texas A&M baseball team was also having a party across the courtyard. The baseball team started yelling at members of our team from their balcony because a lot of the girls were leaving their party and coming to ours. Insults were traded and the usual posturing went on for about an hour.

Later that night, a couple of teammates and I crossed the courtyard to stop by another teammate's apartment. While in transit, the three of us were surrounded by about 12 members of the baseball team. They started pushing us and telling us that we were going to get pounded, when Handz came running over brandishing his gun. The baseball players scattered like cockroaches. We were saved from what was sure to be a severe beating. Handz just laughed and said, "It wasn't even loaded."

Handz wasn't the only one with a gun. Several other teammates had guns and a lot of the people I came across while in Amarillo did as well. It was just a part of life and a part of the southern culture. Guns were like an accessory, like a cellphone or pocketbook. I remember a girl showing us her new gun one time. She had it coated in pink with bedazzled stones. The thing was tiny, maybe the size of a small squirt gun.

Being a Healthy Scratch Sucks

There is nothing more frustrating or humiliating in all of professional sports than being a healthy scratch. Getting healthy-scratched is like having the most important person in your life tell you that you suck, kick you in the balls, and then laugh at you as they walk away. Unfortunately, throughout my career I was all too familiar with this feeling.

The first time I ever got healthy scratched was in college, while I was playing for the Clarkson Golden Knights. I was fresh out of junior and extremely green. I thought I knew it all and was stubborn and resistant to changing my game. I heeded bad advice from the wrong know-it-alls in junior and I was a mile behind the pack when I made the jump to the next level.

In college, we used to find out who was playing each night during or after the morning skate. Usually one of the coaches would pull you aside during the skate and say: "You're not going tonight, kid. Keep your head up and keep working hard. You might be in tomorrow night." Sometimes the coaches might wait until after the skate, while you were getting undressed, and call you into their office to deliver the punch to the stomach. On even more painful occasions, the coaches would tell you to take the warmup that night because one of the regulars was hurt and might not be able to go. They would tell you to prepare as if you were playing while they waited to see if Johnny Banged-Up could go. The worst part was that you knew there was about a one percent chance that Johnny wouldn't be able to go, but you sat around all day with hope in your heart that you'd be in the lineup that night. It made you feel even more insignificant when you saw the injured player dragging a leg around while you sat in the stands, fit as a fiddle. Basically, the coaches were saying that you were so bad that they'd rather have half a player playing in the game than you.

Leading up to the weekend games, there were always tell-tale signs that you weren't going to be playing in the upcoming game. Let's play a little game I like to call "You're Not Going Tonight." Below are the top five signs leading up to a game to tell you that you won't be dressing, in no particular order:

1. If you are practicing all week on a two- man line with mismatched jersey colors…You're not going tonight!

2. If you are a center and you're practicing on a line with two defensemen as your wingers…You're not going tonight!

3. If you are a defenceman and the coach pulls you aside at practice to ask you to take a few rips up on the wing because they might want to use you up front this weekend…You're not going tonight!

4. If you show up for practice and your gear has been moved out of your stall and onto a spare chair in the laundry room, to accommodate a recently acquired player…You're not going tonight!

5. If you walk into the dressing room and see your name on white board beside the third-string goalie…You're not going tonight!

After it is decided that you are going to be a healthy

scratch, the real embarrassment begins. After you find out, there is the call home to your parents to tell them that you won't be playing, so don't bother watching the game on the Internet. Then you head home, where your roommates, who are always in the lineup, are going through their relaxed, well-practiced routine of having a pre-game nap. You are still angry and dejected about not playing, so you try to find ways to not disrupt the routines of others while killing the next four hours.

When it is time to head to the rink for the game you won't be playing in, you prepare yourself for the public humiliation you are about to endure. Firstly, you will spend the next two and a half hours leading up to puck drop working out with the other healthy scratches and staying out of the way of the regulars who are preparing for the game. After that, you might get an assignment from one of the coaches to keep track of neutral-zone turnovers or to keep a special watch on one of your teammates, because he plays the game the right way while you suck.

Once the game starts, you make your way up into the crowd and awkwardly field questions from fans and season ticket holders. You get stuff like: "Jamie? Why aren't you out there playing tonight?"

In the beginning, I was honest and said: "Well, it's just a numbers game and I am one of the odd men out tonight." Or I'd say: "We've got eight defensemen for six spots and I just need to work hard and hopefully get a chance to be in tomorrow night." After one of these responses, the fan would look at you like your parents just died in a fiery crash and rub your back.

Once I became a vet of the healthy-scratch game, I started to take obscure routes up to the press box, walking through rink boiler rooms with hidden ladders and hallways, or I'd just spend the game in the weight room riding the bike and watching the game on TV. I would completely avoid all contact with fans, to spare myself the embarrassment. If we were on the road and I had to sit in the stands, I would walk around with a fake limp or pretend I had one type of injury or another. If a fan intercepted me on the road, asking why I wasn't playing, I'd say something like: "I tweaked my knee in the game last week and Coach just wants to rest me until it's completely healed." This way they think you're not in because you're hurt instead of just being really bad at hockey.

Once you get into the rhythm of being a healthy scratch, you get paranoid about every little thing. When you do get a chance to play and you play well, you are still constantly looking over your shoulder. Every part of your day becomes stressful, especially when you have a paycheque or a scholarship on the line.

On the ice, whether it's a practice or a game, you start to grip the stick a little tighter and overthink every decision. With 28 players (on a typical NCAA roster) battling week in and week out for 20 spots, practices are just as intense and closely scrutinized as games. To put it into perspective, teams even video their practices and analyze certain drills to evaluate players throughout the week.

Below is a week's worth of notes I kept during my freshman year at Clarkson University. To give some background to the situation, we had just played two games at home against Colorado College. I was scratched on Friday and played on Saturday.

Saturday, Nov. 26, 2003

I feel like I played pretty well tonight. I played a lot against Brett Sterling's line and didn't get scored on. I even got some power-play time in the third period and played a lot down the stretch. My legs felt good, and in the third, I drew a penalty on Mark Stuart, after which he called me a "plug". Coming from an NHL first- rounder, I took it as a compliment.

Sunday, Nov. 27, 2003

Spent the day drinking big beers and eating wings at Eben's Hearth with the boys. Sunday, Funday!

Monday, Nov. 28, 2003

We had a two-hour bagger today. Even though we took two of four points from a nationally ranked team, Coach put us through a first hour bag- skating circuit, followed by an hour of battle drills. I tried my best not to end up last in any of the bag skating drills and held my own in the battles, for the most part. During one battle, I dominated and completely owned my man. Coach wasn't watching. The next battle, I got dangled. Coach was watching and I'm pretty sure I saw him shake his head in disgust. I'm totally fucked. I definitely won't be playing on Friday.

Tuesday, Nov. 29, 2003

Another two-hour practice today with a major emphasis on our new defensive zone coverage, which equals a hidden bagger for us defencemen. They've got me paired up with Matt Nickerson today, which is an awesome sign, since he is one of our top defencemen. Or maybe they're pairing me with him to balance out the strong and the weak. I messed up the defensive-zone rotation a couple of times and got reamed out by one of the coaches. I'll probably be paired with the third-string goalie tomorrow.

Wednesday, Nov. 30, 2003

Two hours again today with a major emphasis on forechecks and special teams. On the way into the rink, I walked past Coach in the hallway and I smiled and said "Hi". He grunted and nodded, never looking me in the eye. He hates me for sure. Today I was paired up with Ken Scuderi for practice. Scuds is another one of our top defencemen, so even though I wasn't with Big Nicks today, I was still practicing with one of our top guys. I wasn't practicing on the power play or penalty kill today and spent most of the second half of practice on the bench watching the special teams practice. I just realized that Clarkson had an undefeated season in the '50s! Why haven't I seen that banner before?

After practice, we had a half-hour video session. I was singled out from the Saturday game in three clips, all bad. I overhandled a puck on the first clip and missed my assignment in the defensive zone on the other two. It's amazing how small you can feel when everyone is looking at you as if you just pushed a feeble, old lady down a flight of stairs.

On my way out of the dressing room, Coach intercepted me and told me that I need to do a better job in my own end. He said he expects more from me and that I need to dial it up if I want to play every night. Does this mean that I will be playing Friday? It has to, right?

Thursday, Dec. 1, 2003

Just a one-hour, light practice today with special teams walkthroughs. I kept an eye on the coaching staff for most of the practice and they didn't tip their hand as to if I would be in or not tomorrow night. Since we didn't run any full-strength drills, I'm not sure who they have me paired with at this point. I suspect I won't know if I'm in the lineup tomorrow until after the morning skate. The bus leaves for the University of Vermont tonight after practice.

Friday, Dec. 2, 2003

I found out today at the morning skate that I would be dressing tonight against Vermont. I was paired up with Matt Nickerson and was told to focus on tight gaps and containing guys down low. Overall, I played well and we won in overtime. Nobody from the coaching staff screamed at me during the game and Coach even smiled at me as I passed him in the hallway after the game. Or maybe he was smiling at Big Nicks, who was walking beside me. Either way, we usually don't mess with the lineup when we win, so I might actually get to play again tomorrow night against Dartmouth!

Saturday, Dec. 3, 2003

Today is my birthday and I was told after the morning skate that I would play again tonight alongside Big Nicks. I was pumped to get a chance to go back-to-back nights. My confidence has been down lately, so I kept things simple and played a steady game. I played a bit on the penalty kill but no power-play time. We ended up beating Dartmouth, so the mood was good. If Coach keeps with his philosophy of not changing a winning lineup, I should be back in next Friday against Colgate. I'm pumped to play against Colgate because they snubbed me last year for a punk named J.R. Bria. I've got six buddies on Colgate and I want a chance to show their coaching staff what they missed out on. We left Dartmouth to head back to campus after the game and we'll have tomorrow off.

Fast-forward one week...

I had a bad week of practice. The worse I played and the more the coaches gave me the disappointed, cold shoulder routine, the worse I got. Everything just spiraled out of control and my confidence went in the toilet. I ended up being a healthy scratch against Colgate. We lost and my old roommate from junior lit us up for four goals. I didn't play the next night against Cornell, either.

The funny thing about my freshman year was that when it was over, I felt I had a terrible season and needed to figure out if I was good enough to play at the Division 1 level. That was my mindset at the time.

Looking back on that year, it really doesn't seem that bad. Our team lost in the conference final after upsetting nationally ranked Cornell in a dramatic three-game series. I won Conference Rookie of the Week once, was an honorable mention for the NCAA Rookie of the Month for the playoff month of March, and led our team in plus/minus for the season, while finishing with nine points in 27 games, as a freshman defenceman. Overall, that's a pretty productive year. The problem was I was healthy-scratched 14 times that season. That's just over a third of the games we played. I was never able to find any consistency or confidence, because I knew there was a 34 percent chance that I wouldn't be playing in the next game.

When you turn pro and you're a bubble guy, it's an even more stressful situation to be in. In college, I knew I wasn't getting cut. I may not be in the lineup every night, but my job was safe. In pro, your job is as safe as a snowman in Tahiti.

My first year of pro was an ego-booster. I played in Europe, where I got to be "the man" again. My second year of pro, I signed with Augusta in the ECHL, which was a minor league affiliate of the Anaheim Ducks. Playing for an NHL affiliate has its perks, but if you are a bubble guy not on an NHL deal, you don't have much say in whether you get shuffled out of the mix when guys get sent down. Even if you are lighting it up, if you aren't on an NHL contract, you are the expendable one.

After I made the team in Augusta, I let out a big sigh of relief. A lot of good players who had better college and junior careers than I did were getting cut from ECHL teams, so my confidence was high. Since I came from a college background, I had a false sense of security about my job, at that point. That quickly changed when Portland began sending down NHL-contracted players such as Gerald Coleman (who had already played a few games in the NHL the season before), Ryan Dingle (three-year deal with Anaheim), Bobby Bolt (three- year deal with Anaheim), Matt Christie (entry-level deal with Anaheim), Adrian Veideman (entry-level deal with Anaheim), Geoff Peters (AHL legend) and Shane Hynes (entry-level deal with Anaheim). For every piece of meat that comes in, one goes out.

The hardest part of the process is that there are

always rumors floating around about who is getting sent down and who will get the bullet. Since the ECHL is a Double-A professional league, changes at the NHL and AHL level affect ECHL rosters. The most stressful time as a pro for me came when Scott Neidermayer came out of retirement to rejoin the Ducks in 2007. Since Neidermayer was a defenceman, he would displace a defenceman at the NHL level who would be sent down to Portland to displace a defenseman at the AHL level. The AHL defenseman would then be sent down to boot someone out of a job at the ECHL level. Since I was our most inexperienced defenseman and not on an NHL deal, I was squarely in the crosshairs. The whole process took a couple days for the changes to filter down. Oddly, Portland elected to send down a forward instead of a defenseman and I dodged the bullet.

Since the budgets are significantly lower at the ECHL level, you see a crunch in payroll and, in turn, a reduction in the number of players kept on the active roster. Healthy scratches aren't that common at this level, but, it doesn't mean they don't exist. Often a team will get creative and put a player on the three- or seven-day Injured Reserve (IR). For example, if the ECHL general manager gets a call from the big club saying it is sending a guy down from the AHL for a few games, the ECHL GM might put a player he doesn't want to lose on the 7-day IR. This way, he retains the player's rights while staying under the salary cap. The AHL player plays his four games and is recalled and the ECHL player is reinstated from the 7- day IR. This tricky juggling act happened all the time.

The Midnight Rodeo

My one season playing in Texas was one of the biggest eye-openers of my life. I should have known from the 27-m.p.h. winds and boulder-sized tumbleweeds that playing in Amarillo was going to be a wild experience. After spending my first week with the Amarillo Gorillas on the road in cities such as Odessa, Corpus Christi, Oklahoma City and Albuquerque, I returned home to a much-needed day off and a bonding night out with the boys.

After a few beers on the campus of West Texas A&M, we headed to a big honky-tonk bar called Midnight Rodeo. The building itself was an old corral-turned-saloon and had a big sign with flashing lights. It was an oasis in the middle of a dusty industrial park. Aside from the never ending line of Ford F-150s and Chevy Silverados in the parking lot and the Taco Villa stand out front, you would have sworn you were in Cheyenne, circa 1870.

Walking up to the entrance, you could hear Alan Jackson testing the strength of the brick mortar. A big, burly bouncer, who could only be named Bud, stood beside a cute little blond in Daisy Dukes and a cowboy hat, the Midnight Rodeo's ID check and cover charge tandem.

Through the parlor doors behind Bud's massive frame was a sight to be seen. A massive expanse of a bar awaited us with two-stepping dance partners, ice-cold Budweisers, cowboy hats, dinner plate-sized belt buckles, shit kickers, good ol' boys, dollies and dames. The Midnight Rodeo was a carnival in a western-themed warehouse.

There was a massive, oval-shaped dance floor that

circled around a main bar the size of a school bus. Around the perimeter of the massive dance floor were beer tubs, secondary bars, tables, couches, pool tables and dart boards.

As soon as our small group of six walked in, it was as if someone had knocked the needle off the record player. Everyone looked at us as though we had walked in naked. Here we were, a group of Yankees (which, according to true deep southerners, is what all people are considered north of the Mason Dixon line, Canadian or American), walking into an Amarillo honky-tonk in pastel button-down shirts and tight designer jeans. It would have been like Pauley Shore walking onto the set of "The Good, The Bad and The Ugly."

After the novelty wore off, we settled in and tried our best to mingle. The first big challenge was going to be figuring out how to get to the main bar without getting trampled on the dance floor. The big oval dance floor worked like a merry-go-round. Everyone danced the two-step in an up-tempo, counter-clockwise stream. Getting across that thing was like playing Frogger.

After ducking and weaving our way through the gauntlet, we saddled up to the bar. I decided I'd take the initiative and order the first round for the boys. I signaled the bartender over and he leaned in for my order. "I'll have six rye and gingers," I said while leaning against the bar, trying to look cool.

He looked at me as if I had just farted and said, "Whatchusay?"

"Six rye and gingers," I repeated louder.

"You want bread and ginger ale?" He replied.

"What? No, whiskey and ginger ale," I said, surprised.

"Heck, why didn't you just say that then," he said while shaking his head.

I looked over at my five teammates, who were all

laughing. "They don't call it rye down here, man." Johnny, a three-year veteran, said. "You newbies are gonna learn a few things down here."

"Yeah? Like what?" Nick, a rookie from Red Deer, Alta., asked.

"Well, first thing is, if you want to try to pick up a girl from Texas, you gotta learn how to two-step. It doesn't matter if you look like Brad Pitt. If you can't two-step, you've got no chance." Johnny replied. "All right. seems fair. What else?" I asked.

"The second thing, if you haven't noticed by now, is that you have to dress the part in a place like this. We'd be all right downtown at one of the nightclubs, but out here, it's all about cowboy culture. Right now, everyone in here thinks we're gay. We're more likely to end up with a black eye than a phone number tonight." Johnny replied.

Everyone became silent and looked around the bar, soaking in the atmosphere and thinking about what Johnny had just said. We finished our drinks and headed downtown, where it was more metro, still wishing we were back at the Midnight Rodeo.

Two days later, my roommate and I headed into a big cowboy superstore called Cavender's Boot City. The place was amazing. I mean wall-to-wall, Clint Eastwood-type shit. We walked out of there with bags full of Wrangler jeans, Stetson hats, Texas longhorn belt buckles, studded snap-button shirts, python skin cowboy boots and a new-found swagger. I even learned how to two-step in the aisle with a nice old lady named Darlene, while my roommate was haggling down the price of a gun holster.

A week later, we returned to the Midnight Rodeo, decked out in our new western gear. The only thing I was missing was spurs and twin six-shooters. For some reason, I was squinting more, curling my mouth up at the corners and had developed a drawl. I don't think it was quite southern, but it was a drawl no less. Wearing that getup, I was 10-feet tough. Or at least I felt like I was.

This time around, girls wanted our numbers for dates, not to take them out for shopping and gossip. I ordered whiskey, not bread and our two-stepping would have made John Travolta shed a tear.

If you're gonna make in Texas, ya gotta have swagger.

Meeting a D-List Hero

When I was a teenager, one of my favorite sitcoms was "Titus", which debuted on Fox and was based on the standup comedy of its star and creator, Christopher Titus. The show was a comedic portrayal of a highly dysfunctional family, often showing flashbacks to the childhoods of the main characters. I used to laugh hysterically while watching the show and hardly missed an episode. I later picked up the DVD box sets. Obviously, I was a big fan.

At the start of the 2006-07 season, I was in camp with Bossier-Shreveport of the Central Hockey League. As mentioned in earlier stories, it wasn't the most ideal situation for a kid coming out of college, looking to break into the pro ranks. One thing that I did take advantage of while I was in Shreveport was the terrific nightspots the Louisiana city had to offer.

Shreveport has the feel of a real cultural hot spot, with casino boats and floating restaurants speckled along the winding banks of the Red River. The city is rife with theatre and arts attractions and is heavily involved in cultural celebrations such as Mardi Gras, Cinco De Mayo, and the Red River Revel.

My roommate at the time was Austin Sutter, who I would later play with in Amarillo. Even with all the excitement of a lively nightlife, Suttsy and I liked to frequent a quieter, hole in the wall type spot called The Blind Tiger. The Blind Tiger was a nice, quaint bar and grill. It was the type of place where you could go for dinner and a couple of beers and stay under the radar.

One night, Suttsy and I were having a beer at The Blind Tiger and I got up to get some money out of the bank machine in the corner of the bar. While at the machine, I felt a tap on my shoulder. When I turned around, Christopher Titus was standing there smiling at me. He said: "Sorry to bother you, my name is…"

I completely cut him off and blurted out, "You're Chris Titus! Oh man, I used to watch your show all the time. You're a beauty!"

He laughed sheepishly and said: "Listen, I noticed you were here with a buddy. Would you guys come over and join us and let me buy you a round?" I was stoked. Chris Titus was going to buy me a beer!

I went back to the table and grabbed Suttsy and said, "Chris Titus just invited us over for a beer!"

Suttsy replied: "Who?"

I pointed over at Chris and said: "Remember that show Titus that was on Fox?"

Suttsy recognized him and said: "Oh shit ya! I remember that show. That guy is hilarious."

So we headed over to Chris Titus' table where he was sitting with a group of friends. I felt like I was going over to meet Wayne Gretzky. I almost wanted to ask him if I could run home quickly and get my DVD box sets for him to autograph.

By the time we headed over to Titus' table, we had sucked back a few beers and had a little bit of a glow on. I don't remember much about the other people at the table because I was so focused on Titus. He introduced us to everyone and we grabbed a seat. He asked us where we were from and was noticeably excited when he found out we were Canadians who were playing professional hockey in Shreveport. Turns out he is a huge L.A. Kings fan and asked us if we could get him tickets for the exhibition game we were playing at home in a few days.

Throughout the evening, Titus kept trying to spark up a conversation between me and one of his female friends. Little did I know, she thought I was cute but was too shy to approach me, so Chris took it upon himself to arrange a meeting. As we sat there, I kept bombarding him with my favorite episodes of his sitcom and completely ignored the poor girl seated beside me. I was so enamored at the fact that I was hanging out with Chris Titus that I missed the whole point as to why I was even invited over for drinks.

At the end of the evening, Titus told us to come to his comedy show the next night and bring as many friends as we wanted. Since the next night was another "go night," we rounded up a posse of about seven players and made our way down to the comedy club, where Chris had put us on the VIP list, complete with a front row table. When we arrived at our table, a beautiful girl came over and gave me a big hug and said: "I'm glad you made it. The first two rounds of drinks are on Chris." I stood there dumbfounded, trying to figure out why this girl was hugging me. The rest of the boys were looking at me with wry smiles.

One of the guys said: "Who the hell was that and what does she see in you?"

I couldn't figure it out and said: "I have no clue."

Suttsy piped up and said: "That was the girl who Titus was trying to set you up with last night, you moron. You completely ignored her and treated her like shit the whole time we were there. I'm surprised she didn't just slap you."

After the show, we joined Chris and his entourage for a few more drinks and we left tickets for him and his friends for our upcoming Saturday night home game. I never did get a chance to see the girl again. At least I could have thanked her for the opportunity to meet one of my idols. And apologized for being a dick, of course.

The Player to be Named

I had managed to avoid being traded until after the season ended in my last year playing in North America. During the off-season after the 2008-09 season, the Texas Brahmas traded for my rights. The trade was made in order to settle a deal made earlier in the season. As it turned out, I was the player to be named later in a deal for Alex Greig and Ryan Waldner.

If we hadn't finished dead last in our division and been mathematically eliminated from the playoffs with 16 games left to play, I may have been in the right frame of mind to embrace the trade and push on with my career. At the time, I was completely dejected and exhausted from a season that saw more valleys than Southern California. I was fed up with the grind of the minor leagues and was in the midst of doing what I did at the end of every professional season—questioning where my life was going and why the hell I would spend another year doing this.

The trade made me feel even more useless, if that was even possible. At the time, I felt like I was a cast-off. I didn't look at the potential bright side. In hindsight, I should have been elated with the trade. Texas had just won the league championship (the Ray Miron President's Cup) and its head coach, Dan Wildfong, was a guy I had a tremendous amount of respect for. I had the chance to play briefly with Fonger during my sip of coffee in Bossier-Shreveport a few years prior. Obviously, Fonger thought I had something to add to his already-dominant team, or else he would have declined the player to be named.

One of the shitty things that can happen when trades occur, and it happened with me, is that you don't know you've been traded until well after it has been announced. I can remember the exact moment that I found out I had become property of the Texas Brahmas. I was at my Nana's house (where I spent all my off-seasons), looking under the dining room table for her lost hearing aid, and I got a call from my sister. She said: "Why didn't you tell me you got traded?"

I said: "What?"

She repeated herself, to which I replied: "What are you talking about?"

She said: "I read an article today that said you got traded to the Texas Brahmas."

I quickly opened my laptop and logged onto the CHL website and, sure enough, there was the headline: "Gorillas Complete Trade, Send McKinven to Brahmas." About 20 minutes later, I got a call from Brian Pellerin, head coach of the Amarillo Gorillas. He apologized for me having to find out this way and thanked me for my service last season. I told him that I was exploring options in Europe and thanked him for the call and all he had done for me last season.

About 20 minutes after I got off the phone with Pellerin, Wildfong called me. We had a good chat and I was honest with him about my intentions. I told him about where my head was at and that I was disappointed about the way last season ended. He was supportive and said to let him know if I wanted to sign in Texas.

Fonger was a great hockey guy. He played in the NCAA at Colgate University and then had a very productive nine-year professional career. As a head coach in the CHL, Fonger posted an impressive record of 217-137-36 over six seasons with the Brahmas until they closed their doors after the 2012-13 season.

The next time I talked to Pellerin was a few months later, right after my rights reverted back to Amarillo, at which point he offered me a contract at a reduction of what I made the previous season. I thanked him for the offer and signed in the Slovenian league for a lot more money, less games and much better beer.

Hockey Tidbits

Hockey has a unique culture that comes with a lot of intricacies and traditions. From superstitions to nicknames, when you are a hockey player, you inherit the cultural persona.

Hockey Players Are a Superstitious Bunch

Hockey players are a strange bunch. We like our routines and superstitions and we're meticulous when it comes to preparation. Players will often try to repeat daily routines from days when they played well. After the game, they will retrace their steps and make sure to replicate that routine until they have a bad game. Then it starts all over again.

In my last year of junior, I had the best year of my life. I went to a new team and a new league, playing for the Ottawa Jr. Senators, and didn't really know what to expect. We were a ragtag group with guys from all over. Murray Magill was our captain and, along with defenceman Mike Campaner, called Thunder Bay home. Colin Nicholson and Peter Kennedy were from Dartmouth and Brookfield, N.S., respectively. Jon Smyth was from Markham and Jamie Dagostino from Sudbury. Our backgrounds ranged far and wide, but we all had something special in common—the incredible journey on which we were all about to embark.

That year, we had an up-and-down season, winning in bunches and losing in bunches. We'd go on a tear and rip off 10 wins in a row and then turn around and dump the next six. Our coach was Freddie Parker, who would later go on to coach in the NCAA and OHL and became a scout with the Calgary Flames. Freddie was a great guy, but boy he must have wanted to pull his hair out at times. At the end of the regular season, we finished in fifth place out of 10 teams, really not a great position to be in. Then something magical happened. We clicked at the right time.

In the playoffs, we would eventually go on to defeat the nationally ranked Cornwall Colts 4-1 in the Central Junior Hockey League final series to advance to the Fred Page

Cup. Cornwall had only lost six games all year. We advanced through the Fred Page Cup and qualified for the Royal Bank Cup, Canada's Junior A national championship. In the end, we ended up losing a heartbreaker to the eventual national champion Halifax Oland Exports to close out our miracle season.

As much as I would like to say the reason we achieved so much success was because we banded together and went to war for one another, I have to be honest. The real reason we went on such a streak was because I didn't wash my undershirt or undershorts the entire season. It was to the point when I would pull them off the hook every day and they were crusted in a solid, spear-like shape. The second reason was because I used the same skate lace in my right skate for the whole season without it breaking once. By the end, it was chewed up and held together by strands the width of dental floss in parts, but miraculously it never broke completely. Now that's just me being honest.

If you asked Murray Magill, he might say we won because he ate chicken parmagiana before every game or because he put the left side of his gear on before the right before every game. Jon Smyth might say that we won because he taped his stick at 5:22 p.m. every game day or because he wore an old, ratty necklace that his sister made for him. Maybe these things made a difference and maybe they didn't. But as a hockey player, you weren't going to take the chance of breaking a routine and risk ruining a streak.

Over the years, I've seen some pretty wild superstitions. One former teammate, a goalie, used to pee in his gear every game. When he was younger, he had to pee so bad one game that he just let it go when he was in the net. He ended up standing on his head that game and recorded a shutout victory. Ever since then, he peed in his pads.

Another teammate of mine, Chris Brekelmans, used to drink three Red Bulls and pop about a half-dozen Sudafeds before every game. By the time Breksy hit the ice, he looked like he had just swam 50 laps in a pool. I can remember looking down at him during the national anthem and he'd be grinding his teeth and rocking back and forth like an overworked washing machine. And keep in mind, Breksy was the kind of guy who was born ready to compete, even without the help of a caffeine overdose.

Everyone has their peccadilloes and eccentricities when it comes to the game of hockey and preparing themselves to compete. As in any sport, success and failure often ebbs and flows like waves on a beach. So when you catch that winning wave, you want to make sure you do everything in your power to ride it as long as you can.

Hockey Nicknames

Nicknames in hockey are as much a part of the game as galvanized rubber and the Stanley Cup. As soon as you become a hockey player, the first thing that changes is the name people call you. Most of the time, the nickname that is given is some sort of variation of the actual name itself. For example, if your name is Doug Stewart, you might be called "Stewy". If your name is Lawrence Ramsey, you might become "Rammer". Adding a "Y" or an "ER" at the end of the name is standard operating procedure for deriving nicknames in hockey.

Other times, nicknames will have some form of a meaning or might describe a situation or attribute associated with the player. For example, I played with a guy, Mike Grenzy, whom we used to call "Putters". Grenzy was a big defenceman out of Buffalo, N.Y., who was a Chicago Blackhawks pick. Grenzy had a specific attribute that spawned the nickname "Putters". He had extremely skinny legs with virtually no calves. It literally looked like there were two golf putters hanging out of the bottom of his shorts. One of the guys barked out one day while pointing at his legs: "Hey Grenz, isn't it illegal to carry two putters in the bag?" We all erupted in laughter and from that day on, Mike Grenzy became "Putters".

Over the years, there have been some famous nicknames that carry a meaning. In boxing, it's extremely common. There is "Iron" Mike Tyson, Evander "The Real Deal" Holyfield and "Sugar" Ray Robinson. In basketball, there is "Dr. J" Julius Irving and Clyde "The Glide" Drexler, and in baseball we have seen Randy "The Big Unit" Johnson, George Herman "Babe" Ruth and "Shoeless" Joe Jackson.

Hockey has also had its fair share of publicized nicknames. There is "The Great One" Wayne Gretzky, Maurice "The Rocket" Richard, "Mr. Hockey" Gordie Howe, and a slew of others, including some unique ones like Doug "Killer" Gilmour. Now looking at Gilmour's stature, you may think this is an odd nickname for such a diminutive player. As revealed by Theo Fleury in his book *"Playing with Fire"*, the nickname "Killer" was given to Gilmour by a teammate who stated that Glimour resembled notorious serial killer Charles Manson. So ever since then, Gilmour's nickname was "Killer."

Other nicknames that I've encountered in hockey over the years include playful monikers such as "Boobs," which was a nickname we gave a teammate because he liked girls that had big boobs. Another nickname we came up with for a teammate was "Creep," because when we'd go to a bar and have a few pops, the more he drank, the droopier his eyes would get and he'd start moving in to talk to girls, appearing to have a creepy look about him.

In junior, we had a kid on our team who used to get absolutely nailed every game. We're talking massive open-ice hits. We ended up calling him "Bump," which was a short form for "Speed Bump," because one guy said: "He gets run over more times than a speed bump at the mall on Boxing Day."

Nicknames aren't always given to teammates. One year when I played in Augusta, we drew the South Carolina Stingrays, an affiliate of the Washington Capitals, in the first round of the playoffs. To prepare for the series, our coach, Bob Ferguson, posted their entire lineup on a large whiteboard, complete with each player's tendencies and our keys to success. For example, it might have said:

> "Travis Morin, Center. Morin is highly skilled and will quietly slip in and out of open scoring areas. Make sure to be aware of where he is in our end at all times and finish every check on him, hard."

As the series went on, guys would go up to the board and alter players' names and the descriptions. After Game 2, the aforementioned example of Morin read:

> "Travis MORON, Pussy. MORON is extremely soft and likes to quietly slip in and out of women's clothes in the middle of the night when nobody is watching. Make sure not to break the eggs in his pockets when you play against him."

In that series, we gave one guy the nickname "Tomato Head" because he was clearly on steroids and would turn beet red when you'd chirp him or try to get under his skin.

Giving the opposing players nicknames was a way to add to the chirping that constantly flows on the ice. It's just another way to try to get under their skin and gain any bit of competitive edge you can.

Nicknames are just another slice of hockey culture. It's a way to foster camaraderie and to make personal connections with your teammates. When you're part of a team, you're part of a family. A nickname is just a way for your family to make you their own.

Every Team's Got One

Amid the playful criticism, or chirping, that occurs with most sports teams, there is usually a player or two who are just too easy to pick on. Whether it be for lack of temper control or a lack of intelligence, every team's got a player who shoulders the lion's share of the chirping in the dressing room.

During my years playing in the NCAA, we had a player on our team who always left you scratching or shaking your head when a conversation involving him ended. Let's call this guy "Wild Thing" out of respect to keeping his name anonymous. Wild Thing was a kid who grew up loving hockey, Republican political views and hotdogs. He was a valued student-athlete, who attended a private, top-tier post-graduate educational institution, which had more to do with his athletic ability than intellectual prowess. Wild Thing, to put it kindly, was not going to be wowing anyone with his progressive views on economic reform or theories about quantum physics.

Wild Thing didn't try to hide the fact that he wasn't the sharpest tool in the shed. In fact, he went out of his way to try and prove to everyone that he was indeed smarter than people thought. He would often use sophisticated words and phrases to show everyone that he was on the ball. For example, one of Wild Thing's favorite words to use was "touché". The problem was, Wild Thing didn't know when it was appropriate to use it. He would use it as a general response to a question or a request. For example, someone might say: "Hey, Wild Thing, can I borrow your car today? I have to go get groceries."

Wild Thing would flip the guy his keys and reply: "Touché."

Wild Thing also struggled with common sayings or figures of speech. For example, there might be a casual discussion going on in the dressing room about bad luck. Johnny would be sitting with his head in his hands, griping: "I'm having the worst week ever. I failed my stats test on Monday. Then, on Tuesday coach calls me in and says he's going to pull me off the power play. Then, to top it off, yesterday my laptop died and now I have to buy a new one."

Wild Thing would chime in with a classic Wild Thing-esque figure of speech: "Ya, that sucks pal. You know what they say, the cookie doesn't crumble far from the tree." Immediately, everyone would be looking at him like he had eight heads. All the while he would be obliviously tying up his skates and smiling to himself, inwardly proud of adding what he thought was an insightful comment to the situation.

Another time, we were in the midst of one of our favorite things to do while lounging around the dressing room before or after practice. We were playing a game we called "What the fuck is this?" This was a game that was played with the purpose of diagnosing either injuries and/or possible diseases. On this day, Shifty was complaining about a lingering problem with his shoulder. We had all gathered around him, pulling and yanking on his arm and contorting it in different positions. We were then taking turns telling what we thought the problem was.

Rammer made Shifty lift his arm out to the side and then proclaimed: "You've got a separated shoulder."

Clete pulled the arm back behind Shifty, who winced and grunted in pain, and then said: "Ya, that's definitely a rotator cuff strain."

One of the guys saw Wild Thing sauntering into the room and said: "Hey, Wild Thing, what do you think is up with Shifty's shoulder?"

Wild Thing looked over at the group of wannabe physicians and snapped: "How should I know? What do I look like, a magician?" We all started laughing hysterically.

Rammer blurted out: "Or maybe a doctor? Or physiotherapist?"

The one that I'll never forget happened during a long, rainy road trip to Boston. It was a dull, dingy day and everyone was dead tired. We were on our way to play two games in New England and the bus was quieter than usual. Most of the guys were either sleeping, studying or watching the painfully terrible movie that was playing on the bus micro screens.

The movie, *"National Lampoon's Senior Trip"*, wasn't one of the comedy series' most memorable flicks. I had my chin leaning on my right fist, halfway watching the terrible movie and halfway looking longingly out the window of the bus, wondering where my life journey was taking me.

There was a scene playing in which the two moronic high school kids—who were being played by actors who were probably in their mid-30s—were being disciplined by their teacher to the tune of a 500-word essay. One of the guys on the bus piped up and said: "That's not that bad. I could whip that out in less than an hour."

All of a sudden, Wild Thing jumps in with: "Ugghhh, that depends on whether it is single-spaced or double-spaced." A collective groan from the entire bus followed this comment, which quickly sparked an onslaught of empty Gatorade bottles and pillows. Even the coaches, who hardly ever got involved, looked back at Wild Thing, shaking their heads with scrunched up faces and muttering curse words under their breath.

It wasn't even the ridiculous comments or head-scratching butchering of the English language that made Wild Thing such an easy target. It was his misguided passion and stubbornness. He may not have been making any sense, but he sincerely meant what he was saying. He would argue with you over why Velveeta macaroni and cheese was better than Kraft Dinner, and why Hulk Hogan could beat Muhammad Ali. It didn't matter what the subject was, Wild Thing was passionate and had a firm opinion.

The worst was when people would bring up politics. Any time anyone wanted to rattle Wild Thing's cage, pun intended, they would bring up the subject of politics. The year that George W. Bush was re-elected, I was roommates with Wild Thing. He was a big supporter of the Republicans and had an answer for everything. I remember foolishly asking him who he was going to vote for—John Kerry or Bush. I nearly got spit on during his response: "Bush, you dummy! You think I'm gonna vote for that communist pussy Kerry!"

At this, I put my hands firmly on the cage and gave it

good shake: "Bush, eh? Kerry played hockey, you know. He played at Yale. Why don't you support a good ol' hockey-playing candidate?"

Wild Thing lashed out: "Kerry didn't play hockey! He probably was on the checkers team or something." Ya, Wild Thing, I think Yale has a good checkers team.

So I began poking the beast through the bars: "Why are you going to vote for Bush? Look at the mess he made in his first term."

Wild Thing started to get a bit more testy and defensive: "Because Bush has balls! He doesn't take any shit! Those terrorists tried to bomb us and he's going to stick it up their asses!"

I then began to dangle a raw, 12-ounce steak in front of the bars: "Don't you think they should call a peace truce and end all the violence? I mean do more American soldiers need to go over and give up their lives? Hasn't there been enough death?"

Wild Thing was now launching himself against the cage: "Arrrghhh! Ohhh, you Canadians are a bunch of liberal pussies! Always talking about peace and shit. Bunch of tree huggers and kumbaya-singing wimps!

Everyone hates the U.S. because we're the best! If we don't stick up for ourselves, then everyone will walk all over us like they do to all you Canadian pussies!"

Atta boy, Wild Thing, go get em!

The Legend of Gunner Garrett

For those of you who have read my first book, I may be repeating myself a bit here. In, *"So You Want Your Kid to Play Pro Hockey,"* I spoke briefly about Kenneth "Gunner" Garrett, the legendary minor league trainer.

Considering this, I hemmed and hawed about including Gunner's story in this book until realizing that not including Gunner in a funny book about minor league hockey would be criminal and sacrilegious. Anyone who has had the pleasure of encountering the cantankerous old codger can attest.

The first time I met Gunner, I was sleep-deprived, hung over and in a furious rush. I had just driven 22 hours straight, through the night from Augusta, Ga., to Amarillo, Texas, and I was about to make another four-hour trek to Odessa for my first game as a member of the Amarillo Gorillas of the CHL. When I walked into the Amarillo Civic Center, one of the first things that caught my eye, before I ducked into the dressing room, was a large black banner with a helmet, two crossed hockey sticks and the name "Gunner" embroidered in large bold letters. Immediately, I figured it was a memorial to a former player who died.

After being redirected several times amidst a mad rush of players getting ready for a road trip, I stood nose to nose with the Amarillo team trainer. The man in front of me seemed to have all the prerequisites of a minor league trainer:

Grumpy? Check.
Sarcastic? Check
Quick-witted? Check
Gruff? Check

He reached out his hand and said: "You must be Janine McMuffin. I'm Gunner, the team trainer. Welcome to paradise."

I grabbed Gunner's hand firmly and shook it: "Nice to meet you, Gunner but my name is Jamie." Gunner glared at me, cocking his head to the side: "You look more like a Janine to me. What position do you play?"

"I'm a defenceman," I replied.

"Oh ya? Well you don't look like much," he scoffed while looking me up and down.

"I could say the same about you, but I bet you've already been told that," I jabbed back.

Gunner immediately dropped his grumpy façade and let out a low, bellowing laugh: "You might just be all right, son. Now grab your frickin' gear and come pick out some sticks."

"Hey, Gunner," I asked. "What's with that morbid banner out front?"

"Son, you wouldn't believe it if I told ya. Those bozos thought I was dead and had a banner made up for me," he replied, referring to an incident that occurred during the 2005 season when Gunner was the trainer for the Austin Ice Bats.

Gunner suffered what was thought to be a fatal heart attack at the rink in Austin. He was rushed to hospital and word spread that he had died. Not knowing that he was actually alive, ownership had a large banner made up that was to be hung from the rafters during the next night's game in memory of Gunner. When word came out that he was indeed alive, the banner was given to him as a keepsake and reminder of the close call.

Gunner was a very interesting character, to say the least. He represented a unique perspective. He was straight out of the old guard. It was almost like having Don Cherry walking around your dressing room in a skin-tight Stanfield's hockey underwear jumpsuit, throwing chirps around at all the players and talking about how it was back in the good ol' days.

Gunner's training and equipment managing career spanned 48 years, from 1961 when he started out with the EHL's Johnston Jets right up to his last season with us in Amarillo in 2009. Early in his career, Gunner suited up for 22 games with the New Haven Blades of the EHL over five seasons. Back then, teams usually only carried one goalie and the trainer served as the backup. During that span, Gunner even recorded back-to-back shutouts.

Being plugged into the pro hockey culture for so long meant that Gunner, like all of the players he loved to razz, was a creature of habit. And, like all of the players, Gunner's superstitions and routines were as head-scratching and face-scrunching as anything you've ever heard of. For example, some people say that they love hockey so much they basically live at the rink. In Gunner's case, he actually did live at the rink. In our stick room—a long stretch of open space located under the north-end bleachers—there was an old, fluffy couch with a grungy old blanket and pillow. This was Gunner's bed. A coffee maker, mini-fridge and hot plate served as Gunner's kitchen.

One morning before practice, I got to the rink early in order to prep some new sticks. When I walked into the stick room and flipped on the lights, Gunner nearly bit my head off. "Turn that fuckin' light off before I wrap your nose around the back of your head," he barked while throwing a pillow at me.

Another routine that Gunner had was to wander around before games, chirping players and engaging in playful banter. He especially loved to drift in and out of the medical trainer's room to cut guys up who were getting treatment. He would spit out lines like: "What's going on, son? You tear some heartilage?" or, "What's wrong with him, doc? He tear his motivator cuff?"

Chirping is a major part of the camaraderie in the hockey culture and Gunner was an avid practitioner. It was how he showed his affection for someone. If he was ripping on you, you knew he liked you. If he didn't rip on you, you knew he wasn't a fan.

One of Gunner's funnier peccadilloes was how adamant

he was about certain things and how lax he was about others. For example, Gunner was the only trainer I've ever met who didn't give a shit about the sticks. He literally left the stick room door open all the time. This was unheard of. Usually that room is locked up tighter than Fort Knox.

Players would file in and out of there with bundles of sticks under their arms and he wouldn't even look up from his newspaper. On the flip side, Gunner would fight you to the death and piss on your dead carcass if he ever caught you stealing the 20-year-old, raggedy, used undershirts and long underwear he kept under lock and key in a cabinet beside his desk. It was the weirdest thing. Those raggedy Stanfield's undershirts were from his days tending the end of the bench for the P.E.I. Senators during the early '90s, and he guarded them like it was his daughter on prom night.

One of the reasons Gunner might have been so anal about the long underwear and undershirts might have been the fact that it was all he ever wore. Throughout the entire season, I only saw Gunner in two outfits: One was a matching set of navy blue long underwear and long-sleeved undershirt; the other an Amarillo Gorillas nylon tracksuit (which he wore on the bench during games). You might hear me say this and think, "Well, Jamie, Gunner couldn't have worn that stuff when you went out to restaurants on the road or at fancy team parties," and I'm here to tell you that he certainly did. I still remember the day when one of the guys gave it to Gunner for wearing his tight long johns into an Olive Garden on the road one day: "Geez, Gunner, have some decency. No one should have to see you walking around wearing that. I can see the complete outline of your junk for chrissakes!"

A funny little thing about Gunner was that he absolutely loved ice cream drumsticks. After every game on the road, before bussing out to the next dusty town location, we would stop at a truck stop to gas up. During the pit stop, I would always grab Gunner a drumstick. It was great to see his eyes light up when I'd hand it over to him. He was a like a little kid.

Gunner also loved Christmas. It was the only time I'd ever see him be cheery. He took a lot of pride in putting up decorations and making sure the radio was on a 24/7 Christmas station. He even had his girlfriend make Christmas cookies, which he'd put on display on his desk and promptly slap anyone's hand who tried to sneak in for a quick grab-and-dash.

One day, I told Gunner that he gave my best friend from home, Jordan Reid (who grew up in P.E.I.), his first job as stick boy for the P.E.I. Senators (the AHL affiliate for the Ottawa Senators during the early '90s).

Gunner snapped back at me: "No I didn't!"

I said: "Gunner, I haven't even told you his name yet."

Well, what is it?" he angrily replied.

"Jordan Reid," I said.

"Ohhhhhhhh, I know little Jordie! He's Tom Reid's kid. What a great family. Why didn't you say that's who it was?" he said, with a jolly bounce in his voice.

Confused, I replied: "Ummm, I did, Gunner."

On bus trips, Gunner always sat in the tour guide seat right beside the bus driver. He'd even sleep sitting in that thing. On one particular trip up to Fort Collins, Colorado, Gunner had a pretty serious scare. Just before dawn, Gunner woke up in hysterics. He didn't know who he was, where he was or what the paper items (money) were in his pocket. Gunner was taken to hospital and it was determined he had suffered a mild stroke. Hours later, against stern advice from the doctors, the stubborn old bastard was at the rink, sharpening skates and tossing around chirps.

It's nearly impossible to keep hockey players on the shelf if there is any way that they can play. Grumpy old hockey trainers are no different.

Acknowledgements

A special thanks goes out to all my former teammates for providing me with the material for all the shenanigans described in this book. As teammates, we were family members held together by a sacred bond. For every story that I have shared, there are a hundred others that will go forever untold. I am strictly bound by the code, which makes the bond between teammates iron-clad and unique. Through the good and the bad, teams hold strong, and no matter whether you like the guy sitting next to you or not, you will go through the wall for him.

A special thanks goes out to Helen Brabon for generously providing the rights to use the photograph featured on the cover and to Tim Gordanier for taking the time out of his busy schedule to provide editing support.

TALES FROM THE BUS LEAGUES

Notes:

http://hockeydb.com

http://eliteprospects.com

"So You Want Your Kid to Play Pro Hockey?"
Jamie McKinven, 2012

"Playing with Fire"
Theo Fleury with Kirstie McLellan Day
Triumph Books. Chicago. 2009

Index

A

Abbott, Cam 19
Abbott, Chris 19

B

Ballard, Keith 8
Beauchemin, Francois 205
Beausoleil, Nathan 22
Belak, Wade 247
Bernardo, Paul 199
Bissinger, H.G. 191
Bissonnette, Paul 192
Bitz, Byron 17
Bolt, Bobby 260
Boogaard, Derek 192, 247
Brabon, Helen 288
Brekelmans, Chris 72, 85, 172, 274
Bria, J.R. 259
Brodeur, Martin 152
Brunette, Andrew 204
Bryzgalov, Ilya 153
Burrows, Alex 204

C

Campaner, Mike 272
Campbell, Jason 94
Carkner, Matt 192
Chara, Zdeno 205
Christie, Matt 260
Clitsome, Grant 9
Cole, Erik 46, 47
Coleman, Gerald 153
Conroy, Craig 46, 47
Coolen, Tom 174

Crosby, Sidney .... i, 241
Crum, B.J. 165

D

Dagostino, Jamie 272
Daly, John 159
Deboer, Peter 36
Decaro, John 97
Desharnais, David 204
Desrochers, Jean 66
Dingle, Ryan 260
Divac, Vlade 133
Djokovic, Novak 142, 145
Drechsel, Greg 36, 43, 51
Dryden, Ken 17

E

Eastwood, Clint 53
Ellett, Dave 9
Elway, John 53

F

Farley, Chris 215
Faulkner, Mac 12
Federer, Roger 145
Ferguson, Bob 155, 165, 213, 214, 276
Ferguson, Lorne 214
Fleury, Theo 275
Fournier, Marc-Andre 130

G

Galley, Gary 9
Garrett, Kenneth "Gunner" 281
Gates, Bill 158
Gauthier, Jonathan 130
Giguere, J.S. 153
Gmelch, George i

Godfrey, Josh	205
Goepfert, Bobby	153, 155
Goligoski, Alex	8
Gordanier, Tim	288
Grabner, Michael	205
Gratton, Chris	169
Greig, Alex	268
Grenzy, Mike	275
Gretzky, Wayne	i, 266, 275

H

Halak, Jaroslav	204
Hall, Taylor	205
Handza, Mike	250
Hasselhof, David	45
Hiller, Jonas	153
Hornby, Greg	23
Hynes, Shane	260

I

Iggulden, Mike	17
Immelman, Trevor	190
Irving, Joel	181
Isbister, Matt	22

J

Jacob, Daniel	130
Jagr, Jaromir	202
Jankovic, Beki	90, 109, 145, 146, 147, 150
Jankovic, Bogdan	110
Jankovic, Bojan	90, 145, 146, 147, 150
Jay Latulippe	v, 81
Jones, Bobby	162

K

Kennedy, Peter	8, 272
Kolzig, Olaf	204

Komisarek, Mike 203
Kostadine, Jason 166

L

Lampe, Eric 205
Latulippe, Jay v
Laughlin, Mike 128
Leary, Denis 232
Leggio, David 61
Levasseur, J.P. 153
Lincoln, Abraham 198
Lindros, Brett 169
Lundberg, Eric 166

M

Magill, Murray 272, 273
Marks, John 213
Marsters, Nathan 153
Martin, Paul 8
Maunu, Mitch 9
Mayrand, Dean 192
McCarty, Darren 206
McDonald, Andy 63
McGuire, Molly 189
McKee, David 18, 153
Methot, Marc 9
Mickelson, Phil 161
Milbury, Mike 63
Morin, Travis 276
Morissette, Jake 184
Morris, Mark 36
Moulson, Matt 17, 223
Musatov, Vadim 109, 119, 136
Muscutt, Scott 92

N

Neidermayer, Scott 261
Neilsen, Art 6, 8

Nicholson, Colin ... 272
Nickerson, Matt ... 19, 75, 256, 258
Nieuwendyk, Joe ... 17
Norris, Chuck ... 53

O

O'Byrne, Ryan ... 17
Olson, Clifford ... 199
Ornelas, Jonathan ... 181, 184

P

Parker, Freddie ... 5, 36, 71, 272
Parros, George ... 192
Pellerin, Brian ... 183, 269
Penner, Dustin ... 204
Perowne, Fred ... 130
Peters, Geoff ... 260
Petrovic, Drazen ... 133
Platt, Jason ... 169, 193
Player, Gary ... 190
Porter, Lyon ... 54

Q

Quick, Jonathan ... 204

R

Reid, Jordan ... 286
Reid, Matt ... 98
Reid, Tom ... 286
Reimer, James ... 204
Roche, Sean ... 89
Rodman, Dennis ... 211
Roll, George ... 36, 41, 48, 55, 58
Rose, Axl ... 238
Ryder, Michael ... 204
Rypien, Rick ... 247

S

Scuderi, Ken 257
Sgroi, Mike 191, 192, 193
Shafia, Mohammad 199
Spencer, Brian 200
Springstein, Bruce 190
Sprott, Jim 93
Spurrier, Steve 175
Stamkos, Steven 206
Standbrook, Grant 204
Sterling, Brett 255
Streit, Mark 204
Stuart, Mark 256
Sullivan, John 81
Sutter, Austin 97

T

Thomas, Tim 204
Thornton, Shawn 192
Titus, Christopher 266
Toneys, Nick 166
Tracze, Steve 2
Travolta, John 265
Trukhno, Vyacheslav 205

V

Vanek, Thomas 8
Veideman, Adrian 163
Vesce, Ryan 17
Vorlicek, Frantisek 112, 136

W

Waldner, Ryan 268
Ward, Joel 204
Wayne, John 53
Wharton, Kyle 9
White, Sean 131

White, Todd 13, 47
Wildfong, Dan 269
Woods, Tiger 159
Wright, Scott 94, 99, 107, 110, 120, 122, 130, 141

Y

Yzerman, Steve 53

TALES FROM THE BUS LEAGUES

Other Books by this Author:

"So You Want Your Kid to Play Pro Hockey"

An uncensored peek behind the scenes of hockey's unique culture. Find out how politics unfold at the various levels of hockey. Discover the real issues that are plaguing the game, and what needs to be done now to protect the next generation of up-and-coming hockey hopefuls. Discover what happens on the road, as a team bonds together, and what hockey is like in the Southern U.S. and Eastern Europe. Hockey has its own set of rules, defined within a unique culture. Experience the game of hockey from a new perspective. Strap on the gear and get beneath the helmet.

Tales from the Bus Leagues

Author's Blog:

When in Doubt, Glass and Out

"Hockey and Everything in Between"

Jamie McKinven maintains a blog site for hockey fans, parents, players and critics to get information on everything from tips on mental preparation to hilarious stories about what goes on behind the scenes in the hockey world. If you want to read an interesting article about hockey's unique culture or debate about the newest rule change, chime in and let yourself be heard.

Learn more at:

www.glassandout.com

TALES FROM THE BUS LEAGUES

TALES FROM THE BUS LEAGUES

Tales from the Bus Leagues

Made in the USA
Coppell, TX
21 December 2021

69873363R00184